W9-BAV-195

# Knives and Angels
## Women Writers in Latin America
### edited by Susan Bassnett

PQ
7081
.A1
K55
1990

ST. JOSEPH'S UNIVERSITY

3 9353 00258 5493

*Zed Books Ltd.*

**London and New Jersey**

*Knives and Angels: Women Writers in Latin America* was first
published by Zed Books Ltd., 57 Caledonian Road,
London N1 9BU and 171 First Avenue, Atlantic Highlands,
New Jersey 07716, USA in 1990.

Copyright © Individual contributors, 1990
Editorial copyright © Susan Bassnett

Cover designed by Sophie Buchet
Typeset by Photosetting and Secretarial Services, Yeovil
Printed and bound in the United Kingdom by Biddles Ltd.,
Guildford and King's Lynn

**British Library Cataloguing in Publication Data**

Knives and angels : women writers
in Latin America.
1. Latin American literatures. Women
writers. Critical studies
1. Bassnett McGuire, Susan
860.99287

ISBN 0-86232-874-8
ISBN 0-86232-875-6 pbk

**US CIP is available from the Library of Congress**

# Contents

y sobre todo ángeles,
ángeles bellos como cuchillos
que se elevan en la noche
y devastan la esperanza

('Exilio', Alejandra Pizarnik)

# Contributors

*Marjorie Agosin* is a Chilean poet, author of six collections of poetry and four books of literary criticism. *Scraps of Life*, her book on the Chilean women's *arpilleras* was published by Zed Books in 1988. She teaches Latin American literature at Wellesley College, Massachusetts.

*Susan Bassnett* is a writer, translator and Reader in Comparative Literature at the University of Warwick. She is author of books on translation studies, theatre history, women's poetry and theatre and comparative studies. She has recently completed a translation of Margo Glantz's *Las Genealogias* and a volume of Polish women's poetry. She has four children.

*Catherine Boyle* is Lecturer in Spanish and Latin American Studies at the University of Strathclyde. Her publications include studies of Chilean writing and theatre under authoritarian rule, cultural expression in Latin America, especially popular song and theatre linked to grassroots movements, and women's writing. Her main concern is to create a wider awareness in Europe of the richness of Latin American culture.

*Juan Bruce-Novoa* is Professor of Mexican and Chicano literatures at the University of California, Irvine. He is author of *Chicano Poetry, Response to Chaos*. *'La sombra del caudillo', version periodistica, Inocencia Perversa*. He is a member of the organizing committee of the annual Mujeres de la Frontera conference in Tijuana, Mexico. He is working on a book on Elena Poniatowska.

*Myriam Diaz-Diocaretz* is a poet and Research Fellow at the University of Amsterdam. She has published four collections of her own poetry and compiled and translated an anthology of the poetry of Adrienne Rich. She is author of several books of poetics, translation and critical theory and works in a wide range of languages.

*Chloe Furnival* worked in stage management for four years, then went on to read first and second degrees in Comparative American Studies at the University of Warwick. In 1988 she completed her dissertation on the short stories of Clarice Lispector, Rosario Castellanos and María Luisa Bombal. She lives in Brazil with her husband and small son.

*John King* is Senior Lecturer in Latin American Cultural History at the University of Warwick. He has published widely on Latin American literature, with special reference to Argentina. His books include works on Argentine cinema, on the history and development of Victoria Ocampo's journal *Sur* and on modern Latin American fiction.

*Patricia Murray* is currently working on her PhD in Comparative Literature at the University of Warwick. Her specialist interest is in Latin American and Caribbean writing. Born in Liverpool in 1965, she studied English at Trinity College, Oxford. She has travelled extensively in Central America, and in Colombia, Ecuador and Peru. She does voluntary work at the Nicaraguan Solidarity Campaign.

*Montserrat Ordoñez* is Colombian, but was born in Barcelona, Spain. She has a first degree in Modern Languages from the University of Los Andes in Bogota, and a PhD in Comparative Literature from the University of Wisconsin, Madison. She is Professor of Literature at the Universidad Nacional de Colombia and Universidad de Los Andes in Bogota. In addition to her own poetry, she has published many articles on Latin American literature, especially on women writers and the revision of the canon. Her books include *La voragine: textos criticas* (1987) and *Ekdysis* (poems, 1987).

*Giovanni Pontiero* is Reader in Latin American Literature at the University of Manchester. His critical works include essays on Clarice Lispector, Gabriel García Márquez, the Brazilian poet Manuel Bandeira and the Uruguayan dramatist Florencio Sanchez. His numerous translations of European and Latin American prose and poetry have been published extensively in England and the United States.

*Nissa Torrents* lectures on Latin American film and narrative at University College, London. Her principal research interest is in women's cultural production in Latin America. Her publications include *The Garden of Forking Paths* (London, 1988) with John King and *La Habana* (Barcelona: Editorial destino, 1989).

# Introduction: Looking for the roots of wings

*Susan Bassnett*

In the 1960s and early 1970s, when Latin American literature started to become fashionable and writers like Gabriel García Màrquez, Jorge Luis Borges, Octavio Paz, Mario Vargas Llosa, Julio Cortazar and Carlos Fuentes, to name but a few, became international household names, readers in Europe and the United States might have been forgiven for assuming that all the creative talent in Latin America was male. The list of Great Men, defined by one critic as the 'family' of Latin American writers, contained no women's names at all. The family, as has been pointed out elsewhere, was made up of fathers, brothers and sons; the mothers, sisters and daughters remained absent, relegated in the popular imagination to a life spent somewhere quietly in the house ensuring that their menfolk had time and space in which to create their great works.[1]

Now, in the last decade of the twentieth century, that picture has been radically altered. So much work by women writers, artists, film-makers and critics has appeared, so much has been rediscovered that the map of Latin American creativity has had to be completely re-devised, and the part played by women in the history of Latin American culture can be seen to have very deep roots, which stretch right back into the distant past. The strongest individual voice of seventeenth-century colonial New Spain is that of a woman, Sor Juana de la Cruz, and three centuries later her passionate defence of the right of women to intellectual and creative life is being heard again. Listing those biblical, classical and contemporary women who serve as models to others, Sor Juana comments on one in the following terms:

> Never by a famous man
> have we been shown such victory,
> and this, because God wished through her
> to honour womankind.
> Victory! Victory![2]

From Sor Juana's powerful statements descend a long line of gifted women, some few of whom are discussed in this book. The history of Latin

American countries is a history of colonialism, of revolution, of emergent nationalism, of tyranny and resistance, of genocide, poverty, economic and ecological crises, but also a history of survival, struggle and triumph and it is a history in which women have played a crucial though underestimated role. Their creative work reflects that position, and Montserrat Ordoñez has tellingly entitled her essay on three Colombian women writers 'One hundred years of unread writing', wittily subverting the title of the now classic novel by the well-known Colombian male writer Gabriel García Màrquez. Going even further, in his essay on Elena Poniatowska's novel about Angelina Beloff, an archetypal abandoned woman, Juan Bruce-Novoa suggests that women who write risk rejection by men and yet continue to write because writing is a form of confrontation, a positive gesture in a world that requires them to be silent.

The process of rediscovering lost or neglected women writers owes a debt to developments in feminist literary history which have had an impact throughout the world. Gradually, certain names have begun to surface: Gabriela Mistral, the first Latin American writer to win the Nobel Prize for Literature; Victoria Ocampo, founder of the literary magazine *Sur* that changed the face of Latin American culture in the twentieth century (described here by John King as the great precursor); her sister Silvina Ocampo, friend and member of the circle of writers that include Borges, whose name has eclipsed hers completely until recently; María Luisa Bombal, the Chilean writer whose career is compared by Marjorie Agosin to that of Jean Rhys, the Caribbean writer whose work was ignored for decades; or Alejandra Pizarnik, the poet who died tragically young and whom Octavio Paz held to be one of the greatest writers in Latin America. In some cases, the process of rediscovery is due to chance, or to changes in fashion (the European enthusiasm, in the late 1980s, for Frida Kahlo's paintings is one such example) or to the dedicated enthusiasm of an individual translator, such as Giovanni Pontiero who has played such a crucial role in bringing the works of Clarice Lispector to the English-speaking reader. But regardless of how or why the cultural excavation takes place, what is clear is that now it has begun it is unstoppable. Latin American readers are finding out about their own cultural history and readers in other parts of the world are discovering a little of that neglected heritage through the medium of translation. The mothers, daughters and sisters are no longer confined to the kitchen or bedroom: they have come out into the light.

Describing the role of women writers in Latin America today in an essay entitled 'Whispers and Triumph', Marjorie Agosin comments:

The woman writer in Latin America has taken on the role of witness; she has assumed the burden of the political barbarities of the society and has taken up her position as a deliberate act of defiance against the silence imposed by oppressive governments. The political activism in the literature of Latin American women, like the political actions of the

Mothers of the Plaza de Mayo and similar groups, has become an activity of incalculable force. The image so widespread of the woman writer as someone who escapes real life and dwells in a world of fantasy and dreams, has been replaced by the woman who aims her pen like a rifle and lets fly words of lead and steel.[3]

Marjorie Agosin was writing here about the literature of protest by women such as Isabel Allende, Marta Traba, Elena Poniatowska, Luisa Valenzuela and Cristina Peri Rossi, but she also notes the testimonial quality of so much Latin American women's writing and links this to the practical contribution of women to armed struggle against oppression. The Mothers of the Plaza de Mayo have come to symbolize that contribution, as they stand in the streets holding pictures of their relatives who have been kidnapped and murdered by a corrupt regime. Likewise the Chilean *arpilleristas* embroidered pictures of the same horrors, as they waited vainly for news of their own families, following the right-wing coup of 1973, documented so carefully in Isabel Allende's novel *The House of the Spirits*. In her essay on the Argentinian dramatist Griselda Gambaro, Catherine Boyle reminds us that Gambaro's theatre is built on the need to make people see what death and pain really mean, not only in specific historical situations but existentially, at all times and in all places.

The rediscovery of a cultural legacy of Latin American women has coincided with an upsurge in powerful writing, a process that can be compared with the emergence of both a history and a new output of writing by Black women in the United States. As Patricia Murray points out in her essay on the Nicaraguan writers Giaconda Belli and Rosario Murillo, a key image for both is that of Eve, the new woman in a new revolutionary order. Unlike some feminists in the technologically advanced nations, many of whom have rejected the domestic and the maternal as icons of womanhood, Latin American feminism seems to start from within those boundaries and extend them outwards, creating new images and new parameters. Latin American feminism, as Maria Luisa Bemberg suggests in her interview with Nissa Torrents, is very different in its conception to that of many women in the First World because the problems facing women in the less-developed countries are of a different nature. The silent woman sitting in the room at the end of Clarice Lispector's famous story 'The Imitation of the Rose' is still a depressed, downtrodden housewife to the outward eye, but to herself and to her oppressive husband she is now the holder of a new, inner power, a power that derives from the psychic changes she has undergone in choosing not to choose something (the roses) for herself and realizing the enormity of what she has given up:

She was seated wearing her little housedress. He knew that she had done everything possible not to become luminous and remote. With fear and respect he watched her. Aged, tired, and strange. But he did not even have a word to offer. From the open door he saw his wife sitting upright on the couch, once more alert and tranquil as if on a train. A train that had already departed.[4]

The power of that mysterious inner world of woman's consciousness is a theme that runs through a great deal of work by Latin American women. 'Nobody knows me I speak the night', says Alejandra Pizarnik in one of her *Little Poems*, and in one of her *Fragments to Overcome Silence* she states simply, 'The strongest parts of language are lonely, desolate women, singing out through my voice which I hear in the distance.' The daughter of Russian emigrants, Pizarnik in her poetry takes up another thread that runs through Latin American women's writing – the theme of exile, of not-belonging, the theme that was so central to the poetry of Gabriela Mistral and which has led so many women to identify with minority groups and with the oppressed. Montserrat Ordoñez discusses Soledad Acosta de Samper's novel *Dolores: The story of a leper* as a metaphor for woman's impossible struggle for a better life as a healthy member of a healthy society, while Chloe Furnival shows how Rosario Castellanos's stories exposed the racism as well as the sexism that continued to thrive in post-revolutionary Mexico. For despite the advances gained by women in successive revolutions, fundamental assumptions about the subordinate role of the female still remain, and in her essay, 'Images of Women in the Post-revolutionary Cuban Narrative', Nissa Torrents shows how the colonized female image still persists in the work of male Cuban writers, despite the revolutionary programme to liberate Cuban women.

Luisa Valenzuela has suggested that Latin American women have begun to use a special form of language, which she describes as 'a fascination with the disgusting', adding that she has never noted this in the work of women writers in the United States:

> But South American writers, apparently, are writing this in search of knowledge. The body has to know the disgust, absorb it meaningfully, in order to say all its words. There can be no censorship through the mouth of a woman, so words can finally come out with all their strength, that same strength that has been obliterated from feminine speech ever since the notion of 'lady' was invented by men.[5]

The shock effect on readers created by writers like Marta Traba, Clarice Lispector, Silvina Ocampo, Beatriz Guido and dozens of others lies in their capacity to use this language and through it to emphasize the violence and horror of an imperfect world in which their characters are struggling for survival and for hope in something better. Emblematic of the horrible is Alejandra Pizarnik's Countess Bathory, the woman who murdered hundreds of young girls for the pleasure of watching them die:

> She was never afraid, she never trembled. And no compassion, no sympathy or admiration may be felt for her. Only a certain astonishment

at the enormity of the horror, a fascination with a white dress that turns red, with the idea of total laceration, with the imagination of a silence starred with cries in which everything reflects an unacceptable beauty. Like Sade in his writings, and Gilles de Rais in his crimes, the Countess Bathory reached beyond all limits the uttermost pit of unfettered passions. She is yet another proof that the absolute freedom of the human creature is horrible.[6]

It is not surprising to discover that a major influence on the work of many Latin American women writers has been Surrealism, and as the heritage of hidden work by women Surrealists in Europe begins to be discovered, so also does the surreal come to be seen as more significant than so-called magical realism for generations of women searching for their own language. The world of men, says Griselda Gambaro, in Catherine Boyle's essay, is marked by incomprehension, egoism and injustice, and yet this is the same world in which women also live. So rape, abortion, murder and torture keep reappearing in the work of many Latin American women writers, presented unsensationally and because of that all the more chilling and terrifyingly absurd. Here is Luisa Valenzuela describing the torture and murder of an innocent woman, snatched off the street by the henchmen of the mad tyrant Lopez Rega in her novel, *The Lizard's Tail*:

> She fainted at the climax. Let that serve as one more note of human cowardice. I was left with not only the finger but the ring too. As a keepsake, I let the boys have the damaged blonde – as a keepsake. They would know how to keep her in the shadows for as long as necessary. Until her finger grew back, maybe, or until it was erased from her memory.[7]

In *The House of the Spirits*, Isabel Allende does not shrink from describing the rape and torture of Alba, but nevertheless the novel ends on a note of hope, with Alba confronting the reality of her pregnancy as a positive act of life, despite the fact that the father of her unborn child may be her rapist. She has come to terms with the cycle of violence that relates her to him by blood, through her own grandfather's rape of a peasant woman on his estate half a century earlier. The need to recognize the historical roots of violence is an important step towards freedom.

'There must be a way... another way of being human and free', says Rosario Castellanos in her poem 'Meditation at the Threshold'. In her essay on women poets and the tradition, Myriam Diaz-Diocaretz looks at what she calls the 'matriheritage of the sociotext', the way in which we can read a shared continuity in texts by women from Sor Juana to the present, and it is striking to note how often writers, artists and film-makers from one period draw on the lives of women from a previous period for their inspiration, blending fictional reality with historical fact. The Angelina Beloff of Elena Poniatowska's novel, suggests Juan Bruce-Novoa, is a fusion of the real and the imagined, a combination of two women engaged in a dialogue of female solidarity.

That dialogue recurs in the work of Latin American women, from Sor Juana addressing herself to women from a mythical past to modernist poets. In a poem entitled 'It Could Well Be' from a collection published in 1919, Alfonsina Storni muses on her mother's oppression ('at times my mother was attacked by the whim of liberating herself') and her own newfound sense of freedom:

> And all of that, biting, conquered, mutilated,
> all that she found shut up in her heart –
> without wanting to, I think I've liberated it.[8]

Despite the history of pain and struggle, the life energy remains, handed on from one generation of women to the next. Marjorie Agosin draws our attention to the sensuality and eroticism of María Luisa Bombal's work, while Patricia Murray stresses the same qualities in the work of Giaconda Belli and Rosario Murillo. Giovanni Pontiero quotes Clarice Lispector comparing the activity of writing to the meaningfulness and meaninglessness of loving: 'No one knows why they love just as they do not know why they write.' Violence and sensuality, terror and feeling, the disgusting and the beautiful, knives and angels – these are the dichotomies explored in the works of the women represented here.

The essays collected in this book reflect another kind of passion, that of the writers for their subjects. Passion is an unfashionable and certainly an unacademic word in the field of literary criticism, but it exists for all that, as many feminist critics have recognized. The authors of the essays collected together in this book share a passion for Latin America and a commitment to their material that marks their writing. In some cases, that commitment derives from intense feelings of pride in a cultural heritage, sentiments clearly present in the work of Montserrat Ordoñez and Myriam Diaz-Diocaretz; in other cases it derives from the contact between one writer and another through the medium of translation, as has happened between Giovanni Pontiero and Clarice Lispector or between Susan Bassnett and Alejandra Pizarnik. Some of the writers have enjoyed personal friendships with the women they have chosen to discuss: John King describes how he worked for Victoria Ocampo for a time before her death, while Marjorie Agosin sought out and befriended the ageing María Luisa Bombal, two generations of Chilean writers in exile sharing their lives. Juan Bruce-Novoa, well known for his work on Chicano culture, has a particular fascination for the work of Elena Poniatowska, while Nissa Torrents has studied Cuban writing for many years and also shares with John King a passion for Argentine women's cinema. Further as a testimony to the way in which Latin American women's writing can reach out beyond geographical, cultural and gender boundaries, a younger generation of women is also represented in this book, through the enthusiastic contributions of Catherine Boyle, Chloe Furnival and Patricia Murray, whose commitment to their subject matter arises from a combination of direct contact with Latin America, postgraduate study and political activism.

Another group of writers, with other equally strong passions, would have created a different book, and we are all well aware of how many, how very many superb writers are not represented in these pages, from Claribel Alegria to Isabel Allende, from Luisa Valenzuela to Margo Glantz, from Nancy Morejon to Marta Traba, let alone all those women from previous ages. We console ourselves with the thought that perhaps the very scale of the omissions will lead to further books, to more translations, to new editions and re-publications of neglected material as other readers and writers discover and share their own passions. The days of mothers, sisters and daughters being relegated to the back of the house are finally over. Describing the lot of Chinese women with bound feet Claríbel Alegría says simply:

> It's not that they were useless
> it's that their husbands
> their fathers
> their brothers
> wanted them like that

Now the time for changes has come. She gives advice to women in another place, another age:

> Run along now and play
> don't carry sand for the others
> help your cousins
> to build the castle
> put towers on it
> and walls
> and terraces
> and knock it down
> and rebuild it
> and keeping on opening doors.[9]

The writing, painting, films by women pouring out of Latin America today, newly created on word processors or spilling out of cupboards and musty files, is part of that new process of opening doors. We, their readers, can share that exhilaration of discovery and affirmation.

## Notes

1. See Susan Bassnett, 'Coming Out of the Labyrinth: women writers in contemporary Latin America' in John King (ed.), *Modern Latin American Fiction: A survey*, London and Boston: Faber & Faber, 1987.

2. See Electa Arenal, 'This Life Within Me Won't Keep Still' (a dramatic two-hander comprising texts by Anne Bradstreet and Sor Juana Inez de la Cruz) in Bell Gale Chevigny and Gari Laguardia (eds.), *Reinventing the Americas: Comparative studies of literature of the United States and Spanish America*, Cambridge: Cambridge University Press, 1986.

3. Marjorie Agosin, 'Whispers and Triumphs: Latin American women writers today', *Women's Studies International Forum*, vol. 9, no. 4, 1986, pp. 427–33.

4. Clarice Lispector, 'The Imitation of the Rose', in *Family Ties* (translated from *Laços de família* by Giovanni Pontiero), Manchester: Carcanet, 1985.

5. Luisa Valenzuela, 'The Other Face of the Phallus', in Chevigny and Laguardia, *op. cit.*

6. Alejandra Pizarnik, 'The Bloody Countess', in Alberto Manguel (ed.), *Other Fires: Stories from the women of Latin America*, London: Picador, 1986.

7. Luisa Valenzuela, *The Lizard's Tail* (translated by Gregory Rabassa), London: Serpent's Tail, 1987.

8. Alfonsina Storni, *Selected Poems* (translated by Marion Freeman, Mary Crow, Jim Normington and Kay Short), Fredonia, NY: White Pine Press, 1987.

9. Claribel Alegría, *Luisa in Realityland* (translated by Darwin J. Flakoll), Willimantic, Conn.; Curbstone Press, 1987.

# 1. Victoria Ocampo (1890–1979): Precursor

## *John King*

Victoria Ocampo was the most influential and most notorious woman of letters and cultural patron certainly in twentieth-century Argentina, if not in the whole of Latin America. Her most important legacy was the literary periodical *Sur*, which she financed and edited full-time from 1931 to 1970 and irregularly up to her death in 1979. Her literary output was vast: she wrote a six-volume autobiography, ten volumes of *Testimonios*, a number of critical books on literary figures and translated many works of twentieth-century culture from several languages. Her friendships covered the globe: she travelled incessantly, part literary ambassador, part cultural bridge-builder, part cultural head-hunter. She had the advantages and disadvantages of wealth and an aristocratic background; the advantages and disadvantages of her sex. Her life and work extended the boundaries of what was possible and permitted for women in a closed male society. She constantly recorded herself, her reactions, her impressions and demanded that her readers and the wider society enter into a dialogue with her.

Her notoriety created a series of myths and simplifications around her;[1] she was subject to both demonology and hagiography and, after Eva Perón, was the most talked-about woman of her day. This brief chapter is an attempt to cut through the Manichean judgements and assess her contribution to her cultural milieu. It will take the form of a brief biography, her story within the histories that make up twentieth-century Argentina.

## The early years

The early years, from 1890 to 1929, are the subject of her autobiography which was begun in 1952 and was published, in six volumes, after her death. There are very few autobiographies of women writers in Argentina (Victoria Ocampo, Delfina Bunge, María Rosa Oliver, Norah Lange),[2] in a world of men who constantly wrote about themselves, their usefulness, their representative and exemplary lives.[3] It is interesting that Ocampo felt that she could, late in life, penetrate this male discourse of power. By 1952 she was a well-established public figure, her life was exemplary, and she was writing at a time when Peronism was threatening to undermine the liberal, aristocratic tradition which was her constant frame of reference. The need to reassert a tradition, the 'true' history of Argentina, is present throughout her autobiography.

Her first chapter locates the Ocampo family within this liberal aristocratic tradition – 'Argentine history was the history of our families, it is important to remember this'⁴ – the history of Argentina was synonymous with the development of a few families. She returns insistently to several central houses located in the heart of Buenos Aires (occupying the few blocks from the Plaza San Martín to the Calle Viamonte, in which everything, from political agreements to grand balls, took place: 'The event had taken place in our house, or in the house next door or in the house opposite: San Martín, Pueyrredón, Belgrano, Rosas, Urquiza, Sarmiento, Mitre, Roca, López. . . . All were relatives or friends.'⁵ For Ocampo, this organic sense of culture became lost as the city developed and university faculties, office blocks, ministries and large shops took over the buildings that had been the town houses of the élite.

For a time, however, life was tranquil and settled. The Ocampo girls – there were six in all – were brought up within this close-knit community. Their education, which took place at home and was organized by several governesses, stressed competence in foreign languages. Argentina could supply the immediate concrete needs of the group through the extraordinary wealth derived from the *pampa* region, but the life of the spirit could only be nurtured by contact with European, and in particular French, culture. Spanish was the language of barbarism: the Ocampos were taught French as a first language and Victoria did not feel confident writing in Spanish without the help of a translator until the 1930s, by which time she was forty years old. Her childhood education imposed a linguistic schizophrenia: 'The language of my childhood and adolescence – French – was my language; I could not free myself of it when I tried to write. The drama began there. In order to publish something in my country . . . I had to have my work translated and translations shocked and disgusted me.'⁶ The magazine *Sur* would later address itself to the problems and the advantages of a polyglot education, by making impeccable translation one of its main aims. Victoria had been taught languages as a form of feminine consumption. She would subvert this model by making languages productive.⁷ Families such as the Ocampos would often spend several months of the year in Europe, taking with them not just the entire household, but cows and chickens to provide food for the journey. In Paris they took over entire hotels, or rented apartments in the most fashionable areas: Passy, Neuilly and L'Etoile.⁸ María Rosa Oliver's memoirs recall her family having to change hotels in Paris, since the city was so full of Argentinians.⁹ It was there that she first met Victoria Ocampo, though they lived just across the road in Buenos Aires: she became a lifelong friend and a regular contributor to *Sur*.

Such childhood experiences reveal a fascination with Europe which would be central in the formation of Victoria Ocampo. Another significant aspect of her biography is that she was brought up as part of a large family of girls, in a society and a class that had rigid definitions of a woman's role in the home and in the family. Her early interest in the theatre was not pursued, for this was felt to be a profession unworthy of a lady: theatre in Buenos Aires was perceived as a popular, lower-class form of entertainment, to which immigrants flocked in large numbers. Ocampo's education was limited to languages and Argentinian history; it stressed the attributes and decorum necessary for a young lady to make a good wife. She became a prolific reader, but was aware that this could only be viewed by her family and acquaintances as a frivolous pastime. She wrote in her late teens to a close friend, Delfina Bunge, who would later marry the novelist Manuel Gálvez: 'Writer is a word that can only be defined in a pejorative fashion in our society.... If it is used to describe a woman, it means inevitably that she is a "bas-bleu" or a "poseuse".... By contrast, the word "estate-owner" has prestige. It means... "veau", "vache", "cochon", "couvée".'[10] She began to perceive how stifling were a number of the traditional attitudes of her class, but was trapped within those confines. Women were excluded from male institutions, be they political or cultural: the smoking-room and the club were the spaces in which power resided. *Sur* would later become her 'room'.

The only space for the woman writer was to be a poet: to express the self as the 'yo lírico' was permissible. Pedro Henríquez Ureña, a very sophisticated critic in many respects, could speak for a generation of male critics when he states, 'Perhaps it is worthwhile pointing out the fact that, with very few exceptions, women are absent from the abundant literary movement of the last two decades of the previous century; the movement was probably too impersonal for them.'[11] Victoria's first literary efforts were timid poems in French.

She married early, and disastrously, a scion of the upper classes, Monaco Estrada. It was an attempt to seek freedom from family constraints. The marriage lasted only a few months, though she was forced to live under its cloud for more than a decade, required to hide a longstanding love affair with Julián Martínez (a cousin of her husband) from family and friends in a society where divorce was forbidden. Volumes III and IV of her autobiography talk of this weight of social convention which shaped her existence in the 1910s and early 1920s, as she was caught between passion (in adultery) and the appearances that had to be maintained for her parents. She affirms that she found a way through these dilemmas caused by social control through writing. Interestingly her first published work, an article and a book, was on Dante's *Divine Comedy* ('Babel', *La Nación*, 1920, and *De Francesca a Beatriz*, 1924.) The book is a treble rupture, albeit tentative, with the literary mores of the time. First, she chose the form of the essay, a male preserve since it worked not with feelings but with ideas. Paul Groussac, director of the National Library, attempted to censure her, but she received the support of José Ortega y Gasset, her first intellectual mentor. Second, in her gloss on Dante, she talked fairly openly about her own predicament. How to move from the image of Francesca (Francesca da Rimini trapped, with her lover Paolo, in the second circle of Hell for the sin of sleeping with her husband's younger brother) to that of Beatriz (the pilgrim's guide to Paradise, who shines with holiness, great beauty and wisdom) without sacrificing 'amor pasión'? How to make the profane sacred? This autobiographical analysis, although implicit, was very daring for an aristocratic woman in her early thirties, seemingly happily married. Third, her essay transcended the parochial boundaries of Buenos Aires by being published in Madrid and introduced by José Ortega y Gasset. Here are the beginnings of Victoria's break with her class and with society's network of moral and social prejudices. Beatriz Sarlo correctly states, 'Possessed by her class, by nature and by desire, Victoria Ocampo, at the age of thirty, begins to change the terms of that possession. It is ... a story that takes its toll and her material wealth and traces of snobbery should not overshadow the true significance of her break.'[12]

The pilgrimage towards self-confidence and self-sufficiency in a man's world was punctuated by a series of love–hate relationships with certain male writers. In reality, she had little to do with the literary effervescence of the 1920s. Locked in her complex private life, she did not travel to Europe from the time of her marriage in 1912 until 1928 and therefore missed a most exciting period which other already mature literary patronesses, such as Nancy Cunard and Peggy Guggenheim, had lived to the full. She had also little contact with young Argentine writers (unlike Norah Lange, who became the 'child'-muse of the vanguard poets and later married the best of them, Oliverio Girondo), except for close friends such as Güiraldes. She gave recitals in French and several lectures at the cultural institution Amigos del Arte, but these were *au dessus de la mêlée* of the avant-garde in Buenos Aires, very different to the polemical tone and youthful euphoria of the young writers.

Her first contacts with literary life came not through the turmoil of little magazines, but through her role as hostess to leading foreign intellectuals. *Sur* would later reflect the same interest: the publishing house would extend hospitality similar to that offered by her houses in Palermo Chico, San Isidro and Mar del Plata. In 1924, she invited the Indian poet and mystic Tagore to stay in San Isidro, near her family home, when he fell ill during a lecture tour. Tagore would be the first of several lifelong enthusiasms for great men from the Indian sub-continent, including Gandhi and Nehru.[13] She gave up Catholicism at this time and became increasingly attracted to Eastern religions and philosophies.

Her guest list sometimes confused the truly famous with the charlatan, for she was a compulsive hero-worshipper, and this compulsiveness could blind her for a time to the true nature of a writer's intellectual or even physical inclinations. Such a misunderstanding occurred with Count Keyserling, the founder of the 'School of Wisdom' in Darmstadt, Germany, whom Ocampo had read in the famous Spanish journal, *Revista de Occidente*.[14] She immediately invited him to Argentina and corresponded enthusiastically for over a year, eventually visiting him in Germany. This enthusiasm was misinterpreted by the Count, who was extremely indignant and upset when he found himself physically rebuffed. He took this problem to the celebrated depth psychologist C. G. Jung, who interpreted Victoria's behaviour as that of an anima figure possessed by earth demons.[15] It is ironical indeed that Victoria Ocampo, that most cosmopolitan of women, should suffer on several occasions the indignity of being classified as an 'earth woman'. Ortega y Gasset, another important visitor, attempted a somewhat more subtle description, seeing Ocampo as the fusion of the body of America and the spirit of Europe. She became, in his letters, 'La Gioconda de la Pampa' (the Mona Lisa of the Pampa).[16] These and other remarks made the relationship between Ortega and Ocampo during the 1920s somewhat frosty.

While her encounters with Ortega, Keyserling and the Indian writer Tagore confirmed Victoria Ocampo's belief in the aristocracy of the spirit, and the necessary superiority of literature and art, they also made her aware of the advantages and disadvantages of her sex and marked a further stage in her own, albeit tentative, feminist revolt. Disadvantages, when used as an icon for telluric machismo; advantages, when as a beautiful rich woman in her later thirties, she could visit Paris and England in 1929 and come into contact with the cream of intellectual life. She became the lover of the decadent Pierre Drieu la Rochelle and through him met André Malraux and Aldous Huxley. She visited Adrienne Monnier in her bookshop in the rue de l'Odéon which was stocked with the latest trends in European thought. Thus when she returned from Europe in 1929 and met the North American writer Waldo Frank in Buenos Aires, she was perhaps 'ridding herself of the titans', in Jung's evocative phrase. It was Frank who would persuade her to launch a literary journal, and the time seemed right. She was now living openly on her own, not minding that the small-time machos in Buenos Aires would shout after her 'Machona' or 'Botafogo' (the legendary racehorse of the 1920s, the fastest filly in the world), as she drove her car through the streets, smoking cigarettes. She had emerged from earlier uncertainties to an awareness that she could mix with the great names of literature and art, on some basis of equality. In a literary world of near-starving artists, her wealth cast her naturally in the role of Maecenas, though she was often dismayed by the title, as the biographers of Drieu la Rochelle point out:

When Victoria Ocampo later read in the *Journal* that Drieu classified her among his female Maecenas . . . she became angry and cried. 'How', she wrote to Grover, 'can he talk of Maecenas, for God's sake? The gift was absolutely fraternal.'[17]

Later, however, in different circumstances, she did not hesitate to affirm her financial control of *Sur*: '*Sur* has belonged and still belongs to me materially. Spiritually, it has been shared with a group of writers.'[18] Her formation was in the language and literature of France, but she also had an ambivalent attitude towards her country of origin. Argentina was the patrimony of her family and a few others and she had the right to speak of its advantages and limitations. She was ready to take up the challenge of the South and it was in this optimistic frame of mind that she met the persuasive Waldo Frank. From this meeting, the idea of a literary periodical was voiced. In 1931, it became a reality.

## *Sur* and Company 1930–46[19]

*Sur* has been the most important literary periodical in Latin America in the twentieth century. Victoria sustained it by her wealth, by her European contacts (she saw it as a 'bridge' between cultures), and by her voluminous writings and considerable energy. José Bianco, the managing editor and guiding spirit of *Sur* for some twenty-five years, remarked, 'She was always thinking of different things. She organized lectures and debates, she celebrated the ten years of *Sur*, the fifteen, the twenty, the thirty years, numbers 50, 75, 100, 150. I said to her "Victoria, you really like figures". She carried on, unperturbed.'[20] Instead of offering a detailed analysis of the magazine, which can be found elsewhere,[21] I want to unravel a few strands of Ocampo's political and literary development in this period, which is reflected both inside and outside the pages of *Sur*.

   *Sur* and Ocampo always declared that they had no political motivation – the spirit was always more important than the transitory machinations of politics. Yet we have already analysed Ocampo's declaration of adherence to the tradition of aristocratic liberalism. This tradition was on the defensive in the face of nationalist and authoritarian regimes and Ocampo, for all her disinterested proclamations, demonstrated a firm commitment. Literature was a privileged area of experience and civilization was based on knowing 'how' to read. Those competent in reading literature were particularly qualified, it was felt, to turn their attention to history or politics and, if necessary, make valid statements.

   Victoria knew what to oppose. Despite her love affair with Drieu la Rochelle, who later became a fascist, and the strong fascination for Mussolini she felt on a lecture tour to Italy in 1934, (both incidents are used against her by her detractors), by the Spanish Civil War and the meeting of the PEN Club in Buenos Aires in 1936 she had declared herself a convinced anti-fascist. Her support of 'personalist' Catholic philosophers in *Sur* in the mid-1930s incurred the wrath of the traditional, reactionary Argentine church. Ocampo was a threat to stable moral codes in several respects: she lived openly as a separated woman, flaunting the sacred vows of matrimony; she opposed the 'sacred crusade' of France against the Republic; she published dangerously progressive Catholic ideas; she herself had given up Catholicism in favour of Eastern philosophies. Also, with the advent of World War Two, she was a fervent supporter of the Allied cause in a country that had many Nazi sympathizers (her friend Waldo Frank was badly beaten up by fascist thugs in Argentina in 1940 as a 'Jewish bolshevik'). She was one of the key intellectuals wooed by the Nelson Rockefeller's Coordinators Office as part of the United States's craze for Pan Americanism during the war. She was one of an increasingly large sector of the Argentine oligarchy that realized that the old links with the British Empire were not enough and that Argentina should have closer links with North American capital (this was the basis of the Pinedo Plan of 1940). In all this she was clear: it was the duty of the civilizing minority to maintain 'standards' in a world gripped by autarkic nationalism.

And yet at the same time, she had no clear political model to follow. She opposed the thuggery of the Infamous Decade implicitly, and campaigned actively for women's rights until she felt that the women's movement was being hijacked by left political groups. She actively opposed what she saw as fascism within, the advent of Peronism, yet could not adhere to any credible political alternative: liberalism could best be defended by claiming it to be above or beyond politics and reconstituting it in eternal terms and on a purely cultural level. Literature could demonstrate the superiority of art over life and set up an alternative tribunal against which events could be judged. Even in literature, however, an ideological filter worked: Marxists and fascists were excluded. There was little defence of her choices and her obsessions: standards were 'known' rather than defined. She often asserted that the virtues of literature were inaccessible to the masses; cultural standards could only be maintained by a few. Her *Testimonios* were a dialogue between friends, friends who knew how to read.

Yet it would be wrong to imply that Ocampo's writings were merely a display and a withholding of that cultural wealth which nobody should do without. Her friendships, her translations, her writings were in the public domain and had a wide influence. Let us take one example – her relationship with Virginia Woolf. If she can be said to have a literary model in the 1940s and 1950s, it was to be found in the works, and particularly in the example of Virginia Woolf. Personal contact played an important role: Ocampo met Woolf on several occasions, wrote her enthusiastic letters, tried in 1936 to persuade her to travel to Buenos Aires, and finally succeeded (much to the annoyance of Woolf) in capturing her image by commissioning the beautiful photographs by Gisèle Freund. For Ocampo, the whole Bloomsbury group was fascinating, and *Sur* could strive to maintain the same standards across the Atlantic. Both groups came, at least in part, from a narrow educated sector of the upper classes, who had wide and sustained contacts with that class as a whole. There were in both cases elements of contradiction between some of these educated people and the ideas and institutions of their class, especially with regard to the rights of women. And both responded to the general tensions of a period of social, cultural and intellectual crisis.[22]

Ocampo's relationship with Virginia Woolf was very one-sided. After they met at an exhibition of Man Ray's photographs in November 1934, Victoria sent Virginia a box of orchids as a visiting card. Several lavish presents followed, roses and a display case of butterflies, a reference to Woolf's literary conception of Latin America: 'Those immense blue grey lands with the wild cattle, the pampas grass and the butterflies.'[23] The presents pleased and embarrassed Woolf. She was attracted to wealth – 'She [Victoria Ocampo, whom she calls Baroness Okampo (sic) in a letter to Hugh Walpole] is a generous woman who sheds orchids as easily as buttercups'[24] – and was mildly glad that Victoria was interested in publishing her books in Spain, though she read no Spanish. 'The Lawrence has come – a magnificent looking book, though I can't read a word of it and I shall be proud to see *A Room* look like that.'[25] Woolf used Victoria, her amorousness and her wealth, to make Vita Sackville-West jealous. She wrote in a letter dated 19 December 1934: 'I am in love with Victoria Okampo [sic]', and again on 29 December: 'I have had to stop Victoria Okampo [sic] from sending me orchids. I opened the letter to say this, in the hope of annoying you.'[26] But this was a time when the Woolf–Sackville-West love affair was really at an end, and Woolf often wrote teasing or snubbing Sackville-West. Ocampo was not a close friend. Woolf described her thus to Sackville-West in January 1939:

> A woman, Victoria Okampo [sic], who is the Sybil [Colefax] of Buenos Aires, writes to say she wants to publish something by you in her Quarterly Review *Sur*. She is in Paris.... She's immensely rich, amorous; has been the mistress of Cocteau, Mussolini – Hitler for anything I know: came my way through Aldous Huxley; gave me a case of butterflies; and descends from time to time on me, with eyes like the roe of codfish phosphorescent: what's underneath I don't know.[27]

This cruel appraisal notwithstanding, Victoria recognized the importance of Woolf's writing for women in Latin America. Even though *A Room of One's Own* (1929) is a fairly light sarcastic text – taken from lectures she gave to a Cambridge undergraduate audience – it expresses Woolf's strong conviction that women writers were placed at a great disadvantage because of men. She developed these views in two further works *The Years* (1937), an account of a Victorian childhood, and *Three Guineas* (1938, published by *Sur* in 1941), an attack on war as a form of male posturing, and on militarism which glorified the male principle and prevented woman from receiving an adequate education. The men of Bloomsbury have always made light of the potential radicalism of Woolf's views. Nigel Nicholson states, 'She confined her argument to the daughters of educated men, who came from comfortable homes and she thought the working classes pitiable but uninteresting.'[28] Leonard Woolf called her the least political animal that lived since Aristotle invented the term. This view has been contested by feminist historians and literary critics who see her writing as an essential part of a specifically female literary tradition and her criticism as a necessary attack on male patriarchal values. This debate cannot be analysed here. What is important for our argument that Ocampo disseminated Woolf's work in Latin America at a very early date and thus helped to place on the agenda the problems of women in general (Argentine women still did not have the vote), and women writers in particular. Ocampo could thus use 'a publishing house of her own' to help combat some of the injustices revealed by Woolf's analyses. Also, on a purely literary level, Woolf was a consummate artist and Ocampo was lucky to find Borges as a translator for two of her works: *A Room of One's Own* and *Orlando*. She was an example of what a woman could achieve and, as such, Ocampo held her in awe.

*Sur* published *Un cuarto propio* [A Room of One's Own] over four months (*Sur*15–18, December 1935–March 1936). Victoria took to heart in *Sur* Woolf's declaration that, to write, a woman must have money and a room of her own. If Victoria could solve the economic problem, she would still have to fight with institutionalized masculine power, in cultural institutions as well as society at large. The pages of her magazine would therefore attempt to assess women writers and offer them a forum for discussion. Shortly after *A Room of One's Own*, the Sur publishing house brought out *Orlando*. This was followed in 1938 by *To the Lighthouse* (1927), an extract of which appeared in the magazine in April 1939. Latin American women writers closely associated with Ocampo's enterprise in the 1930s and 1940s were the Chileans Gabriela Mistral and María Luisa Bombal, and Victoria's sister Silvina.

If Virginia Woolf could be seen as the ideal European woman writer, Gabriela Mistral was her South American equivalent. In her speech accepting entry to the Argentine Academy of Letters in 1977, Victoria Ocampo talks of her friendship with both writers. Gabriela Mistral spent time at Villa Ocampo:

> In 1938, she lived in my house throughout her stay in Argentina and after a few days she wrote to me (we used to write to each other from our rooms): 'You have done me a lot of good: I needed to know, to *know* (she repeats) that a completely white person can be a genuine American.' ... And afterwards she added 'I have been enormously surprised to find you just as criollo as I am.'[29]

It seemed at first an unlikely friendship: Gabriela Mistral was half Indian, half Basque and was brought up in rural Chile, in the valley of Elqui. She began as a rural teacher, and later – like so many other Latin American writers – became a diplomat. Her poems deal with the problems of the Indian, the landscape of Latin America, the joys of childhood, and talk of a mystic communion between God, men and nature. Victoria Ocampo synthesized for her the best of Latin America:

> I love you . . .
> Because you resemble the forms of nature
> The abundant maize of America. . . .[30]

Such judgements helped to justify Victoria's assertion that to be Argentinian was to be a blend of Europe and Latin America, a view shared by many. Perhaps nobody apart from Victoria, however, would have attempted to link Proust with the Mapuche Indians: 'Gabriela, the "aubépines" inhaled by Proust . . . are neighbours of your almond trees. There is not such a great distance believe me, between Combray and your Valley of Elqui. My heart has measured the distance.'[31] Mistral published several poems and articles in *Sur* and the Sur publishing house brought out her book of poems *Tala* in 1938.

The most frequently published woman creative writer in the early volumes of *Sur* is Silvina Ocampo. The two sisters could not have been more dissimilar, as Silvina desired neither the public personality nor the high profile of Victoria. It was Silvina's friendship with Borges and her marriage to Adolfo Bioy Casares that helped to forge a most interesting and eccentric *cénacle* which revolutionized Argentinian letters in the late 1930s and early 1940s. They always remained outside the main orbit of *Sur*, laughing at many of its pretensions, especially Victoria's cultivation of the great names of contemporary letters, but they did publish their major work in *Sur* and thus benefited from Victoria's dynamism. There is no space to analyse the *oeuvre* of Silvina Ocampo, perhaps the most underrated of all Argentinian writers, whose mature work can stand comparison with that of Borges, but it is no exaggeration to state that from the 1930s, the Ocampo sisters, in their different ways, opened up new spaces in the cultural field for women writers, which would greatly benefit subsequent generations.

## From Perón to Perón, 1946–1976

Perón emerged as Argentina's political leader in 1946, despite the best but rather paltry efforts of the opposition parties who held a pre-election rally on 12 October 1945, a rally which included Victoria Ocampo. Her presence was immortalized in the doggerel of the Brazilian poet Augusto Federico Schmidt:

> I saw you, people of Buenos Aires
> I saw Victoria Ocampo, splendid in time,

Mingling with the masses
[...]
I heard the song of the people
Born in the heart of the people
Clamouring for freedom.[32]

But it was during the mass Peronist rally of 17 October (celebrated in Peronist iconography) that the real *voz del pueblo* was heard, sweeping Perón to an election victory a few months later. Within Argentina, the ten-year period of the first two Peronist presidencies can be seen as a deliberate assault on the aristocratic and liberal values which were embodied in Ocampo's life and work. Peronism claimed for itself a new synthesis of democracy, rationalism, anti-imperialism and industrial development, and railed against the undemocratic, dependent Argentine oligarchy. Whilst Perón's aggression remained at the level of rhetoric – he stopped short of class confrontation – his use of symbolism and mythology was deliberately populist. The image of Evita, the studiously cultivated resemblance of Perón to the great tango singer Carlos Gardel, the *descamisado*, the *cabecita negra* and the rhetorical manipulation of Perón's speeches and his use of radio and the press, all of these made up a new style which was anathema to Ocampo.

Ocampo has become inscribed in the hagiography of anti-Peronism both as a saintly victim of the regime and as a true feminist, as compared to Eva Perón. The comparison is revealing. Ocampo made almost no reference to Evita, living or dead. There was no obituary in *Sur* following her death in 1952, only a small black border line placed on the cover of issue numbers 213–14 (July–August 1952), to comply with the government decree on national mourning. For all her interest in the rights of women, Ocampo could not recognize or debate with the woman who gave women the vote and held such an extraordinary power in the country as a political figure and as a symbol. In a brief reference in Volume VIII of *Testimonios*, 'El derecho de ser hombre', Ocampo denies that Evita was interested in women's rights:

Read the dismissive declarations that appear in *La razón de mi vida* ... I quote this book because its badly informed author had such an extraordinary power in our country. But of course she was not interested in the battle for the rights of women.... The vote for women was important to her, mainly as an instrument for the leader of her political party.[33]

She repeated these sentiments in an article called, significantly, 'La trastienda de la historia' [The Back-room of History], published in a special issue of *Sur* on women (1971), the first issue after *Sur* had ceased regular publication. Here Evita is attacked for her lack of recognition for suffragettes and for delivering the women's vote to Perón, rather than fighting for the defence of women in general.[34]

All these observations were published many years after Evita's death. In the late 1940s and early 1950s, Ocampo's attacks were more indirect but quite clear: civilization had to be defended in the face of the chaotic, primitive and stupid forces unleased by mass Peronism. One of the great problems of these years was that liberal groups, even of the left, could not see beyond this vision of Peronism. Even though Ocampo waged a constant campaign against Perón, it was hardly the stuff of which martyrs are made. But she was one of perhaps a thousand people taken in for questioning in April 1953, during troubled weeks that saw a bomb attack on Perón and violent reprisals during which the Jockey Club was looted and burned down and the offices of the Socialist and Conservative parties were wrecked. Both Victoria Ocampo and the Jockey Club were symbols of the oligarchy and she was arrested at her house in Mar del Plata. Unlike many other prisoners, however, she had the range of contacts to become a *cause célèbre* and her friends throughout the world organized protests. Ironically, the most persuasive and influential plea came from Gabriela Mistral, a voice of America, rather than one of *Sur*'s foreign friends, and Perón found in her appeal an excuse for freeing Ocampo, whose meddling in politics had never stretched to bomb conspiracies. She would later write movingly on her prison experiences.

When Perón was ousted in a military coup in 1955, Ocampo brought out a special issue of *Sur*, entitled *For National Reconstruction*, which included her prison memoir. The feeling of relief was great, summed up in Borges's lapidary terms: Peronism was literally bad art, a substandard music-hall act. 'There were therefore two stories: one of a criminal nature, made up of prisons, torture, prostitution, robbery, death and fires; the other, more theatrical, made up of stupid actions and stories for the consumption of louts.'[35]

Ocampo was not in the vanguard of the process of 'reconstruction', of modernization which took place in Argentina in the 1960s and early 1970s, and which her magazine and her life had helped to create. Her organic sense of culture, which was formed in the 1920s and 1930s, found it difficult to adjust to the new conditions of Latin American literary modernism, the enlarged marketplace, the importance of the Cuban revolution, the boom in culture.[36] Her world had been based on an intimacy among élites. In the 1960s, as these friends were dying and new forces – the 'swinging' 1960s or the radicalization of Peronism – were wresting hegemony from the world she knew and increasingly attacking her in crude analyses of cultural dependency, she became defensive and perplexed: how could Julio Cortázar, a writer she had promoted in the 1940s, become a best-seller?

At the same time, a strange fact, the common people are buying works by Cortázar (by Cortázar!) and read him on the underground or on the bus. However Cortázar is clearly an author for minorities, not for readers who must become fabulously bored . . . because they do not have the necessary preparation to digest and savour him. Let no one take offence. When faced with machines (let's say the car that I drive), I am also totally at a loss.[37]

By the late 1960s, working-class unrest fused with student radicalism in a series of revolts in Argentina (the most important of which took place in Córdoba in May 1969) and eventually brought the military government down. The anti-government alliance was aided indirectly by the spectacular successes of the Peronist and Marxist guerrilla groups which sprang up and began a series of raids on military targets and banks. Guerrilla violence, nationalist, radicalized middle-class sectors, a combative trade-union movement, the likely return of Perón: all these elements struck at the heart of Ocampo and her magazine and caused her finally to give up her unequal struggle against the tide of time. She closed *Sur* in 1970, because 'The diffusion of culture does not seem to me to be the path chosen by the majority of the turbulent young people of today.'[38] When she wrote these words, she was eighty years old.

The events of the 1970s, the return of Perón, the interregnum of Isabelita, the near civil war of the 1970s, the military coup of 1976, were even more bewildering and tragic. She became very ill in later years and was perhaps thus spared the worst of the reports of atrocity, which had Borges emerging in tears from the trials of military dictators in the mid-1980s declaring that the reality of violence had been much worse than he could ever have imagined.

She was elected to the Argentine Academy in 1977, the first woman to receive this recognition. It proved the occasion of a typically pugnacious speech. Even in her mid- to late eighties, while her health was good she remained extraordinarily active. I was working in her offices: she always arrived many hours before me, grilled me on my previous day's work, organized my life, rang me and kept up a flow of anecdotes in several languages, from which she switched without noticing – French to her secretary, English to me and Spanish on the telephone, without pausing for breath. She had an overwhelming personality.

## By way of conclusion

In his visit to Argentina in 1929, Waldo Frank described the interior of Victoria Ocampo's house, a description that can be extended to her life's work from a 'room of her own'.

In this conglomerate of borrowed fineries... stands a simple house – back to back with the rhetorical Embassy of Spain.... The walls of this house are white lime over brick... at the foot of the stairs is a cactus in a mirrored box.... The owner of this house is a daughter of the conquistadores named Victoria Ocampo. 'What did I want to do', she says, 'I wanted to make the sky and the trees come into my rooms. They do come in. I wanted space ... emptiness ... walls naked white; a background so neutral and clear that the colored cover of a book, a yellow hat on a table, a flower in a vase, a spot of blue sky reflected in the mirror, should be a sudden holiday for the eyes ...' One may go deeper. Doña Victoria has borrowed lavishly from Europe. The rugs are by a Frenchman and a Spaniard of the day; the tables are English; the vast globe in the hall is Renaissance; the architectural lines owe much to schools of Germany and France. But all these details have been transfigured and composed by an Argentinian – an American will ... Victoria Ocampo ... in her cult of light, in her work of structure within the chaos of the pampa nation, has learned that she must clasp the bitter cactus in her hand, clasp it against her breast. She has prophesied for her country.[39]

Ocampo perceived her role as that of spokesperson of a civilizing minority in the literary and ideological 'chaos of the *pampa*', attempting to maintain standards of literary decorum throughout troubled periods such as World War Two, Peronism and the growth of alternative cultural activity. As a reflection of Argentinian culture, 'a cactus in a mirrored box', she offered the fragmented, selective reflection of her origins, but she also changed this culture as a proto-feminist, writer and editor. Her practice involved an opening to the world, in an attempt to break away from cultural provincialism, and from the moralism and restrictions of her class. ('I wanted space ... emptiness'). This entailed bringing many writers from Europe and 'arranging' them with her Argentine friends. The arrangement provoked a bitter controversy. Critics have seen her strategy as that of whitewashing Argentine culture so that the objects of value – European – could be shown to better effect ('walls naked white', a 'neutral background'). For Waldo Frank and many others, including this writer, the organization proved harmonious, not just a copy of foreign styles, but a real process of transformation. She can rightly be said to have 'prophesied for her country'.

## Notes

1. For a balanced, if slightly hagiographic account of her life, see Doris Meyer, *Victoria Ocampo: Against the wind and the tide*, New York: George Braziller, 1979. For a caustic, populist attack, see Blas Matamoro's two works, *Oligarquía y literatura*, Buenos Aires: Sol, 1986.

2. The following paragraph is based on the research of Sylvia Molloy. See Molloy, 'Dos proyectos de vida: Norah Lange y Victoria Ocampo', *Filología* vol. XX, no. 2, 1985, pp. 279–93.

3. Adolfo Prieto, *La literatura autobiográfica argentina*, Buenos Aires: Jorge Alvarez, 1966.

4. V. Ocampo, *Testimonios* vol. V, Buenos Aires: Sur, 1957, p. 28.

5. V. Ocampo, *Autobiografía* vol. 1: *El archipiélago*, Buenos Aires: Sur, 1979. p. 10.

6. V. Ocampo, *Testimonios* vol. V, p. 20.

7. Beatriz Sarlo, *Una modernidad periférica Buenos Aires 1920 y 1930*, Buenos Aires: Nueva Vision, 1988.

8. V. Ocampo, *Autobiografía* vol. II: *El imperio insular*, Buenos Aires: Sur, 1980, pp. 65–75.

9. María Rosa Oliver, *Mundo mi casa*, Buenos Aires, 1965.

10. V. Ocampo, *Autobiografía* vol. II, p. 104.

11. Pedro Henríquez Ureña, *Las corrientes literarias en la América hispánica*, Mexico: Fondo de Cultura Económica, 1964, p. 183. Quoted in Molloy, p. 93.

12. Sarlo, p. 93.

13. In her recent fascinating study of Ocampo and Tagore, Dr Ketaki Dyson argues convincingly the deep mutual respect between the two personalities. Victoria would become Tagore's muse for the rest of his life. See Ketaki Kushari Dyson, *In Your Blossoming Flower-Garden: Rabindranath Tagore and Victoria Ocampo*, New Delhi: Safutya Akademi, 1988.

14. Ocampo's account of their relationship is to be found in Victoria Ocampo, *El viajero y una de sus sombras*, Buenos Aires: Sur, 1982. In *Figuras simbólicas, Medida de Francia*, Buenos Aires: Sur, 1983, she recounts her meetings with remarkable men in this period.

15. Jung's interpretation reads as follows: 'Your excellent description of the fateful intermezzo with X [Ocampo] clearly shows that it is an encounter with an "earth woman" fraught with meaning. Concealed and revealed in it is one of the most beautiful animus-anima stories I have ever heard ... X's longing for identification refers to the animus which she should like to possess in you, but she mixes it up with you personally and then of course is deeply disappointed. This disappointment will be repeated always and everywhere, until man has learned to distinguish his soul from the other person. Then his soul can return to him. This lesson is a hellish torture for you both, but extremely useful, *the* experience one would have wished for you, and assuredly the most important torture of all for X, who is still possessed by her earth demons. Perhaps she prefers to be torn to pieces by the titans, as happens in many such anima figures' (C. J. Jung, *Letters I*, Princeton: Princeton University Press 1973), pp. 72–3.

16. V. Ocampo, *Autobiografía* vol. III: *La rama de Salzburgo*, Buenos Aires: Sur, 1981, p. 115.

17. Pierre Andreu and Frédéric Grover, *Drieu la Rochelle*, Paris: Hachette, 1979, p. 220.

18. Victoria Ocampo, 'Despues de cuarenta años', *Sur* 325, July–August 1970, pp. 1–5, here p. 1.

19. *Sur y Cía* [*Sur* and Company] is the final volume of Ocampo's autobiography, Buenos Aires: Sur, 1984.

20. José Bianco, 'Victoria', *Vuelta* 53, April 1981, pp. 4–6, here p. 6.

21. J. King, *Sur: An analysis of the Argentine literary journal and its role in the development of a culture, 1931–1970*, Cambridge: Cambridge University Press, 1986.

22. Raymond Williams, 'The Bloomsbury Fraction', *Problems in Materialism and Culture*, London: Verso, 1980, p. 162.

23. Virginia Woolf, *The Sickle Side of the Moon: The letters of Virginia Woolf 1932–1935*, Nigel Nicholson (ed.), London: Hogarth Press, 1979, p. 439.

24. *ibid.*, p. 350.

25. *ibid.*, p. 358.

26. *ibid.*, pp. 355 and 359.

27. Virginia Woolf, *Leave the Letters Till We're Dead: The letters of Virginia Woolf 1936–1941*, Nigel Nicholson, (ed.), London: Hogarth Press, 1980, p. 310.

28. Introduction to Woolf, *The Sickle Side*, pp. xv and xviii.

29. V. Ocampo, 'La mujer en la academia', *La Prensa*, 17 July 1977, cultural supplement, p. 1.

30. Gabriela Mistral, 'Recado a Victoria Ocampo en la Argentina', *Sur* 43, April 1938, p. 32.

31. V. Ocampo, 'Gabriela Mistral en mi recuerdo', *Testimonios* vol. III, Buenos Aires: Sur, 1946, p. 181.

32. A. F. Schmidt, '12 de octubre de 1945', *Sur*, 137, March 1946, pp. 74 and 78.

33. V. Ocampo, 'El derecho de ser hombre', *Testimonios* vol. VIII, Buenos Aires: Sur, 1971, p. 190.

34. V. Ocampo, 'La trastienda de la historia', *Sur*, 326–8, January–June 1971, pp. 11 and 17.

35. Jorge Luis Borges, 'L'illusion comique', *Sur*, 237, November–December 1955, p. 9

36. See J. King, *El Di Tella y la cultura argentina en la década del sesenta*, Buenos Aires: Editorial de Arte Gaglianone, 1985.

37. V. Ocampo, 'Despues de cuarenta años', *Sur*, 325, July–August 1970, p. 1.

38. *ibid.*, p. 5.

39. Waldo Frank, *South of Us*, 3rd edn, New York: Garden City Publishing Co. Inc. 1940, pp. 126–7.

# Works by Victoria Ocampo

## Autobiography, criticism and articles

*De Francesca a Beatrice* (postscript by Ortega y Gasset). Madrid: Revista de Occidente, 1924; es: Sur, 1963.

*La laguna de los nenúfares* (scenic fable). Madrid: Revista de Occidente, 1926.

*Testimonios* vol. I. Madrid: Revista de Occidente, 1935.

*Domingos en Hyde Park*. Buenos Aires: Sur, 1936.

*Testimonios* vol. II. Buenos Aires: Sur, 1941.

*San Isidro* (with a poem by Silvina Ocampo and 68 photographs by Gustav Torlichent). Buenos Aires: Sur, 1941.

*338.171.T.E.* Buenos Aires: Sur, 1942 (reprinted 1963).

*Testimonios* vol. III. Buenos Aires: Sudamericana, 1946.

*Soledad sonora* (*Testimonios* vol. IV). Buenos Aires: Sudamericana, 1950.

*El viajero y una de sus sombras* (*Keyserling in mis memorias*). Buenos Aires: Sudamericana, 1951.

*Lawrence de Arabia y otros ensayos*. Madrid: Aguilar, 1951.

*Virginia Woolf en su diario*. Buenos Aires: Sur, 1954.

*Testimonios* vol. V (1950–7). Buenos Aires: Sur, 1957.

*Habla el algarrobo* (*Luz y sonido*). Buenos Aires: Sur, 1960.

*Libro de cumpleaños* (*R. Tagore*). Edited and translated for *Sur*, Buenos Aires, 1961.

*Tagore en las barrancas de San Isidro*. Buenos Aires: Sur, 1961.

*Testimonios* vol. VI (1957–62). Buenos Aires: Sur, 1962.

*Juan Sebastian Bach: el hombre*. *Sur*, August 1964.

*La bella y sus enamorados*. *Sur*, September 1964.

*Testimonios* vol. VII (1962–7). Buenos Aires: Sur, 1967.

*Diálogo con Borges*. Buenos Aires: Sur, 1969.

*Diálogo con Mallea*. Buenos Aires: Sur, 1969.

*Testimonios* vol. VIII (1968–70). Buenos Aires: Sur, 1971.

*Roger Caillois y la cruz del Sur en la Academia Francesa*. Buenos Aires: Sur, 1972.

*Testimonios* vol. IX (1971–4). Buenos Aires: Sur, 1975

*Testimonios* vol. X (1975–7). Buenos Aires: Sur, 1977, 2nd edn 1978.

*Autobiografía* vol. I. *El archipiélago*. Buenos Aires: Sur, 1979.

*Autobiografía* vol. II. *El imperio insular*. Buenos Aires: Sur, 1980.

*Autobiografía* vol. III. *La rama de Salzburgo*. Buenos Aires: Sur, 1981.

*Autobiografía* vol. IV. *Viraje*. Buenos Aires: Sur, 1982.

*Autobiografía* vol. V. *Figuras simbólicas. Medida de Francia*, Buenos Aires: Sur, 1983.
*Autobiografía* vol. VI. *Sur y Cía.* Buenos Aires: Sur, 1984.

## Translations

Albert Camus, *Calígula.* Buenos Aires: *Sur*, March–April 1946.
Colette and Anita Loos, *Gigi.* Buenos Aires: Sur, 1946.
Dostoevsky, Camus, *Los poseídos.* Buenos Aires: Losada, 1960.
William Faulkner, Albert Camus, *Réquiem para una reclusa.* Buenos Aires: Sur, 1957.
Graham Greene, *El cuarto en que se vive.* Buenos Aires: Sur, 1953.
Graham Greene, *El que pierde gana.* Buenos Aires: Sur, 1957.
Graham Greene, *La casilla de las macetas.* Buenos Aires: Sur, 1957.
Graham Greene, *El amante complaciente.* Buenos Aires: Sur, 1959.
Lanza del Vasto, *Vinoba* (in collaboration with Enrique Pezzoni). Buenos Aires: Sur, 1955.
T. E. Lawrence, *El troquel*, Buenos Aires: Sur, 1955.
Dylan Thomas, *Bajo el bosque de leche* (in collaboration with Félix della Paolera). Buenos Aires: Sur, 1959.
Graham Greene, *Tallando una estatua.* Buenos Aires: Sur, 1965.
Jawaharlal Nehru, *Antología* (edited with a preface by Victoria Ocampo). Buenos Aires: Sur, 1966.
John Osborne, *Recordando con ira.* Buenos Aires: Sur, 1958.
Mahatma Gandhi, *Mi vida es mi mensaje.* Buenos Aires: Sur, 1970.
Graham Greene, *La vuelta de A. J. Raffles.* Buenos Aires: Sur, 1976.

## 2. María Luisa Bombal: Biography of a story-telling woman
### *Marjorie Agosin*

In order to enter into the cosmogony and magic of the stories of María Luisa Bombal, one has to explore the city of her birth, Viña del Mar, on the Chilean coast. Viña del Mar is a city of water. During the peaceful winters a constant, faint drizzle hangs along the seashore; in the autumns each dawn comes laden with determined dew. The constant fog is a sure sign that we are approaching Viña del Mar; it appears over and over again in the writings of María Luisa Bombal: 'The fog presses closer and closer against the house each day. Already it has made the araucarias disappear whose limbs drummed against the balustrade of the terrace. Last night I dreamed that it invaded the house, slowly seeping through the cracks around doors and windows, causing the colour of the walls to vanish.'[1]

A pure geography, crafted in words with the skill of a sculptor, an ambience that calls to mind Gothic heroines of English novels or fairy tales by Nordic writers: these elements form part of the essence of María Luisa Bombal. She was a writer both visible and invisible, one who burst upon the literary scene during the effervescent epoch of a Buenos Aires dominated by the personalities of Victoria Ocampo and Jorge Luis Borges, yet at the same time a writer who remained submerged in the nebulous mist of her own being.

María Luisa Bombal was born in the city of Viña del Mar on 8 June 1909. In her memoirs she writes, 'Even with my eyes blindfolded, even if someone took me around the world and tried to make me lose myself in some by-way, even with my eyes blindfolded, all I would have to do is to take a deep breath, just once, to know that I was in Viña del Mar.'[2]

She was born in Montaña Street, a steep avenue that still exists today. From the highest part one can see the distant hills of Valparaíso, as well as the wide sea that she describes in such familiar terms: 'I know a lot of things that no one else knows. I know an infinity of small, magical secrets about

*Translated from the Spanish by Cola Franzen

the sea, the earth and the sky. This time though I will tell only about the sea. In the waters below, far below the deep, dense zone of darkness, the ocean again becomes luminous.'[3]

She grew up in the company of her twin sisters Blanca and Loreto. Their mother read them Andersen's fairy tales, full of princes and princesses. These characters were to play a very significant role in Bombal's novels; the women she imagined in her books were always searching for Prince Charming, like the anonymous woman in *La última niebla* (The Last Fog), sunk in a dream world, absorbed in the memory of a single night of love:

> Patiently, without despairing, I still await his coming. After supper I go down to the garden and furtively open one of the Venetian blinds of the living room. I open it just a crack. Night after night, if he so wishes, he would be able to see me sitting next to the fire or reading in the circle of the lamplight. He could follow every one of my movements and enter at will into my inmost life. From him I have no secrets.[4]

In 1922 María Luisa went to live in Paris where she stayed until 1931. In those years she wrote in French but she always, she said, kept a strong link with her native Spanish. It is easy to imagine María Luisa wandering through the streets of Montmartre, attending classes in dramatic art with Charles Dullan and finishing her studies at the Sorbonne with a thesis on Prosper Merimée. No wonder that when she returned in Chile in 1933 Neruda called her affectionately 'Madame Merimée'.[5]

María Luisa came back to Chile wearing elegant clothes and large stylish hats; she was an immediate success in the Bohemian circles of the capital. One of her childhood friends described her thus: 'María Luisa now has the brilliance that comes from a combination of intelligence, culture, humour, and few years.'[6] Another writer of the time told the following story about María Luisa and her arrival in Chile:

> I had recently arrived in Santiago from Imperial. I found myself with Pablo (Neruda) in a café in Bandera Street, a café that was clean, formal, bourgeois, different from the ones we usually frequented. Pablo said to me, I'm waiting for a girl. Kiss her hand because I've told her that you are a very traditional gentleman. María Luisa arrived alone: an elegant and gracious princess, above all, gracious.[7]

This grace and sparkle made her one of the most popular figures of the Chilean literary scene. More important, she was part of Neruda's intimate circle: he was one of the few who perceived that behind the constant laughter was a serious writer, the creator of tragic stories and lonely women. As she wrote:

> Why is the nature of women such that there always has to be a man to form the axis of their life? Men manage to put their passion into other

things. But the destiny of women is to keep stirring up the sorrow of love in an orderly house, before an unfinished tapestry.[8]

The life of María Luisa unwinds like the tangled threads of an uncompleted tapestry. She worked as an actress in the theatre, went out with Pablo Neruda and Marta Brunet; nevertheless a strange sadness was always with her. She was unhappy in love and her passion for the aviator Eulogio Sánchez was not returned. María Luisa Bombal finally left Chile in 1935 and from that time on she was a perpetual exile. She travelled through the United States and Europe for decades, only to return to die in the city of fog and sea, to Viña del Mar.

She stayed in Buenos Aires from about 1933 to 1941, a period in her life that was very important to her for various reasons. She became part of the group around *Sur*, and formed close relationships with Norah Lange, Alfonsina Storni and Victoria Ocampo. 'Georgie', as she called Jorge Luis Borges, was a great friend. In Borges's austere bedroom, next to the head of his bed, was a photograph of María Luisa.

In Buenos Aires she wrote her first great novel, *La última niebla*, published in 1935. She wrote it in the kitchen of the flat of Pablo Neruda and his Dutch wife, Maria de Haagenar. María Luisa was living with them and said she wrote in the kitchen because 'it was a pretty room with white walls and plenty of light'.[9]

The story begun in her first novel was elaborated and re-elaborated, over and over again, in the pages of her next novel, *La amortajada* [The Enshrouded Woman], published in 1941, and then in her famous short story, 'El árbol' [The Tree].[10] These brief, intense narratives all describe the alienated and anxious existence of a woman whose sole passion is to find a way to live completely and fully. Bombal's two novels highlight the ruptures existing in a world filled with repetitious rituals. Here are a few lines from *La última niebla*: '"Why did we get married?" "Just to get married," was the response.'[11]

*La última niebla* caused a lot of excitement in literary circles in Buenos Aires and Santiago. This novel, so pared down and so intense, never loses its emotional intensity. Its hundred pages are kept focused on one single memory, one single obsession – one night of love with a stranger.

Bombal's success continued with *La amortajada*. Here she began to experiment with one of the most contemporary ways of writing, three years before Borges published *Ficciones*. I refer to the interweaving of reality and fantasy that has come to be called magical realism. *La amortajada* is spoken by a dead woman, who reminisces about her life from infancy to death, and describes her death, wake, funeral and burial. (It is interesting to note that *Pedro Páramo*, the brilliant experimental novel by the Mexican writer Juan Rulfo that prefigured the great boom in American prose writings, was not published until 1955.)

Like her first novel, *La amortajada* is a poetic soliloquy spoken by a woman who yearns for love. In fact, the dream of a Prince Charming like those in the fairy tales of Andersen and Hensen pursued María Luisa Bombal always, in both her writings and her personal life. Both the life and the writings were tapestries where reality and fiction were interwoven.

The search for ideal love was the leitmotif of a large part of Bombal's literary production. In her personal life her attempts to find love always ended in failure, like her passion for Eulogio Sánchez, the young Chilean industrialist and aviator she met after she returned to Chile in the 1930s. Her marriage to the Argentinian painter Jorge Larcos was also a failure. She herself said, 'I never had the knack of love. That is a fact. Every time I fell in love I lost a friendship and replaced it with a tragedy.'[12]

The tragedy continued when María Luisa Bombal, back in Santiago after her stay in Buenos Aires, shot Eulogio Sánchez on a city-centre street, leaving him gravely wounded. Sánchez did not press charges against her, and because of this, and the efforts of Argentinian and Chilean writers, she was released by the Chilean authorities after a few months and left Santiago for New York. She arrived there in 1941 and she worked at various jobs. She wrote film scripts, worked as a translator, drank a lot and wrote very little. In 1944 she married the French count, Phalle de St Phalle, in a ceremony in Stamford, Connecticut. She continued to live in New York until 1973, when her husband died.

In New York María Luisa Bombal lived the life of a permanent exile. Although she was acquainted with writers such as Sherwood Anderson and painters such as the Chilean Nemesio Antúñez, she was lonely, and remained in a state of permanent sadness. She said to me many times, 'I find life so very hard.' The stay in North America was an extremely dark period for her, and she became more and more reclusive and anxious. Her own description of Ana María in *La amortajada* comes to mind: 'She spent years withdrawing and becoming more limited and more wretched day by day.'[13]

Her attitude of indifference, of giving in to the delirium of drink became a major problem, and after her last *nouvelle*, *La historia de María Griselda* (1946), which might be considered a continuation of *La amortajada*, she wrote no more. Her friends in New York said they remembered her in those non-writing days, standing a little bent, her gaze downcast.[14] She said to me many times, 'I only write when I have something to say.' There is prophecy in her words in *La última niebla*: 'The suicide of an old woman, how repugnant and useless!'[15] These words, from her first novel, decribe with amazing intuition a desolation like that of her own life in later years. The life story of this invisible writer is fascinating for all those interested in the connections between literary biography and theories of reception.

This silence of so many years might seem surprising, but we note that her life story is similar to that of many women writers, particularly that of Jean Rhys, whom Bombal resembles in her life as well as in her work. During the 1930s and 1940s both were creating feminine characters who were helpless, lost in old hotel rooms, desperately looking for love. And in their personal lives there are many parallels. Both emigrated from the countries of their birth; both spent time in Paris and then disappeared into the most complete oblivion until they were rediscovered in their seventies. At the age of 76, Rhys published *Wide Sargasso Sea* and public interest in her work was reawakened, with the result that her earlier books began to be reissued. Something similar happened with María Luisa. Both women were premature perhaps in their artistic creation. Both excelled in the creation of characters with a deep psychological dimension, and all the women in the works of both writers seem to be one woman. In her autobiography, Jean Rhys says, 'The characters (in my books) have always been shadows for me. I have never known other people. I have only written about myself.'[16]

Djuna Barnes is another similar case:

– Tell them almost anything, but give them facts.
– Facts – I said slowly –My God have we come to that?
– Oh indeed – he said scornfully – Are you going to be purely personal?
– I am, everyone is who writes well.[17]

María Luisa Bombal, sunk in the shadows, said to me, 'I am my characters and I will die with them.' I remember taking beautiful walks with her along Marina Avenue of Viña del Mar, our arms linked. One day when we returned to her house, María Luisa turned to me and said, 'The day they cut down this tree next to my window I will die too.' And indeed the tree was cut down some time later and María Luisa died a week later in a hospital in Santiago, on 6 May 1980. She died without having received the highest honour of her country, the National Prize for Literature. Some blame her small output, a crude charge to make against one of the most innovative writers of contemporary prose in Spanish.

But the story of pioneering women writers keeps on being repeated and perhaps María Luisa Bombal became engulfed in silence during her long exile because she was ahead of her time. She broke with the *criollismo* common for the period, and spoke of the body and of desire without euphemisms; her lyrical and luminous prose knits together stories of desire, memory and the emptiness of remembering. It is enough to recall the startling scene of a naked woman contemplating her own body in *La última niebla*. I say startling because earlier women spoke only from behind a veil. María Luisa unveils herself and defines herself, discovers and dis-covers herself, in celebrating her own erotic nature:

I didn't know I was so white and so beautiful. The water lengthens me and my limbs take on unreal proportions. Before, I never dared look at my breasts; now I look at them. Small and round they resemble diminutive corolas suspended over the water.[18]

Sensuality, pleasure and desire, so evident in the narratives of Bombal, are in fact the central co-ordinates of her writings. On the surface her well-known works such as *La última niebla*, *La amortajada* and 'El árbol' represent the life of a woman circumscribed by the perimeters of home and bourgeois environment. In the heart of the writing, or rather, in the inner space of the narrative, the works present a poetical articulation of erotic desire. In *La última niebla*, for example, a clandestine lover is created, and re-created over and over with such obsession in the imagination that the imagined story of the lover becomes much more real than the real story of the husband. These early texts are concerned with the search for an outlet of desire, or perhaps it would be more accurate to say they represent the writing of desire. They also coincide with the period in her life when María Luisa was searching for an ideal amorous union. By the period of her exile, however, Bombal's concerns had shifted. Agata Gligo gives a true picture of María Luisa when she says that from the beginning of 1941, the period of her stay in New York, 'the years of the past had left more interior traces than exterior ones. The fact that others belonged to certain concrete worlds reminded her that she belonged to none.'[19] The anomaly of being an outsider, manifested in her physical exile from her country, as well as the life she lived in New York, constantly moving from one hotel to another, found an echo in her story, 'Las islas nuevas', in which the protagonist Yolanda searches for a state of non-desire, the physical ambiguity of the feminine. Yolanda is a woman with a strange wing growing on her left shoulder, a woman who refuses to belong to a man. She rejects her suitors and thus consciously chooses a life without erotic pleasure, without this 'other', without the Prince Charming who haunted the dreams of heroines of long ago.

In 'Las islas neuvas' the rules of love operating within *La última niebla* and *La amortajada* are overturned to show an anomalous woman exiled from the realm of the erotic, a woman mutilated, belonging to herself alone, no longer conceiving of love as the centre of her existence.

The last work of María Luisa Bombal, *La historia de María Griselda*,[20] is a sequel to *La amortajada*, in that María Griselda is the daughter-in-law of Ana María, of *La amortajada*. María Luisa said that she had left María Griselda so alone that she had decided to create a story especially for her. The weaving together of the two texts is the central motif of this work. It is interesting to note that María Luisa said once that she felt invaded by her characters, that they never left her in peace, and that yes, they were connected with one another.[21]

Like Yolanda, María Griselda is beyond erotic desire and does not respond to that 'other', the husband who keeps her imprisoned because he is jealous of her magnetic beauty.

How can one capture, know and exhaust each of the movements of this woman? If he had been able to wrap her in a tight net of patience and memory, perhaps he would have been able to understand, comprehend the reason for her beauty and for his own anxiety.[22]

María Griselda, like Yolanda, does not belong to any order of the rational, nor can she accept any imposed restrictions. Nobody could possess her or cage her as her parents, settled in the great house in the south of Chile, wished to do. 'And thus it was that like hunters of a skittish gazelle, they had begun to follow the tracks of María Griselda.'[23] The metaphorical chase is unsuccessful and María Griselda, like Yolanda, is beyond possession by the 'other'. These women invent an alternative to love: refusal to accept it.

During her last years in Chile, after her return from New York following the death of her husband in 1973, until the day of her death in 1980, María Luisa never allowed herself to be possessed. She fled like María Griselda from literary reunions, from social gatherings. Following the republication of *La historia de María Griselda* many people came forward to meet her again, to pursue her; the young generation became acquainted with her. But she remained silent, reclusive. She preferred to shut herself up in her room in her house in Viña del Mar and to gaze at the far-off hills of Valparaíso, and smell the sea of her childhood. She preferred to wander through the well-kept parks of the city in a solitary reverie, lingering now and then beside big, leafy trees where trunks bore the carved names of lovers. I believe that she partly turned herself into one of her own characters. She ended by sinking more and more deeply inside herself and inside the bottles of wine drunk so many nights in the solitude of insomnia. I believe she knew that she was rejected and misunderstood as a writer and that the accusation of being sparse in her literary output was a constant torment to her. She said that in order to write well one had to write poetically. Her texts are surely some of the most poetical of any in the Spanish language.

In spite of her life as a recluse, remaining in deep silence within the walls of her house, María Luisa never lost the spark that characterized her in her youth. We spent quite a lot of time together at one period, and during that time I would go to see her every morning. We laughed a lot in those days, all the time, about anything and everything. We found everything funny, from the zigzag flight of flies to the beet-red nose of Alfonsina Storni or the crazy chatter of María Luisa's three female cousins who lived in her house. Everything that happened was a possible story, possible literature, but not in the sense of *Literatos*, written with a capital *L*. She never spoke of her work in an analytical or critical way, quite the contrary. Each one of her characters was alive inside her and sometimes when we said goodnight, she would say, 'I'm going to chat a little while with María Griselda and Ana María.'

To know María Luisa was to be filled with her free and luminous spirit. Perhaps this is why Pablo Neruda used to call her 'the Fire Bee': she had the capacity to kindle passions and illusions, to arouse hope, despite her own feelings of depression. I remember small details about her, such as the regular monthly letter she sent to a prisoner in the south of Chile who had written to her many years earlier to tell her that *La última niebla* saved him from committing suicide.

Pablo Neruda used to retell stories about her, adding his own fire to the telling. Let's put on masks, she suggested one day, and they did, and went out into the streets, into the best-known and busiest areas. Remaining completely serious, calm and distinguished behind their masks, they took a long walk through downtown Santiago.

How can one forget this María Luisa with her sudden changes of humour, her fresh laugh or her tragic daylight awakenings? How can one forget her advice, her critical comments on your writing, while she still admired what you wrote? How can one forget those glasses of wine filled with memories but never with forgetting?

And it seems I am seeing her right now as I write and that these words validate her death, because she did not believe in death and always preferred the other side. As I remember her, her presence bursts through the pages. I see her with her black suit, her subtle elegance, her black hair cut straight across her forehead, to borrow Ezra Pound's description of the River Merchant's Wife in *Cathay*. I see her when she invites me to go on ahead and we climb a flight of magical, narrow stairs, full of omens, as the life of this woman was, and as it continues to be. An invisible writer, whose life and work lie in silence but nevertheless a writer who with two short works changed the course of the literature of Chile and Latin America.

## Notes

1. María Luisa Bombal, *La última niebla*, Santiago: Editorial Orbe, 1968, p. 46. Originally published in 1935.

2. *El niño que fue: recuerdos de infancia*, Valparaíso: Ediciones Universitarias, 1975, p. 15.

3. 'Lo secreto', published in the fourth edition of *La última niebla*, 1968, p. 139.

4. *La última niebla*, p. 61.

5. Much of the biographical information for this study comes directly from my personal knowledge of María Luisa Bombal, the rest from the biography of Bombal by Agata Gligo (*María Luisa*, Santiago: Andrés Bello, 1984). The story about Prosper Merimée comes from one of my conversations with María Luisa.

6. Gligo, *op. cit.*, p. 45.

7. This story is told by the Chilean poet Juvencio Valle in Gligo, *op. cit.*, p. 48.

8. María Luisa Bombal, *La amortajada*, Santiago: Editorial Univertaria, 1978, p. 78. This work was published for the first time in Buenos Aires in 1938 by Editorial Sur.

9. Conversation with the author in August 1977.

10. 'El árbol' was published originally in *Sur*, no. 60, September 1939.

11. *La última niebla*, p. 35.

12. Gligo, *op. cit.*, p. 90.

13. *La amortajada*, p. 78.

14. *ibid*, p. 115.

15. *La última niebla*. p. 82.

16. Jean Rhys, *Smile Please*, New York: Harper & Row, 1979.

17. Djuna Barnes (quoted in Andrew Field, *The Formidable Ms. Barnes*, Austin: University

of Texas Press, 1983).

   18. *La última niebla*, p. 43.

   19. Gligo, *op. cit.*, p. 110.

   20. This work was published in *Norte*, no. 10, August 1946, pp. 34–54, and published in Chile by Ediciones Universitaria de Valparaíso in 1977.

   21. Conversations with the author.

   22. *La historia de María Griselda*, Valparaíso: Ediciones Universitaria, 1977, p. 61.

   23. *La historia de María Griselda*, p. 55.

# Bibliography

## Works by María Luisa Bombal

*La última niebla*. Buenos Aires: Francisco A. Colombo, 1935; Santiago: Editorial Orbe, 1968.

*La amortajada*. Buenos Aires: Sur, 1938; Santiago: Editorial Universitaria, 1978.

*La historia de María Griselda*. *Norte*, no. 10, August 1946, pp. 34–54; Valparaíso: Ediciones Universitaria, 1977.

'Las islas nuevas'. Buenos Aires: *Sur,* no. 53, 1939, pp. 13–34.

'El árbol'. Buenos Aires: *Sur,* no. 60, 1939, pp. 20–30.

'*Mar. cielo y tierra*'. Buenos Aires: *Saber Vivir*, no. 1, 1940 pp. 34–5.

'Trenzas'. Buenos Aires: *Saber Vivir*, no. 2, 1940, pp. 36–7.

'Washington, ciudad de las ardillas'. Buenos Aires: *Sur*, no. 106, 1943 pp. 28–35.

'La maja y el ruiseñor'. Viña del Mar: *Revista Viña del Mar*, no. 7, 1960, pp. 8–12.

'Lo secreto', included in 4th edn of *La última niebla*. Santiago: Editorial Orbe, 1969, pp. 175–83.

## Translations into English

*House of Mist*. New York: Farrar, Strauss & Co., 1947; London: Cassell, 1948.

*The Shrouded Woman*. New York: Farrar, Strauss & Co., 1948; London: Cassell, 1950.

*New Islands and Other Stories*. New York: Farrar–Strauss–Giroux, 1982, translated by Richard and Lucia Cunningham, with a preface by J. L. Borges. Includes *The Final Mist* [*La última niebla*]; 'The tree' [El árbol]; 'Braids' ['Trenzas']; 'The Unknown' ['Lo secreto']; 'New islands' ['Las islas nuevas'].

## Selected studies on the work of María Luisa Bombal

Adams, M. Ian, 'María Luisa Bombal: Alienation and the poetic image', in *Three Authors of Alienation: Bombal, Onetti, Carpentier*, Austin: University of Texas Press, 1975.

Agosin, Marjorie, *Las desterradas del paraíso: protagonistas en María Luisa Bombal*, New York: Senda Nueva de Ediciones, 1983.

Cortés, Darío, 'Bibliografía de y sobre María Luisa Bombal', *Hispanic Journal*, vol. 1, no. 2, 1980, pp. 125–42.

Guerra-Cunningham, Lucia, *La narrativa de María Luisa Bombal: una visión de la existencia femenina*, Madrid: Ed. Playor, 1980.

Vidal, Hermán, *María Luisa Bombal: la feminidad enajenada*, Barcelona: Hijos de José Bosch, 1976.

## Articles

Agoni Molina, Luis, 'El motivo de la frustración en *La última niebla* de María Luisa Bombal', *Cuadernos Hispanoamericanos*, no. 363, 1980.

Agosín, Marjorie, 'Conflictos y resoluciones parciales en *Believe Me, Love* de María Luisa Bombal', *Chasqui*, vol. 9, no. 1, 1979.

Agosín, Marjorie, 'Un recuerdo de María Luisa Bombal', *Revista Interamericana de bibliografía*, vol. 30, 1980.

Agosín, Marjorie, 'María Luisa Bombal, una escritora invisible', *Literatura Chilena: creación y crítica*, no. 21, 1982.

Agosín, Marjorie, 'Mysticism and Antimysticism in María Luisa Bombal', *Circulo-Revista de cultura*, vol. X, 1982.

Agosín, Marjorie, 'Intertextualidades en la niebla', *Letras femeninas*, vol. IX, no. 2, 1983.

Campbell, Margaret, 'The Vaporous World of María Luisa Bombal', *Hispania*, vol. 44, no. 3, 1961.

Castellanos, Rosario, 'María Luisa Bombal y los arquetipos femeninos', in *Mujer que sabe latín...* Mexico: Sepsetentas, 1972.

Cortés, Darío, 'El arte poética en la novelas de María Luisa Bombal', in *Hispanic Literatures: 5th annual conference*, Indiana: University of Pennsylvania, 1980.

Debicki, Andrew P., 'Structure, Imagery and Experience in María Luisa Bombal's *The Tree*', *Studies in Short Fiction*, vol. 8, no. 1, 1971.

Fox-Lockert, Lucia, 'María Luisa Bombal: *La Amortajada*', in *Women Novelists in Spain and Spanish-America*, Metuchen, New Jersey: Scarecrow Press, 1979.

Levine, Linda Gould, 'María Luisa Bombal from a Feminist Perspective', *Revista Interamericana*, vol. 4, no. 2, 1974.

Nelson, Esther W., 'The Space of Longing: *La Última Niebla*', *The American Hispanist*, vol. 2, no. 21, 1977.

Orlandi, Claudia W., 'Mist, Light and Libido: *La Última Niebla*', *Kentucky Romance Quarterly*, vol. 26, 1979.

Pacífico, Patricia, 'A Feminist Approach to Three Latin American Women Writers', in *Una historia de servicio: 66 Aniversario de la Universidad Interamericana*, Río Piedras, Puerto Rico: Inter American University Press, 1979.

Rodriguez-Peralta, Phyllis, 'María Luisa Bombal's Poetic Novels of Female Estrangement', *Revista de estudios Hispánicos*, vol. 14, no. 1, 1981.

Valdiviesco, Mercedes, 'Social Denunciation in the Language of 'El arbol' ('The Tree') by María Luisa Bombal, *Latin American Literary Review*, vol. 4, no. 9, 1976.

Valenzuela, Victor, 'A New Generation of Chilean Novelists and Short Story Writers', *Hispania*, vol. 37, no. 4, 1954.

# 3. Speaking with many voices: The poems of Alejandra Pizarnik
## Susan Bassnett

Whenever Shelley found his flow of poetic inspiration flagging, he would sit down and translate a text written by someone else, and in this time-honoured way would both settle down to serious work again and, by structuring poems based on other poems, reawaken his own poetry. Shelley's system of using translation as a means of unblocking his own poetic impulse can be taken a stage further: in my own case, translating another poet most often means producing a poem that I would like to have written myself, and so the activity of translation is not only far from being the secondary art that some critics have dismissed it as, it is an intrinsic part of certain writers' development. Translation scholars have never established clear explanations of why some writers choose to translate, and the question of personal empathy is one that has never really been explored, despite the testimony of poets including Ezra Pound, who invented the notion of the translation as 'homage' and saw the role of the translator as to bring the dead back to life.

In the case of Alejandra Pizarnik, who died tragically young in 1972, that process of resurrection entails bringing to light a great poet whose work has been so neglected that it is difficult to obtain. Briefly, before Britain and Argentina went to war in 1982 over the Falkland Islands (Malvinas), there was a possibility that her diaries might have been purchased by a British university. Her name, thus, might well have begun to be known by more than the small number of people able and interested enough to read her work in Spanish, but that enterprise failed. Those who discover Pizarnik's writing usually stumble across it (perhaps in a pirate edition such as the one I first encountered) and then remain enchanted by the power of a poet who said so simply, 'Poetry begins with a man or a stone or a tree...'[1]

Alejandra Pizarnik was first pointed out to me as a parallel case to Sylvia Plath – a woman writer who committed suicide, a woman with a sense of cultural displacement (she was Argentinian, of Russian parentage) whose distressed self-image provided her with a central theme and who was fascinated by images of death and silence. Like Plath, she had a strong pictorial sense (she studied painting for some time in Paris) and used key words throughout her writing. Like Plath's poetry, her works – her seven collections of poems, her essays, her short fiction and her diaries – can be seen, indeed need to be seen, as a unified whole rather than as a series of separate entities. Ted Hughes pointed out that Sylvia Plath effectively wrote a single poem in many fragments, and the same argument can be made for Pizarnik's work. This is not to deny her poetic development, rather to emphasize the consistency of her poetic craftsmanship.

For me, having encountered Pizarnik in this comparative manner, the next task was to read her complete works. This proved extremely difficult: some texts are out of print, some virtually unobtainable, and some anthologized and varying considerably from edition to edition. In short, there is no authoritative body of Pizarnik texts in the way that there now is a body of Plath texts. Reading Alejandra Pizarnik's work is a voyage of discovery fraught with difficulties. A voyage of discovery, even though Octavio Paz wrote the preface for her 1962 collection *Arbol de Diana*, which ought to have ensured her greater public recognition. In that preface, Paz wrote lyrically about the magic tree, the tree that is 'transparent and gives no shade . . . that gives off its own brief, sparkling light, that is born in the dry lands of America, that has no roots . . . whose trunk was considered by the ancients to be the (female) sex organ of the entire cosmos . . . that is both masculine and feminine.' Here Paz, in his usual blend of the real and the marvellous, was writing about a fusion of elements in the poems but most of all about Alejandra herself, the writer. His preface concludes with the following:

> Some people who are considered intelligent complain that despite all their learning they can't see anything. To remove this error, all one has to do is remember that the Tree of Diana is not a physical thing that can be seen. It is an (animate) object that enables us to see further, a natural part of the seeing process. Furthermore, the slightest test by experimental criticism will effectively and definitively dispel the prejudices of contemporary exposition: placed in front of the sun, the Tree of Diana reflects the sun's rays and brings them together in a central flame called poem, which produces a luminous warmth that can burn, melt down, vaporize unbelievers. This test is recommended to our own literary critics.[2]

Poetry, then, is to be experienced and received, not analysed. Nevertheless, Paz tells us a great deal about Pizarnik's poetry, and his insights perhaps explain why she has been so little appreciated and why now, in another time, when feminist criticism has come into being as a serious discipline, her work can have such appeal. Paz stresses the ancient sources of Pizarnik's inspirational flow, her honesty ('the product does not contain a single false particle'), the antagonism she encountered, the archetypal symbolism of her imagery and her hermaphroditism, her blending of the primal elements of masculine and feminine. Again, the similarity with

Sylvia Plath can be seen in the way in which both writers refer back to myths of antiquity, to the Great Goddess figure who is all things in one and whose primordial colours recur through the poetry of both women – red, white and black. In 'Fragments to Overcome Silence' Pizarnik writes:

> The strongest parts of language are lonely, desolate women, singing out through my voice which I hear in the distance. And far away, lying on black sand, is a girl filled with ancestral music. Where is real death? I wanted to illuminate myself in the light of my lack of light. Branches die in my memory. The girl nestles down in me with her she-wolf's mask. She who could go on no longer and pleaded for flames and we burned together.[3]

Alejandra Pizarnik was born in 1936, and died just 36 years later in Buenos Aires. She was the same tragically young age as Byron, another poet whose work was misunderstood in his own lifetime. When she was seventeen years old she began to keep a diary, and from the extracts available to us, together with her poetry, details of her biography can be roughly traced. The daughter of Russian immigrants, like so many other women in the Americas she grew up with a sense of cultural uneasiness, puzzled by the culture of her parents' past and not fully assimilated into the culture of her present. In a poem entitled 'Suspicion' she summarizes that uneasiness in a simple childhood image:

> Mother used to tell us about a white forest in Russia . . . 'and we'd make little snowmen and put hats on them that we took from great-grandfather . . .'
> I would look at her with suspicion. Whatever was snow? Why make men out of it? And above all, what was a great-grandfather?[4]

In another poem, dedicated to Olga Orozco, she summarizes her childhood in the following terms:

> All I know of my childhood
> is a glow of fearfulness
> and a hand pulling me over
> to my other side.[5]

In a poem called 'Fiesta' she speaks about her 'orfandad', saying 'I unfurled my homelessness/across the table, like a map.'[6]

Childhood, homelessness, loneliness and loss recur throughout Pizarnik's poetry, expressed through a series of powerful visual images that remind us of her training as a painter (after beginning her studies in Buenos Aires, she moved to Paris and there from 1960 to 1964 she studied painting, heavily influenced by the Surrealists and by artists such as Paul Klee). The terseness of her poems and the sharpness of their imagery recall the Japanese *haiku*, and like Oriental poets (and again like Plath) she uses key words that connect her earliest poems to the very last ones, reinforcing the view that her opus is a single entity consisting of many fragments. Prominent among her keywords are: *el silencio* [silence], *el náufragio* [shipwreck], *la ausencia* [absence], *la orfandad* [the state of being an orphan, homelessness, not belonging], *la inocencia* [innocence], *la muerte* [death], *el cuerpo* [body], *el espejo* [mirror], *el viento* [wind], *el centro* [centre], *el tambor* [drum], *la luz* [light], *el tiempo* [time], *la lila* [lilac], the three colours red, white and black and *el ángel y el cuchillo* [angel and knife]. 'I don't hear the orgasmic sound of certain precious words,' she confesses, in a fragment written not long before her death,[7] but the conciseness of her imagery, the way in which her poems spiral outwards from their tightly wrought structure can be seen clearly in an earlier piece, 'Signs':

> Everything makes love with silence.
>
> They promised me a silence
> like fire, a house of silence.
>
> Suddenly the temple is a circus
> the light a drum.[8]

Characteristic of Pizarnik's poems is their brevity. She experimented with a range of styles, and her critical essays are witty and elegant, while her short prose (heavily influenced by the Surrealists) tends towards the grotesque. Writing about poetry in 1962, she declared:

> The poem is the place where anything can happen. Like love, laughter and suicide, it is a profoundly subversive activity and poetry has nothing to do with its freedom or its truth. Talking about freedom and truth and using these words to refer to the world we inhabit is to utter a great lie. But not when we use those words in poetry... the place where everything is possible.[9]

Pizarnik saw poetry as an activity that needed careful craftsmanship, so precise that it might almost be described as ritualistic. She continually changed the order of her words, played with lines, reducing the size of her texts so that each poem became smaller and smaller, closer to the bones. The technique is reminiscent of the sculptor Giacometti. In her diary, she writes about her dread of poetry, the form that sentences her to abstraction. She is obsessed with the idea of a pure language and of the tainted quality of the language she is forced to use. 'If writing were for me,' she wrote on 25 July 1965, 'I would not always feel with certainty that the principal thing in each of us is unsayable.'[10] Once her poems were written, she claimed, she abandoned them to their readers, whose task was then to create their own poem. In this notion of the poem as unfinished, rewritten by each new reader in the act of reading, she anticipates post-modernist reading strategies. The communication process is perceived not as between poet and eventual readers, but rather any communication that occurs happens within the boundaries of the text. In a diary entry for 29 May 1965, Pizarnik describes words as scalpels, silence as skin that covers and shelters. The act of writing, in this metaphor, is an act of barbarity, of tearing open the skin of silence and exposing the wounded flesh beneath.

The diaries reveal a constant search for literary models. She relates strongly to Artaud, to Kafka, reads Ungaretti, another poet of the skeletal text, Eluard, Nerval, Isak Dinesen. In the late 1960s she began to experiment increasingly with the prose-poem, fascinated by the need, in that form, for white spaces. 'Prose poems,' says the entry for 17 July 1967, 'necessity of double spaces. At least for my "style".'[11] In an entry for 1 May 1966, she describes the difficulty of finding a model:

> I would like my misery to be translated into the greatest possible beauty. It's strange: in Spanish no one exists who can serve me as a model. Octavio himself is too inflexible, too steel-like, or, simply, too virile. As for Julio, I don't share the free and easy manner in writings in which he employs oral language. I like Borges but I don't want to be one of his many followers. Rulfo enchants me, at times, but his rhythm is his alone, and furthermore he is excessively Mexican. I don't want to write an Argentine book but rather a tiny book resembling Nerval's *Aurelia*. Who, in Spanish, has achieved the extremely fine simplicity of Nerval?[12]

When Alejandra Pizarnik died in 1972, the impact of the new feminism was beginning to be felt strongly in the United States and Europe and was spreading out also into the rest of the world. Although Pizarnik was in no way a feminist writer, her work reflects many of the fundamental concerns of feminist aesthetics, just as Sylvia Plath's poetry anticipated many of them a decade earlier. In his preface to *Arbol de Diana*, Octavio Paz talks about the process of reading and seeing, about the magic tree that cannot be seen at all if approached only with the intellect. He suggests that poetry is part of a process that, although linked to the intellect, is nevertheless in essence outside it, beyond it, with a starting point in the realm of feeling. Those feminist writers who have struggled with the idea of a culture that gives pre-eminence to the rational and intellectual have pointed out that this culture decrees the irrational to be less acceptable. Furthermore, in industrialized societies the irrational elements are generally held to be those who, at the margins of acceptability, behave and think in ways that deviate or subvert – the mad (and suicides are generally held to be mad, to have the 'balance of their minds disturbed'), children (who have not yet learned to reason), artists and poets who reject the idea of being 'socially useful', homosexuals (who do not conform to accepted categories of sexual behaviour) and women, who so easily become 'hysterical' (that word which equates the womb with madness) and whose emotions run too close to the surface for comfort. Alejandra Pizarnik falls into all these domains, as a woman writing poetry full of intense emotion, a woman struggling to control her own sexuality, an artist and a poet, a writer fascinated with the world of childhood, a suicide. She does indeed stand at the edge of the world of rationality, and her texts reflect that.

According to Hélène Cixous:

A feminine text cannot fail to be more than subversive, it is volcanic; as it is written it brings about an upheaval of the old property crust, carrier of masculine investments.[13]

Cixous also attempts to define the specificity of women's writing:

Her writing can only keep going, without ever inscribing or discerning contours ... She lets the other language speak – the language of 1,000 tongues which knows neither closure nor death. Her language does not contain, it carries; it does not hold back, it makes possible.[14]

This is uncannily close to Pizarnik's own attempts to define feminine writing, the new language she is trying to forge out of her own pain, in her awareness that existing models are inadequate for her needs. 'I cannot speak with my voice, but with my voices,' she states in 'Foundation Stone'. 'Something in me cannot give in to the ashes which rain down, which well up inside the woman who is me, with me being her and being myself, unspeakably separate from her.'[15] Reading Pizarnik's poetry today, in a post-feminist period, it is possible to see that she was wrestling with what have come to be perceived as some of the fundamental concerns of feminist aesthetics. She refused to own her poems, claiming that the many voices within them were just part of what she described as the triangular relationship involving writer, poem and reader, and she also refused to write specifically for any particular reader, hoping in this way to encounter readers who would understand her writing instinctively.[16]

Throughout her writing career, Pizarnik returned again and again in her poetry to the problems of writing. She wrote many poems about making poetry and about the impossibility of true communication through language. In the symbolically entitled 'Useless Frontiers', she says:

> A place
> I don't mean a space
> I'm talking
>             about
> I'm talking about what is not
> I'm talking about what I know

not time
but all those instants
not love
no
    yes
no
a place of absence
a thread of hopeless unity.[17]

A series of recurring images is connected to childhood, to the time when the woman is a little girl and the father is all-powerful, a girl–father relationship prefiguring the powerlessness of women in adult male society. Pizarnik's poetry and prose are full of references to dolls, tiny female figures that can be so easily broken and torn apart, but which are also sinister, because in their silence there is a sense of knowledge. In a prose piece entitled 'On Time and Not', Pizarnik sketches an encounter between Death, a girl, a Mad Queen and a doll. The Mad Queen asks her son to bring 'the precious blood of your daughter, her head and her entrails, her femurs and her arms' and the doll listens, with its eyes wide open. Later, as the girl worries about how much the doll might have overheard, the narrator tells us that 'the doll was smiling, although rather too innocently perhaps'.[18] Pizarnik was fascinated by the fairy tale, the realm of forests and wicked queens, witches and enchantments, handsome princes and wild beasts, the realm of Alice in Wonderland adrift in a world of dark shadows and atrocious monsters lying in wait for her. Her writing is full of images that recall the Russian folk tales she heard as a child, archetypal images that disturb in the way that Angela Carter's reworking in her novels of folktale elements also disturbs, making readers aware of the primeval origins of those tales and drawing attention to the position of women and girls as either victims or destroyers, a variant on the Madonna–whore dichotomy of contemporary patriarchal society.

Pizarnik's fascination with the magical led her also to experiment in her poetry with incantatory effects. Many of her poems are like riddles or spells, and none more obviously so than the tiny poem 'Only a Name' which is a word-play on her own name:

alejandra alejandra
debajo estoy yo
alejandra[19]

The childhood poems are marked by a great sense of sadness. In 'Childhood' she says simply:

.The hour when grass grows
in the horse's memory.

> The wind makes naive statements
> in praise of lilacs,
> and someone goes into death
> with eyes wide open
> like Alice in the land of second sight.[20]

Her father, after his death, inhabits the dark forest too:

> And then it was
> that with his cold, dead tongue in his mouth
> he sang the song they never let him sing
> in this world of obscene gardens, of shadows ...
>
> Then from the highest tower of absence
> his song rang out through the gloom of concealment
> through the silent spaces
> filled with uneasy hollows like these words I write.[21]

In Sylvia Plath's poetry, the figure of the dead father rises up like a Colossus, and later fuses with the figure of her husband in poems like 'Lyonesse'. Similarly, Pizarnik's father figure in his tower of absence is fused with the figure of the lover, whether male or female, who always goes away, always betrays, never fully materializes to become real. In 'Exile', one of her most powerful expressions of the sense of failed love, she writes:

> Sinister delirium of loving a shadow.
> The shadow cannot die.
> And my love
> can only clasp that which flows
> like lava out of hell:
> a hidden lodge,
> phantoms deliciously erect,
> priests of foam,
> and above all angels,
> angels beautiful as knives
> that rise up in the night
> and tear hope apart.[22]

In 'Privilege 2' she uses biblical language to describe the loss of the beloved:

> Oh my beloved
> most handsome of the men
> who leave by night,
> endless is your never turning back
> you will be shadow until the day of days.[23]

The themes of loss and of hope betrayed are, however, only a part of Pizarnik's writing. There is another side to her work, one which is described by Ines Malinow in an introduction to a collection of Pizarnik's poems. Noting that Pizarnik felt, shortly before her death, that she was writing her best poetry (another extraordinary parallel with Plath), Malinow discusses her sense of humour, her irony and self-deprecatory wit, her fighting spirit and her refusal to give in. 'Poetry like Alejandra's was not meant to communicate but to not-communicate [*incomunicar*],' she says, reinforcing Pizarnik's own statement about the life of the poem and its relationship with subsequent readers.[24] Pizarnik may have written in *Arbol de Diana* about letting life fall and suffer, be bound with fire in the house of the night[25] but she could also write, as in the little poem 'Undoing':

> Someone wants to open a door somewhere. Her hands
> hurt as she grips her ill-omened prison of bones.[26]

Growing up in the 1940s and 1950s meant that Pizarnik lived through the years of Peronism and the military coup of 1955. In the late 1960s there were student riots in Argentina. Her parents and grandparents had been members of the Russian nobility, whose power was destroyed with the October Revolution, and so both in her family background and in the society around her the prison, the knock on the door by night, the tortured body in a ditch, armed conflict and sudden death had a meaning beyond the fairy tale. She claimed to have no interest in politics, but moved in leftist circles in Paris and could not but have been affected by the changes in Argentinian society during her lifetime. As a Latin American of Russian origins, the cruelties of the folk tale, of Czarist Russia and of the Revolution were mixed with the cruelties of a continent with a history of violence, oppression and revolution. García Márquez, so often hailed as a principal exponent of that very Latin American mode known as magical realism, in his novel *One Hundred Years of Solitude* wrote under the guise of fiction about a massacre of protesting workers that was subsequently denied by the very people who actually saw it happen. He presents this episode as a culmination of the absurdity of reality, where a horror can take place and then be dismissed as a fabrication. With horrible irony, during the writing of this essay the massacre of young people in Peking's Tiananmen Square in June 1989 has also been dismissed as fiction by the forces of authority, and the television images of tanks cutting a path through unarmed crowds have been repudiated. Reality, it would seem, is more absurd than any art, and this feeling is at the heart of Pizarnik's vision and leads to her sense of despair and to the rage in her writing. That sense of rage at the absurdity of the human condition also led her, like many Latin American writers both male and female, towards Surrealism, to the terrifying images of violence and monstrosity that were intended to reflect the real.

The text that gives the clearest example of Pizarnik's attempt to explore the violence she believed lay within human beings is *Acerca de la condesa sangrienta* [The Bloody Countess], a story divided into twelve sections inclusive of a preface. 'The Bloody Countess' tells the story of a sixteenth-century Central European noblewoman, Erzebet Bathory, who tortured over six hundred young girls to death and who, after being tried and condemned to being walled up in the castle where she had carried out her murders, 'never showed the slightest sign of repentance ... never understood why she had been condemned'.[27] The symbol of this horror is the Countess's white dress, which turns red with the blood of her victims, and later her white body, which she bathes in blood in a vain attempt to keep at bay the ravages of time.

In the opening section, Pizarnik refers to the book on the Countess by Valentine Penrose, the French Surrealist writer, and notes that Penrose concentrated on 'the convulsive beauty of the character'.[28] The calmness of the Countess contrasts throughout with the appalling nature of her crimes, which are described in detail, all the more terrible because carried out by a woman upon other women. A thread of autobiography runs as a subtext through the story – the Countess has a noble ancestry but the family have decayed and become corrupt, she has transformed her desire for passion into a love affair with death, she sits in front of a great dark mirror, she suffers from melancholia. Section VII, whose language echoes many of Pizarnik's poems, makes that autobiographical element very clear:

> An unchangeable colour rules over the melancholic; her dwelling is a space the colour of mourning. Nothing happens in it. No one intrudes, it is a bare stage where the inert I is assisted by the I suffering from that inertia. The latter wishes to free the former but all efforts fail, as Theseus would have failed had he been not only himself, but also the Minotaur; to kill him then, he would have had to kill himself.

Sexual pleasure can briefly help the melancholic to feel alive, but afterwards the pain is worse than before:

> Melancholia is, I believe, a musical problem: a dissonance, a change in rhythm. While on the *outside* everything happens with the vertiginous rhythm of a cataract, on the *inside* is the exhausted adagio of drops of water falling from time to tired time. For this reason the *outside*, seen from the melancholic *inside*, appears absurd and unreal.[29]

Just as the Marquis de Sade became a Surrealist hero, so the Countess Bathory is a Surrealist heroine: not because of any approval of their crimes, but rather because they represent the ultimate subversion, and their actions challenge every established social rule known to mankind. Octavio Paz, in one of his best-known poems, sang the praises of the ultimate unfettered freedom of de Sade, and Pizarnik states simply in the conclusion to her story that the Countess 'is yet another proof that the absolute freedom of the human creature is horrible'.[30] In this statement lies the paradox – if absolute freedom is so unspeakable, then it follows that freedom itself must be undesirable, and what passes for freedom is merely illusion. In this, Pizarnik comes close to Sartre, who saw suicide as a statement of affirmation, or to Genet with his praise of criminals, or to Georges Bataille. In an interview with Martha Moia, Pizarnik tried to explain her attraction to Surrealism:

> I believe that signs, words, hint at things, they suggest things. This complex way of feeling language leads me to believe that language cannot express reality; all we can do is speak about the obvious. That's where my desire comes from to make poems that are terribly precise, despite my innate Surrealism, and I want to work with elements from the inner shadows. That is the main feature of my poetry.[31]

The word as sign that can only hint at what is concealed in shadow is how Pizarnik thought of language. That sign is a complex one, sometimes symbolic, sometimes iconic, most often indexical, referring to something other, somewhere else. This is indeed an innately surreal way of thinking and of shaping a poem; Pizarnik's works as a whole comprise a network of signs that are cross-referenced between poems and prose texts over the years of her writing career. In the third verse of 'Ancient History', for example, she writes:

> Someone is singing a song the colour of birth:
> the madwoman moves through the chorus with her silver crown.
> They throw stones at her. I never ever look into the heart
> of songs. Down at the bottom, there is always a dead queen.[32]

The mad, dead queen at the heart of song exemplifies Pizarnik's vision of creativity. She seems to have understood implicitly what other women were shortly to state explicitly – that culture and language, phallocentric as they are, conceal the bodies and suppress the voices of women. The queens of folklore have their origins as deposed pagan goddesses, the woman writer has to accept that the very act of writing is sacrificial:

> A savage struggle between syllables and spectres, broken verses, ragged poems, sentences like amputated arms, desires that nobody under the sun could imagine, stars without light, waves without sea, words and ancient lips caress me, unimaginable beings and things.[33]

Like Jean Rhys, a writer whose heroines are always betrayed, always in search of the unattainable, Pizarnik claimed that she wrote out of unhappiness and, had she been happy, would not have needed to write at all. She was a highly individualistic writer, who understood that poetry is an art but also a craft, like music or painting, and requires great care and attention to detail. In her recurrent themes many of the principal concerns of overtly feminist writers can be found – she explores the duality of woman's role as helpless child on the one hand and as Our Lady of Death on the other, reminding us that the sweetly pretty Alice in Wonderland clashed with the murderous Queen of Hearts at the end of the dream and reminding us also that the murderous queen was dreamed by Alice in the first place. Pizarnik offers no comfortable view of woman. She writes about the plight of the woman artist with no models in her language, about the woman without children, about the eternal child-woman under the shadow of the great father figure, about the woman struggling to define her own sexuality, about the woman betrayed in love, but she also writes about the woman who kills and desires to kill, the woman who descends kicking and screaming into darkness and death. All these women, and the line of Russian princesses from her own ancestry, speak in her poems, in the many voices that are always hers.

In her diary entry for 29 December 1962, she wrote:

I change the colour of paper, the colour of ink. I write laughing. I write to ward off coldness and fear. I write in vain. Silence has corroded me: some poems remain like a dead person's bones that chisel into my frightened nights. The meaning of the most obvious word has been lost. I still write. I still throw myself urgently to narrate states of astonishment and rage. A very slight pressure, a new recognition of what's stalking you, and you will no longer write. We're just a few steps away from an eternity of silence.[34]

In this passage the 'I' of the speaker merges with 'you' and 'we', another example of Pizarnik's many voices speaking through the same text.

Pizarnik took her own life, but the fascination with death that recurs throughout her writing is not a morbid obsession but rather a profoundly philosophical questioning of the meaning of life and death. In her diaries she refers to dreaming of herself as both victim and murderer simultaneously, and her prose and poetry explore that dualism: she is both bloody countess and butchered young girl, mad queen and child, avenging angel and passive endurer. Her friends (like Sylvia Plath's friends) remember her wit, her irony, her energy and her sense of life rather than any death wish, though in her writing she explored death in its many aspects. In a diary entry for 27 April 1966, three months after the death of her father, she says simply, 'How I should like to be far from madness and death.'

It would be a misreading of her work to see it all as a prefiguration of her suicide; rather her fascination with images of death and violence reflects her Latin American origins, her Slavic ancestry, her existentialist present and her innate Surrealism. The last lines of the title poem of her collection *The Final Innocence* stand as a fitting epitaph to a writer whose poetic gift is still waiting to be recognized fully:

> I have to leave
> no more inertia in the sunlight
> no more discouragement in the blood
> no more queuing up for death.
> I have to leave
> So forward, woman, on your way![35]

# Notes

All English translations are by Susan Bassnett, unless otherwise specified.

1. 'Piedra fundamental', from *El infierno musical*, 1971.
    Es un hombre o una piedra o un árbol el que va a comenzar el canto.
2. Preface to 1962 edition of *Arbol de Diana*, reprinted in Alejandra Pizarnik, *Poemas*, Medellin: Editorial Endymion, 1986.
Algunas personas con reputación de inteligencia, se quejan de que, a pesar de su preparación no ven nada. Para disipar su error, basta recordar que el árbol de Diana no es cuerpo que se pueda ver: es un objeto (animado) que nos deja ver más allá, un insrumento natural de visión. Por lo demás, una pequeña prueba de crítica experimental desvanecerá, efectiva y definitivamente, los prejuicios de la ilustración contemporánea: colocado frente al sol, el árbol de Diana refleja sus rayos y los reúne en un foco central llamado poema, que produce un calor luminoso capaz de quemar, fundir y hasta volatilizar a los incrédulos. Se recomienda esta prueba a los criticos literarios de nuestra lengua.
3. 'Fragmentos para dominar el silencio', from *Extracción de la piedra de locura*, 1968.
Las fuerzas del lenguaje son las damas solitarias, desoladas, que cantan a través de mi voz que escucho a lo lejos. Y lejos, en la negra arena, yace una niña densa de música ancestral. Donde la verdadera muerte? He querido iluminarme a la luz de mi falta de luz. Los ramos se mueren en la memoria. La yacente anida en mí con su mascara de loba. La que no pudo más e imploró llamas y ardimos.
4. 'Desconfianza', from *Textos de sombra y ultimos poemas*, 1982.
    Máma nos hablaba de un blanco bosque de Rusia . . . 'y haciamos
    hombrecitos de nieve y les poniamos sombreros que robabamos
    al bisabuelo . . .'
    Yo la miraba con desconfianza. Que era la nieve? Para que
    hacian hombrecitos? Y ante todo, que significa un bisabuelo?
5. 'Tiempo', from *Las aventuras perdidas*, 1958.
    Ya no sé de la infancia
    mas que un miedo luminoso
    y una mano que me arrastra
    a mi otra orilla.
6. 'Fiesta', from *Los trabajos y las noches*, 1965.
    He desplegado mi orfandad
    sobre la mesa, como un mapa.
7. Fragment from *Textos de sombra* (1982), with a note stating that this was copied in a green notebook and marked 'for correction', 1972.
No oigo los sonidos orgasmales de ciertas palabras preciosas.

8. 'Signos', from *El infierno musical*, 1971.
>    Todo hace el amor con el silencio.

>    Me habían prometido un silencio como un fuego, una casa
>    de silencio.

>    De pronto el templo es un circo y la luz un tambor.

9. 'El poeta y su poema', *Prologos a la antología consultada de la joven poesia Argentina*, 1968.
>    La poesia es el lugar donde todo sucede. A semejanza del amor, del humor, del suicidio y de todo acto profundamente subversivo, la poesia se desentiende de lo que no es su libertad o su verdad. Decir libertad o verdad y referir estas palabras al mundo en que vivimos o no vivimos es decir una mentira. No lo es cuando se las atribuye a la poesia: lugar donde todo es posible.

10. English text only, quoted in his own version in Frank Graziano, *Alejandra Pizarnik: A profile*, Durango, Colorado: Logbridge-Rhodes, 1987.

11. *ibid.*

12. *ibid.*

13. Hélène Cixous, 'The Laugh of the Medusa', in E. Marks and I. de Courtivron, *New French Feminisms*, Brighton: Harvester, 1981.

14. *ibid.*

15. 'Piedra fundamental', see note 1 above.
>    No puedo hablar con mi voz sino con mis voces.
>    Algo en mi no se abandona a la cascada de cenizas que me
>    arrasa dentro de mi con ella que es yo, conmigo que soy
>    ella e que soy yo, indecibilmente distinta de ella.

16. 'El poema y su lector', 1967.

17. 'Fronteras inutiles', from *Los trabajos y las noches* (1965).
>    Un lugar
>    no digo un espacio
>    hablo de
>    >    qué
>    hablo de lo que no es
>    hablo de lo que conozco

>    no el tiempo
>    sólo todos los instantes
>    no el amor
>    no
>    >    sí
>    no

>    un lugar de ausencia
>    un hilo de miserable unión

18. '*A tiempo y no*', 1968.
>    traeme la preciosa sangre de tu hija, su cabeza y sus entrañas, sus femures y sus brazos la muñeca sonreia, aunque tal vez con demasiado candor

19. 'Nombre', from *La ultima inocencia*, 1956.

20. 'Infancia', from *Los trabajos y las noches*, 1965.
>    Hora en que la yerba crece
>    en la memoria del caballo.
>    El viento pronuncia discursos ingenuos
>    en honor de las lilas,
>    y alguien entra en la muerte
>    con los ojos abiertos
>    como Alicia en el país de lo ya visto.

21. 'Poema para el padre', from *Textos de sombra*, 1982.

> Y fue entonces
> que con la lengua muerta y fria en la boca
> cantó la canción que no le dejaron cantar
> en este mundo de jardines obscenos y de sombras…
>
> Entonces, desde la torre más alta de la ausencia
> su canto resoñó en la opacidad de lo ocultado
> en la extensión silenciosa
> llena de oquedades movedizas como las palabras que escribo.

22. 'Exilio', from *Las aventuras perdidas*, 1976.

> Siniestro delirio amar a una sombra.
> La sombra no muere.
>
> Y mi amor
> sólo abraza a lo que fluye
> como lava del infierno:
> una logia callada,
> fantasmas en dulce erección,
> sacerdotes de espuma,
> y sobre todo ángeles,
> ángeles bellos como cuchillos
> que se elevan en la noche
> y devastan la esperanza.

23. 'Privilegio' from *Extracción de la piedra de locura*, 1968.

> El más hermoso
> en la noche de los que se van,
> oh deseado,
> es sin fin tu no volver,
> sombra tú hasta el día de los días.

24. Ines Malinow, preface to *Poemas*, *op. cit.*: '… una poesía como la de Alejandra no era para comunicar, sino para incomunicar.'

25. See *Arbol de Diana*, Poem no. 35.

26. 'Desfundación', from *Extracción de la piedra de locura*, 1968.

> Alguien quiso abrir alguna puerta. Duelen sus manos
> aferradas a su prisión de huesos de mal agüero.

27. 'Acerca de la condesa sangrienta', 1965. The translation is by A. Manguel, included in his collection of stories by Latin American women writers *Other Fires*, London: Picador, 1986. 'Nunca demostró arrepentimiento. Nunca comprendió por qué la condenaron.'

28. 'La belleza convulsiva del personaje'.

29.   Un color invariable rige al melancólico: su interior es un espacio de color de luto; nada pasa allí, nadie pasa. Es una escena sin decorados donde el yo inerte es asistido por el yo que sufre por esa inercia. Este quisiera liberar al prisionero, pero cualquier tentativa fracasa como hubiera fracasado Teseo si, además de ser él mismo, hubiese sido, también, el Minotauro; matarlo, entonces, habria exigido matarse.

Creo que la melancolía es, en suma, un problema musical: una disonancia, un ritmo trastornado. Mientras *afuera* todo sucede con un ritmo vertiginoso de cascada, *adentro* hay una lentitud exhausta de gota de agua cayendo de tanto en tanto. De allí que ese *afuera* contemplado desde al *adentro* melancólico resulte absurdo y irreal.

30. 'Ella es una prueba más que la libertad absoluta de la criatura humana es horrible.'

31. *Algunas claves de Alejandra Pizarnik*, interview with Martha I. Moia, 1967.

Siento que los signos, las palabras, insinuan, hacen alusión. Este modo complejo de sentir el languaje me induce a creer que el lenguaje no puede expresar la realidad: que solamente podemos hablar de lo obvio. De allí mis deseos de hacer poemas terriblemente exactos a pesar de mi surrealismo innato y de trabajar con elementos de las sombras interiores. Es esto lo que ha caracterizado a mis poemas.

32. 'Historia antigua', from *Los trabajos y la noches*, 1965.

Alguien canta una canción el color del nacimiento:
por el estribillo pasa la loca con su corona plateada.
Le arrojan piedras. Yo no miró nunca el interior de los
cantos. Siempre, en fondo, hay una reina muerta.

33. From *Zona prohibida*, 1982.

Lucha feroz entre sílabas y espectros, versos rotos, poemas en harapos, frases como brazos amputados, deseos que nadie imaginó bajo el sol, estrellas sin luz, olas sin mar, me abrazan palabras y labios viejos, seres inimaginables y cosas.

34. Diary entry, translated in his own version in Frank Graziano, *Alejandro Pizarnik*.

35. 'La ultima inocencia', from *La ultima inocencia*, 1976.

Hé de partir
no más inercia bajo el sol
no más sangre anonadada
no más formar fila para morir.

He dé partir

Pero arremete, viajera!

# Alejandra Pizarnik: a select bibliography

*La tierra mas ajena*. Buenos Aires: Botella al Mar, 1955.

*La ultima inocencia* and *Las aventuras perdidas*. Buenos Aires: Botella al Mar, 1976.

*Arbol de Diana*. Buenos Aires: Sur, 1962.

*Los trabajos y las noches*. Buenos Aires: Editorial Sudamericana, 1965.

*Extracción de la piedra de locura*. Buenos Aires: Editorial Sudamericana, 1968.

*Nombres y figuras*. Barcelona: Colección La Esquina, 1969.

*El infierno musical*. Buenos Aires: Siglo XXI Argentina, 1971.

*Los pequeños cantos*. Caracas: Arbol de Fuego, 1971.

*Acerca de la condesa sangrienta*. Buenos Aires: Lopez Crespo Editorial, 1971.

*Zona prohibida*. Veracruz, Mexico: Ediciones Papel del Envolver/Colección Luna Hiena, 1982.

*El deseo de la palabra*. Barcelona: OCNOS/Barral Editores, 1975.

*Textos de sombra y ultimos poemas*, edited by Olga Orozco and Ana Becciú. Buenos Aires: Editorial Sudamericana, 1982.

## In English

Frank Graziano (ed.), *Alejandra Pizarnik: A profile*. Durango, Colorado: Logbridge-Rhodes, 1987.

# 4. Confronting myths of oppression: The short stories of Rosario Castellanos

## Chloe Furnival

Rosario Castellanos (1925–74) was born into a white, wealthy landowning family in Mexico City and grew up on the family's estate in the southern, predominantly Indian-populated state of Chiapas. In 1941, President Cárdenas's land reforms[1] finally reached this traditionally closed-off state, dramatically scaling down the Castellanos family's land-ownership there and causing the family's migration to Mexico City. Rosario Castellanos studied philosophy at the national university in Mexico City, presenting her Masters thesis in 1950 entitled 'On Feminine Culture' ['Sobre cultura femenina']. Later she returned to Chiapas (1956–57) and worked in San Cristóbal de las Casas for the Instituto Nacional Indigenista (INI) on projects that unashamedly aimed at integrating Indians into the mainstream culture.[2] Elements of these various stages in her life can be detected in much of her prose and poetry. The thematic focus of her first novel, *Balún Canán* (1957)[3] – the lives of Indians and women (both Indian and white/mestiza women) in a provincial town in Chiapas –was one that came to dominate subsequent works, in particular her first two collections of short stories, *Ciudad Real* [1960, *Royal City*] and *Los convidados de agosto* [1964, *Guests in August*], and her second novel, *Oficio de tinieblas* [1962, *Tenebrae*]. Her final anthology of short stories, *Álbum de familia* [1971, *Family Album*], narrows the concern down to the position of Mexican women. This brief study sets out to show that her short fiction can be seen to provide a critical insight into the bourgeois male 'utopia' that emerged from the Mexican Revolution; her stories expose the racism, sexism, opportunism and hypocrisy that continued to thrive in Mexico's Revolutionary 'utopia'.

Rosario Castellanos's wholehearted acceptance of INI's ideologically unsound project of working towards the elision of all difference between the races, of asserting 'individual humanity' above all else (Castellanos herself believed that, 'The Indians are human beings who are absolutely equal to whites, only that they live under special and terrible conditions'[4]), has to be seen as symptomatic of her reaction against both the widespread perception of Indians as 'exotic creatures' and against an entrenched and oppressive hierarchical system in which differences – between whites, mestizos and Indians, and between men and women – were *exaggerated* in order to keep an archaic, colonial system of oppression intact, a system of which she had first-hand experience in her childhood. Castellanos arrived at an identification of the woman question with the Indian one, chiefly through her readings of the social theories of the French philosopher Simone Weil. Weil had formulated theories of power and oppression in capitalist, technological societies, one of her main tenets being that power debilitates and dehumanizes those who wield it as much as those who are oppressed by it.[5] Castellanos applied this idea to white–Indian, man–woman relationships in Mexico, in which the roles are forever alternating:

> At first glance, one has the impression that the role of victim corresponds to the Indian, and that of victimizer to the other. But human relations are never so schematic, and social ones even less so. The masks sometimes change, the roles alternate.[6]

As will become evident, the dichotomies present in her *indigenista* stories – between victimizer and victim master and slave, linear, historical time and circular, mythical time – are ones that also underpin her later stories that focus on the lives of Mexican women. In some of her essays, Castellanos discusses the way that in Mexican history, both women and Indians have been perceived as 'communities of interpretation' (Edward Said).[7] Historically, both groups were the subject of theological enquiries, the conclusions of which dictated that both women and Indians needed to be placed under the authority of a superior (male) being, which in the case of the Indian was the *encomendero* (white landowner), and in the woman's case, a husband or father.[8] A situation emerged therefore by which the colonial discourses variously used to describe Indians were permeated with the very same terms that were used to describe women, and vice versa. Because both so-called 'minority' groups occupied a position marginal to the dominant centre, they were seen to constitute the boundary between order and chaos, either being seen as representatives of irrationality and 'chaotic' sensuality (which meant that the Indians were variously labelled 'barbaric' or 'savage', and the women lustful 'whores'), or being elevated to representatives of 'a higher and purer nature than men'[9] (so that in this schema, the Indians are 'noble savages', while women were seen as morally superior to men). In short, the Indian and the Mexican woman have, over the centuries, been made the subjects of a set of reductive, crippling myths denying them choice and an autonomous identity. The word 'myth' here refers to the myth-making that underlies systems of oppression, which justify the denigration and exploitation of certain sectors of society. It is myth, by which 'bourgeois ideology continuously transforms the products of history into essential types',[10] that Barthes exposed in *Mythologies* as the delusive element that pervades the discourses of society. In *The Labyrinth of Solitude*, Octavio Paz analyses some of the myths that pervade Mexican culture, one example being his exposition of how 'the Mexican' (which in his text, always means the Mexican *man*) never opens himself up to the world, always viewing life as combat (*lucha*).[11] Set up against the forever pugnacious 'Mexican' is the Mexican woman, who is an enigmatic and passive being; like all women, the Mexican woman is

> a symbol . . . of the stability and continuity of the race. In addition to her cosmic significance she has an important social role, which is to see to it that law and order, piety and tenderness are predominant in everyday life. . . . Thanks to woman, many of the asperities of 'man-to-man' relationships are softened.[12]

Paz explains that because the Mexican way of life is constructed as a mask designed to hide the most intimate feelings of Mexicans, it would be inconceivable to allow woman to cast aside her symbolic role and express herself as an autonomous being, for this would cause the mask – i.e. the whole Mexican way of life – to crumble.[13] So the pressure on the Mexican woman to conform is a formidable one. It could be said that Paz's self-conscious function as the 'unveiler' of the many myths that structure Mexican culture banishes him to a theoretical realm in which his ability to understand and acknowledge the full weight of the Mexican myths does not contribute to their elimination. Rather, the project of deciphering myths signifies a degree of complicity with them; the very process of demythification restores the object under scrutiny to its mystified state. This, according to Barthes, is the paradox that dogs every mythologist[14] (Barthes uses the word 'mythologist' to describe the person who *studies* the myth, the person who creates it being the 'myth-maker'), and in some respects it is a paradox that can be detected in much of Castellanos's non-fiction that takes as its project the unveiling of the myths that surround the Mexican woman.[15] If Octavio Paz was one of the first to draw attention to the masked nature of the Mexican character, then Castellanos was one of the first to show in her fiction and non-fiction alike that those masks were very suffocating indeed for Mexican women.

Reading of some of the stories of her first (*indigenista*) anthology, *Ciudad Real* (1960), demonstrates how Castellanos prepared the ground for her fictional treatment of the myths that impair Mexican women's lives. The stories of this anthology focus on critical points of interaction between white/mestizo culture and Indian culture. Most of the stories focus on the repeated cycles of aggression and exploitation that Indians have suffered at the hands of the whites over the centuries since the Conquest. For example, the first story, 'The Death of the Tiger'[16] traces the downfall of the once-dominant and belligerent Bolometic tribe, reduced by the white invaders to a defeated, bedraggled group who, after centuries of living timidly on sparse, unyielding land beyond the margins of the white settlers' towns, are finally forced to descend to Ciudad Real in search of a livelihood. The only white prepared to communicate with the Bolometic is the *enganchador* (agent), who sees in them welcome prey for his business of supplying cheap labour to white landowners. The *enganchador* and his assistant are appropriately depicted as grotesque, Dickensian caricatures:

> Don Juvencio drummed his fingers on the curve of his stomach, at the height of the waistcoat button where the watch chain should have hung. Remembering that he did not yet own a watch chain made him dig his spurs into the conversation . . . [p. 213] Don Juvencio's assistant showed his teeth in a wicked little smile. [p. 214]

These two mercenary whites work from a circular office that contrasts with the geometrical layout of the city's streets, but which reflects on their business of perpetuating time-tested patterns of exploiting Indians. The narrative suggests that the tragic plight of the Bolometic can largely be put down to the Indians' lack of means of communicating with the whites: the *enganchador* is easily able to exploit them because he can speak their dialect. The ominous description 'silence spread upon them like a stain' (p. 213) suggests the immediacy of his domination of them through language, for although he speaks to them in their own dialect, they are still rendered silent and therefore powerless. In other stories, however, the whites are depicted as being intolerant of the existing linguistic diversity, forcing the Indians into the straitjacket of the Spanish language, condemning them to be 'foreigners in their own land'. For example, the Indian protagonist of the story 'Aceite guapo', Daniel Castellanos Lampoy, seeks consolation from his loneliness in his new job as *mayordomo* (caretaker) to an alabaster saint, Santa Margarita, in a local Catholic church. For hours each day, Daniel sits pathetically talking to the saint at her altar, but the comfort he derives from these 'chats' is quickly dampened when the white sacristan assures Daniel that his words have 'fallen on deaf ears':

> Look at Saint Margarita's face. She's white, she's *ladina*, the same as Saint Juan, Saint Thomas, the same as all the rest of them. She speaks proper Spanish. How do you think she's going to understand the tzotzil dialect? [p. 47]

The sacristan assures him that only by purchasing and drinking some expensive 'aceite guapo' (alcohol) from a white settler's chemist (i.e. only by further subjecting himself to the economic system that exploits him), will Daniel miraculously attain instant access to the Spanish language, and therefore to the saint. On following the sacristan's advice, Daniel arrives at the church in a drunken stupor, babbling to the saint in what he pathetically believes to be Spanish. Predictably, he is expelled from the church forever. Clearly, this story amounts to a harsh critique of the Catholic Church and its role in the Indian communities. It points to the way that the perpetuation of a type of folk-Catholicism is only to the

Church's advantage, for it ensures the devotion of the mass of the Indians, which leaves them at the mercy of hypocritical Church officials. Daniel's turning to white religion as a source of comfort is therefore a paradoxical choice, for the religion forms an integral part of the social structure that victimizes and degrades him. In other stories in this collection, the author's attack on the Catholic Church's treatment of the Indians is extended to include a harsh critique of Catholic missions (see especially the stories 'Arthur Smith salva su alma' [Arthur Smith Saves his Soul] and 'La rueda del hambrimento' [The Wheel of Hunger].

In all of the *indigenista* stories, any interaction between whites and Indians is filtered through the various stereotypes that each race has formulated for the other, dictating the nature of the confrontation with one another. The stereotypes of the Indians formulated by the whites of San Cristóbal are all pejorative, but they also reveal the whites' fear of the Indians, who, after all, in a state like Chiapas, are in a majority. This fear is clearly demonstrated in the story 'La suerte de Teodoro Méndez Acubal' [Teodoro Méndez's Luck], in which a white jeweller is convinced that the Indian (Teodoro) peering into his shop window is about to rob him, simply because, in the white settlers' parlance, all Indians are thieves:

> The Indians are a race of thieves! . . . the man with the nose pressed against the window of his shop was a thief. There was no doubt about it. [pp. 58–59].

The paralysing effect of stereotypes grounded in myth also dictates the Indians' perception of the whites, in a way that in Castellanos's stories, more often than not, perpetuates their feelings of inferiority to whites, a phenomenon that arguably has its roots in the Conquest (when the Indians' belief that the *conquistadores* were gods whose arrival had been prophesied, put them at a distinct disadvantage in the subsequent battles).[17] The chaos that sometimes arises from the Indians' synthesis of their own myths and legends with the history of their oppression at the hands of the white settlers is dramatized in the story 'La tregua' [The Truce], in which a dying white man who stumbles into an Indian village is identified by the Indians as the dangerous, legendary spirit *el pukuj* who periodically appears 'now in the guise of an animal, now in the dress of the white man' (p. 30), and who is always the harbinger of disaster to the tribe. The now prostrate and weak *pukuj* of the story therefore offers the tribe not only an opportunity to wreak their revenge against this mythical spirit, but also a chance to avenge themselves of all the brutality that they have suffered at the hands of the whites. The narrator describes the bloody murder of the white man:

> Then the fury was unleashed. A stick used to beat, a stone used to crush his skull, a machete used to slice off his limbs. The women shouted from behind the walls of their huts, urging the men on to complete their criminal job. [p. 35]

The white man becomes the fated scapegoat of the Indians' syncretic myth system. What is perhaps interesting to note here is that, notwithstanding her support for INI's integrationist projects, her belief in the Indians' essential sameness to the whites, Castellanos does not shy away from depicting the Indians engaged in a seemingly spontaneous act of barbaric primitivism.[18] Significantly, the very description of this bloody murder once again points to the inhumanity of white rule, for this act was by no means a spontaneous abberration, but the result of centuries of abuse at the hands of the whites, whose organized system of oppression was no less barbaric.

'Modesta Gómez' is a story which reveals that the same forces have caused both the Indian's and the Mexican woman's oppression. Tracing the life of the lower-class mestiza protagonist, Modesta Gómez, the narrative reveals how in a social system grounded in racism, sexism, opportunism and intolerance, each act of brutality engenders another, and that predictably, it is the Indians who ultimately bear the brunt of all the accumulated cruelty of the system. Having been rejected by her family as a young child – the first harsh act in a long chain of them ('One mouth less to feed was a relief for everyone' [p. 65]) – Modesta takes up the position of nanny to Jorgito, the son of an upper-class white family. Modesta and Jorgito are the same age, but Jorgito is taught by his mother on numerous occasions that it is acceptable to punish Modesta physically. The outcome of such indoctrination is that in his adolescent years, Jorgito regularly rapes Modesta, and although aware of the nature of her son's nocturnal antics, Jorgito's mother convinces herself that they are 'natural' for his sex:

> Doña Romelia suspected something of her son's antics.... But she decided to play ignorant. When all was said and done, Jorgito was a man, not a saint, he was just the age when men feel the urge. [p. 68]

(Needless to say, when Modesta is visibly pregnant by her son, Doña Romelia throws her out onto the street rather than acknowledge any responsibility for her son's behaviour.)[19] Years later, after the death of her drunken, violent husband, Modesta is forced to become an *atajadora*, a job which consists of snatching from the Indians the products they bring to sell in the market, paying them a meagre sum that is only a fraction of what the produce will be worth in the market.[20] The graphic description of the *atajadoras* (all mestizas) in action points to the desperation of these women as they are forced to literally scrabble around for a livelihood:

> The *atajadoras* threw themselves wildly at the Indians. They struggled, suffocating shouts, to get hold of any object that wouldn't be damaged. Finally, when a woollen blanket or a bag of vegetables or a clay pot were safely in the hands of the *atajadora*, she would rummage in her blouse for a few coins, then toss them to the ground without counting them, leaving the defeated Indian to snatch them up. [p. 73]

Modesta over-enthusiastically participates in this degrading ritual, singling out a young Indian girl as her first victim:

> Modesta fought until she was on top of her. She pulled the girl's plaits, she slapped her cheeks, she dug her nails into her ears.... Inflamed, panting, Modesta grappled with her victim. She didn't want to let her go even when the girl gave her the woollen blanket that she had hidden. Another *atajadora* had to intervene. [pp. 73–4]

Looking at her bloodied fingernails, Modesta felt satisfied: 'She looked at her bloodstained fingernails. She didn't know why. But she was happy' (p. 74).

Although the Indians are not introduced until the climax of the narrative, their presence is felt throughout, for their very existence on the margins of Ciudad Real determines the nature of the rigid social hierarchy that is completed at the story's close. Modesta and the other *atajadoras*, all of them, as women, the victims of repeated acts of brutality that the system throws up, can only find consolation by entering into another exploitative relationship that ultimately only further entrenches their acquiescence to the system that degrades them. (The same can be said of Jorgito's mother, who compensates for her lack of self-esteem by cruelly exploiting her servants.) The final horrific image of Modesta's bloodstained fingernails explicitly points to the way that the mechanisms of oppression barbarize the oppressors. Modesta's inability to explain her exhilaration indicates the way that a type of fragmented vision is inscribed into the hierarchical social structure, for the system works to ensure that women like Modesta will never be able to assemble the fragments of their experiences into a whole that would unveil the workings of the system. (Undoubtedly, Modesta's final feeling of satisfaction is the effect of a kind of *unconscious* synthesis of the fragments, for it clearly stems from the fact that she feels that she has avenged herself of all the violence that the system has inflicted upon her.) The importance of this story in the anthology lies in its exposure of the multidimensional nature of the oppression suffered by both Modesta and her Indian victim, for as non-white, working-class women, they are both exploited (in the economic sense), and oppressed (in the sense that their sex and race is constructed as inferior to those of the dominant group).[21] The story shows how women in particular are susceptible to the brutality of the power hierarchy, and because of the nature of the system, the possibility of any form of positive interaction between the women of the different social groups is ruled out.

In some of the essays of *La mujer que sabe latín* [*The Woman Who Knows Latin*, 1973], Castellanos seeks to expose the myths that victimize and impair the Mexican woman. Her project was clearly indebted to her reading of Woolf's essays – particularly *A Room of One's Own* – and of Simone de Beauvoir's *The Second Sex*. Although today, the 'demythification' project is regarded as a well-trodden path, in her time, Castellanos was undoubtedly a pioneer in this area within Mexico. She exposed the sexism intrinsic to the Mexican cultural tradition, which stems largely from the way that women's lives are refracted through the national feminine symbols of La Malinche, the Virgin of Guadalupe, and Sor Juana Inés de la Cruz, so that in Mexican society, a woman is pigeonholed resembling either the supposed treacherous whore or the self-abnegating mother or the socially deviant scholar.[22] Castellanos was what today would be termed a liberal-reformist feminist, a stance that advocates the idea that women need to challenge the distorting stereotypes of conventional femininity, and fight for legislation and reform in order that they might take up their rightful and 'equal' places in the linear (masculine) time of project and history.[23] Such a stance can be criticized for its veiled aspirations for women to be able eventually to act and choose on the same terms as men without actually challenging the patriarchal structure,[24] yet it is important to remember that Castellanos was formulating her feminist ideals at a time when Mexican women had only recently (in 1953) gained national suffrage, so women's insertion into existing public life still seemed to be the priority for Mexican feminists.[25] Castellanos admired the work of the North American liberal-feminist Betty Friedan,[26] and like Friedan she eventually grappled with the phenomenon of why women -- in Mexico, educated middle-class women in particular -- were prepared to limit their horizons and accept marriage and motherhood as their sole vocation in life. Castellanos was aware of how society weighted the odds against the educated woman, for once trying to practise a profession she found herself in a social no man's land: '... in the place where Sor Juana was born: Nepantla, the land of inbetween, the place without identity. Up until now, that still small group of professional women has tended to consider itself as mutant creatures.'[27]

Castellanos called for consciousness-raising among women, so that they might begin to redefine themselves beyond the terms of patriarchy: 'construir la imagen propia, autorretratarse' ('construct their own image, depict themselves').[28] Such exhortations to women seem to be informed by an idealism in which her vision of women's emancipation located in change at the level of individual subjective consciousness, with no direct reference to the need for change in the structures of society at large. However, this idealism is modified by the pessimism of many of her narratives, in which women (and Indians) come up against much more formidable barriers even when they do attempt to break out of the treadmill of oppression.

In the stories that focus on the lives of women, the status of the *solterona* (spinster) become paradigmatic for the confined status of women in general. Dismissed as an abberation by patriarchal society because of her status and sex, the *solterona* epitomizes in the extreme the position of all women forced to live by the stringent codes of patriarchy. In Castellanos's stories, the *solteronas*' marginalized position does not endow them with more freedom to challenge the social order simply because they devote much of their energy in attempting to integrate into the hostile society that stigmatizes them. Their ultimate aim is usually integration into the world via the 'respectable' path of marriage. That is, the *solterona*'s entry into society is contingent on a man to act as social mediator. The title story of *Los convidados de agosto* [*Guests in August*] focuses on an anomalous day in the life of a middle-aged, upper-class spinster, Emelina – anomalous because it is a day of fiesta in her provincial home town. Elements associated with fiesta in Mexico – life and death, dream and reality, the halt of the flow of time and the abrupt break with routine – therefore become integral to, and in many respects determine, Emelina's experiences on this 'exceptional' day in her dreary life. Emelina is first described as waking from a dream (in which she is passionately embracing her fantasy lover) to the knell of the town's funeral bell. This seems to suggest that the life/death dichotomy is inverted in Emelina's case, with activity – life, passion – being confined to her dream world. Reflecting on the scandals of past *fiestas*, it emerges that Emelina harbours a deep fascination and envy for the daring and so-called 'loose' women who were able to exploit the riotous *fiesta* atmosphere to the full: the *toreras* of the previous year with their brassy outfits and provocatively defiant gestures, the women of the *barrios* who got pregnant by strangers and were forced to live in shame. In Emelina's view, the *fiesta* had given these women the much sought-after opportunity to shed 'the burden of spinsterhood' (p. 62). But Emelina too is weighed down by the restrictions of her class, for unlike her those women 'did not have much honour to lose and no surname to safeguard' (p. 62).

Emelina's spinsterhood keeps her in a state of constant anxiety about the passing of time. Her daily ritual of inspecting her naked body for wrinkles is just one manifestation of this. (Significantly, and in harmony with the timeless atmosphere of *fiesta*, Emelina detects no new wrinkles on this day.) Her dislike for the 'sterile lushness' (*verdor estéril*) of the quequextle plant she glimpses from her window, which thrives in 'shady places' (pp. 67–8), symbolically reflects her discontent both with her own sheltered life as a spinster in wealthy surroundings, and with her still-intact virginity. Yet when she picks a branch of the quequextle and attempts to unwind a tight, new shoot, it ominously reverts to its 'natural' position: 'But it was flexible and vigorous. Hardly was it loose when it sprung back to its natural position' (p. 68). (Again, when she impulsively opens the door of her canary's cage, the bird prefers the safety of the cage to the unstructured space of freedom [p. 68].) Later, at the end of the *fiesta* bullfight, in the pandemonium created by the customary collapsing of the wooden spectators' stadium, Emelina faints and is thrown into the arms of a total stranger, and soon afterwards, defying the scandalized stares of the townsfolk, she proudly enters a *cantina* (bar) with the stranger. She is soon very drunk, and allows the stranger to lead her from the *cantina*. But they are intercepted by Emelina's brother, Mateo, who assaults the stranger while her brother's best friend, Enrique, drags the humiliated Emelina home in front of intrigued spectators, unceremoniously dumping her on her doorstep and shouting accusations at her: 'You have brought shame to your family's name! And with a nobody! With an unscrupulous stranger!' (p. 95). The narrative closes with two resonating images: Emelina howling in the street, 'like a madwoman, like an animal', while Enrique abandons her, to go and hammer on the door of a brothel.

Clearly, what is being exposed in this ending are the double standards of a moral code that has as its priority the preservation of 'gentlemen's honour' (enshrined in the family's name) at all costs. The control of women's supposed boundless sexuality is considered to be the mainstay of the system of preserving male honour; women not already under the tutelage of male authority are considered to be replete with latent desires that are incompatible with the smooth functioning of patriarchal society. (Only within the walls of the brothel can this female sensuality be legitimately unleashed for men's pleasure.) Just as the narrative had opened with the rupture of routine that the *fiesta* celebrations bring, so it closes with another rupture, which is this time the total severance of Emelina's already fragile, spinster's hold on the external world. The fact that she is finally reduced to a 'howling animal' suggests that she has now been banished to the realms of absolute marginality. This final animalistic depiction of Emelina confirms an underlying association between her and the bull of the bullfight, for the bull had leapt over the barriers of the stadium only to be skilfully and quickly killed by the *matadero*. Both the death of the bull and the humiliation of Emelina are needed to ensure that male honour and prowess remain intact; both 'deaths' are approved by the community to ensure that tradition is observed. The collective interest in, and approval of, Emelina's punishment is highlighted in the way that it is deemed to be any man's prerogative – not necessarily a relative of Emelina's – to censure her for her transgression of social protocol. The fact that a man with only a casual connection with her family (her brother's friend) is able to take charge of what amounts to her destiny points to the decisive role that the social *milieu* plays in shaping the parameters of a woman's life. The equation is made explicit in this story: the preservation of male domination in such communities implies the confinement or social death of women.

The stories of Castellanos's final anthology, *Álbum de familia* (1971), move out of the enclosure of the provincial town and into the more impersonal world of Mexico City's suburbia. Castellanos's assessment of the conditions of the lives of urban middle-class women in these stories undermines assumptions about the supposed progressive, liberal values of the city; rigid definitions of femininity are proved not to be limited to Mexico's provincial towns. However, the fragmentary nature of life in the metropolis mystifies the mechanisms of power and oppression; the city – like patriarchy – is not a seamless, monolithic structure. The complex web of power relations that constitute patriarchal systems coincides with the fragmented incoherency of urban life, and so the fact that the success of the patriarchal economy is still contingent on confining women to certain roles can be more effectively masked. The first story of the anthology, 'Lección de cocina' [The Cooking Lesson],[30] analyses the way in which the asymmetrical relations between the sexes in patriarchal societies are sustained by the process of naturalization – the discourse of common sense. Underpinning the entire narrative is the discord between the vitality of the woman's concrete existence (symbolized in the text by a piece of meat) and the rigidity of abstract and stereotypical social prescriptions of femininity (symbolized by the recipe). The narrative is structured around the interior monologue of a newly-wed woman as she prepares a piece of meat for supper. The opening lines describe the kitchen in which the 'action' of the narrative takes place:

> The kitchen is shining white. It's a shame to have to get it dirty.... Looking closely, this spotlessness, this pulchritude lacks the glaring excess that causes chills in hospitals. [p. 158]

The narrator's very denials that the kitchen's sterile ambience recalls the deathlike atmosphere of a hospital ironically establishes the association between the kitchen and death. At the very least, the kitchen's almost blinding whiteness indicates a nullification of all that has preceded it – poignant when combined with the new wife's realization that her assumption of the role of wife has effectively invalidated her active past as an independent woman. The skills she acquired then are now secondary to the new, 'wifely' ones: 'For example, choosing the menu' (p. 158).

As the narrator follows a recipe to prepare a piece of meat, a pattern emerges by which the discrepancy between the reality of an inexperienced and incompetent (by patriarchal society's standards) wife cooking the meat and the ideal, finished product that the recipe promises is a discrepancy which is paralleled by the discrepancy existing between the woman's expectations of marriage and domesticity (expectations themselves constructed by various social discourses) and the reality of the situation: rather than find herself in the domestic bliss that society promises of marriage, she is confined to an orderly, impersonal kitchen, performing chores presumed to be the wife's vocation. Part of her dilemma arises from her awareness that she has *already* complied with the myth-making that surrounds marriage: for example, her sexual relations with her husband fall far short of the myths surrounding marital sex, yet she masochistically assists in their perpetuation.

> But I, self-sacrificing little Mexican wife, born like a dove to the nest, smiled like Cuauhtémoc under torture on the rack when he said 'My bed is not made of roses', and fell silent. Face up, I bore not only my own weight but also his on top of me. The classic position for making love. And I moaned, from the tearing and the pleasure. The classic moan. Myths, myths. [p. 159]

The narrator explicitly draws an analogy between the meat's metamorphosis through the various stages as she prepares it and her own changing condition from woman to wife. Just as the frozen meat was unrecognizable 'under its icy coating' (p. 159), so too was she once anonymous in society's eyes as a 'frigid' spinster. And just as the meat's 'offensive redness' (p. 160) can be toned down by rubbing spices into it, so too the woman's 'dense, viscous and turbid' (p. 160) vitality and individualism can be tempered by the demands of marriage and domesticity. In this way, the shrivelling up and burning of the piece of meat is ominous, foreshadowing the way in which traditional married life will eventually deform her if she is to meet the standards of the socially prescribed 'recipe' for a 'successful' marriage. ('The meat lies there silently, faithful to its deceased state' [p. 163]. Attention is drawn to the artificiality of both marriage and the recipe/text in this repeated juxtaposition of reality and myth; both are exposed as narrative codes that artificially construct worlds in terms of a particular ideology that upholds the status quo. The commonsense, patronizing language of recipes (which Virginia Woolf once referred to as 'a charming directness'!)[31] – like the patriarchal concept of the marriage union – presents the ideology of female submissiveness to (male) authority as natural and eternal. But because the narrator takes offence at the recipe's presumptuous tone, and goes out of her way *not* to identify herself with the unified and knowing subject whom the recipe addresses, its collusive tone is exposed and therefore undermined:

> Well, just who do you think you're talking to? If I knew what tarragon or *ananas* were I wouldn't be consulting this book, because I'd know a lot of other things too.... But you all start from the assumption that we're all in on the secret and you limit yourselves to stating it. I, at least, solemnly declare that I am not, and never have been, in on either this or any other secret you share. [p. 159]

In the narrator's refusal to recognize herself as the obvious, unified, but contradictory subject that the recipe constructs and addresses, lies the possibility for change, which may be detected in her defiance of convention:

> From today on, I'll be whatever I choose to be at the moment.... From the very beginning I will impose, just a bit insolently, the rules of the game. My husband will resent the appearance of my dominance. [p. 164]

This defiance is symbolically paralleled by the way that the meat remains raw 'in a few obstinate places' (p. 163). The narrator discovers that it is this 'obvious' and contradictory stance that she is expected to adopt if she hopes for a (conventionally defined) successful marriage. Although she recognizes that the contradictions in the recipe's terms of address correspond to her own experiences as a woman living by patriarchal codes, the recipe's final closure (which is based on an illusion that has no bearing on the reality of the burnt-up meat) works to smooth over these contradictions. By contrast, the narrator's text remains open-ended (the last line being: 'And yet . . .' [p. 165]). Because of the text's de-familiarizing of the conventional, the ironic tone used throughout is appropriate, highlighting as it does the incongruity and contradictory nature of reality.[32] Finally, although the story draws on the metaphor of the wife's world as a recipe, the story's message is not just a feminist one, for it also points out that reality lived day by day is a constructed reality.[33]

Although the title story of *Álbum de familia* does not read well as a short story (its long, dense monologues bear witness that it was originally intended to be a stage play)[34], it is important, for it explores a theme that was arguably uppermost in Castellanos's mind in the wake of the boom in Latin American literature: the 'problem' of the woman writer. The boom clearly provides the context, for the story also explores the phenomenon of literary superstardom and how this affects the 'exceptional' woman writer who joins the select group of male boom writers. Matilde Casanova, an internationally acclaimed writer, returns to Mexico after just having won the (fictitious) Premio de las Naciones (this detail, along with the description of her Indian appearance and the reference to her past as a schoolteacher suggests that Gabriela Mistral was the model for this character,[35] although Mistral was clearly pre-boom). Her secretary, Victoria, has arranged for her to meet some of her ex-pupils from her university-teaching days, and also two young students. The problem of the glamour that comes with a writer's fame is explored at great length in the first section of the narrative in a conversation between Victoria and a newspaper reporter of the popular press. Most of the population, like the reporter, have not even read Matilde's work, but the reporter unashamedly and cynically declares that the whole nation is bathing in the glory of her literary prize because, in her view, 'The champion disappears behind the halo of glory and the merit/prize is shared amongst all her compatriots' (p. 69). This journalist can be seen as a representative of both the general public's views of Matilde's achievement, and also, more significantly, of the widespread opinion of women's role in Mexican society. Toeing the party line, the journalist predictably dismisses Victoria's feminism as outdated and irrelevant in revolutionary Mexico where, she declares, 'there no longer exists any position that is inaccessible to Mexican women'. She adds that the requirements for women to 'get on' in Mexico are that they be discreet and accommodating ('do not make any display, nor adopt a defiant attitude' [p. 77]). This strategy is dismissed by Victoria as having for centuries been proved ineffective: 'But that position is the one that our grandmothers adopted! Dissimulation, deceit. What originality!' (p. 77).

Matilde's first entry shows her to be a distraught and anxious woman, unfulfilled by her profession, and suffering because she regards her writing as effective only as a palliative and disguise of the 'crime' of her sterility (p.

82). Matilde therefore displays the exaggerated 'symptoms' of the woman writer who, as Mary Eagleton notes, 'finds herself at a point of tension, aware that her writing both challenges the conventional view of what is appropriate for women and encroaches on what some see as a male preserve'.[36] Her anxiety over this conflict of roles surfaces despite the fact that she is a writer for whom the material obstacles to writing have been solved; she is economically independent, has 'a room of her own', and most important, has the invaluable services of Victoria, who in many respects protects Matilde from the world. Through this relationship between the two women, Castellanos examines the important roles that other women can often play in the lives of successful women writers; Victoria is the substitute 'literary wife' who channels her own creativity into the life of a successful writer.[37] Indeed, towards the end of the narrative, Victoria confesses to have sacrificed her own vocation as a writer and the precarious existence that comes with it so that she might hide 'behind a mask that amplifies my voice', a role that she believes endows her with 'absolute liberation' (p. 150). As Beth Miller notes, Matilde suffers from the syndrome Borges alludes to in 'Borges y Yo' [Borges and I]:[38] she feels that she has become trapped in a duplicitous situation in which the public image of herself becomes confused with her private self. But whereas in Borges's case, the legend and the man turn out to be inextricable, in the case of Matilde the existence of social expectations of a woman's 'true' role determines that this tension will never be resolved for her. Through the other characters of the story – three women writers, Matilde's ex-students – Castellanos reveals the different ways in which women of the same class (i.e. upper-middle and middle class) have attempted to resolve this dilemma. One writer, Elvira, has given up her marriage to continue her career; another, Josefa, has compromised her career for her children, and is obliged to write soap-opera scripts and journalistic pieces to make ends meet; and Aminta is a successful, unmarried writer who has prostituted herself to the commercial side of the business in her quest for fame – her public image is more important to her than the quality of her work. Out of these three writers, Josefa is convinced that she is the only one who has successfully resolved the conflict: 'I am the only one of us who has fully assumed her responsibilities as a woman and mother' (p. 124). But, according to Victoria's interpretation of *machista* Mexican ideology, even Josefa is a 'mutilated' woman by dint of the fact that she has chosen to be a writer as well as a mother:

> In Mexico the alternatives and circumstances for a woman are very limited and precise. Any one who wants to be more or less than daughter, wife and mother, can choose between becoming a black sheep or an immoral woman. [p. 149]

Matilde's notable absence for much of the narrative contributes to the mythologizing of her, but it also points to the extreme isolation and withdrawal from society that a successful writer can often endure, and that unlike her male counterparts, the woman writer's chosen solitude is in this case tainted by visions of what she lacks as a woman in society's eyes. It could be said that the opening description of the sea's waves symbolically condenses the story's pessimistic message, namely, that this conflict between women's powerful, individual urges and social expectations will be an eternal one:

> ... the waves stopped at the point at which – why? – they gave up their strength and began to pull back, as if regretful of the impetus that had carried them so far, only to regret their hesitation and start again. [p. 65]

In another essay, Castellanos subscribes to Virginia Woolf's view that out of all the professions, writing is the one that has been considered most suitable for women to follow because 'The family peace was not broken by the scratching of a pen. No demand was made upon the family purse.'[39]

Just after Castellanos's death in 1974, the Mexican author José Emilio Pacheco wrote in *Excelsior*:

> When the shock of her death passed and her books were re-read, one could see that none of us had in our time such a clear understanding of what the double condition of woman and Mexican meant. . . . Naturally we did not know how to read her.[40]

Her tragic and rather bizarre death (she died after accidentally electrocuting herself while serving as Mexico's Ambassador to Israel) undoubtedly inspired a wave of re-reading of her fiction, some of which used the texts as a means of arriving at the woman behind the work. For example, 'Cooking Lesson' has been referred to as a description of the author's own personal experiences as a newly-wed;[41] the torment that the young narrator–protagonist of *Balún Canán* [*The Nine Guardians*] experiences after the death of her brother Mario is invariably discussed as a direct reference to Castellanos's own devastating experience of overhearing her mother lament the fact that her son, Benjamin, had died and not the young Rosario.[42] Perhaps this mythologizing of Castellanos the woman is almost inevitable given her sudden death, but one of the effects of giving primacy to tracing in her fiction elements of the personal events of her life is that the fiction itself is neutralized: confined to the realm of the writer's private life, which has 'traditionally been the only life any "safe" woman may be presumed to lead'.[43] This does not mean that the formidable influence that certain formative events of the author's life brought to bear on her work should be denied (it is impossible to ignore the author's experience of working with Indians, or her childhood in a provincial town, or, indeed, her experience as a woman living under patriarchy), but it needs to be rejected as the central informing factor of the work. Castellanos was not a 'safe' woman; through her writing, she tackled what she considered to be the major social concerns of her time: the systematic denigration and oppression of women and Indians. In the light of more recent feminist literary theory this unproblematical movement from the text to the world beyond it can be criticized for its unquestioning acceptance of the *patriarchal* view of literature as representation, when the unveiling of the myths circumscribing women's lives is seen to be the most pressing need (as was arguably the case with Castellanos), but this type of social realism is often regarded as the most effective style to adopt.[44]

The influence of Rosario Castellanos's work on twentieth-century Mexican feminism was formidable. From the time of her Masters thesis of 1950 – a work which the writer Elena Poniatowska regarded as 'the point of departure for the contemporary women's movement in Mexico'[45] – Castellanos kept up a dialogue with the major trends in international feminist thought, filtering them through Mexican reality to come up with her unique and often satirical critique of contemporary social codes (see especially her play *The Eternal Feminine*).[46] Her advocacy of a type of integrationalist, liberal feminism, her unswaying conviction (conveyed in many of her essays) that women will be 'liberated' once they have access to study, work and sexual freedom, on the same terms as men – on a par with her belief that the Indians should be integrated into mainstream society in order to 'progress' – is a vision that is counterbalanced by the bleaker one that her short stories engender in focusing on the deeply entrenched values of Mexican society, which would clearly require more than social reform to eradicate. Rosario Castellanos used writing not only as a means of apprehending Mexican reality but also as a means of survival; in her own words, the act of writing realizes

> the desire to survive on a page, surrounded by all that we have loved, by all that we have found to be intolerable and painful, by what has excited us, aroused us to rebellion, brought us peace. Grasping that momentary lightning, we discover in its brief clarity, beauty and order, the laws and meaning of the world and of our own lives.[47]

The fact that Castellanos consciously set out to expose the darker side of the patriarchal 'laws and meaning of the world' in her prose and poetry makes all the more ironic the place of her burial: Mexico City's Rotunda of Illustrious Men.[48]

## Appendix: Spanish quotations that appear roughly translated in this chapter

p. 53 'A primera vista se tiene la impresión de que el papel de víctima corresponde al indio y el de verdugo al otro. Pero las relaciones humanas nunca son tan esquemáticas y las sociales lo son aún menos. Las máscaras se cambian a veces, los papeles se truecan.'

p. 55 'Fíjate en la cara de Santa Margarita. Es blanca, es ladina, lo mismo que San Juan, que Santo Tomás, que todo ellos. Ella habla castilla. ¿Como vas a querer que entienda el *tzotzil*?'

p. 56 '¡A los indios, una raza de ladrones! . . . el hombre que aplastaba su nariz contra el cristal de su joyería era un ladrón. No cabía duda.'

p. 56 'Entonces la furia se desencadenó. Garrote que golpea, piedra que machaca el cráneo, machete que cercena los miembros. Las mujeres gritaban, detrás de la pared de los jacales, enardeciendo a los varones para que consumaran su obra criminal.'

p. 57 'Doña Romelia sospechaba algo de los tejemanejes de su hijo. . . . Pero decidió hacerse la desentendida. Al fin y al cabo Jorgito era un hombre, no un santo, estaba en la mera edad en que se siente la pujanza de la sangre.'

p. 57 'Las *atajadoras* se lanzaron contra los indios desordenadamente, Forcejeaban, sofocando gritos, por la posesión de un objeto que no debía sufrir deterioro. Por último, cuando el chamarro d'elana o la red de verduras o el utensilio de barro estaban ya en poder de la *atajadora*, ésta sacaba de entre su camisa unas monedas y, sin contarlas, las dejaba caer al suelo de donde el indio derribado las recogía.'

p. 58 'Modesta luchó hasta quedar encima de la otra. Le jaló las trenzas, le golpeó las mejillas, le clavó las uñas en las orejas. . . . Enardecida, acezante, Modesta se aferraba a su víctima. No quiso soltarla ni cuando le entregó el chamorro de lana que traía escondido. Tuvo que intervenir otra *atajadora*.'

p. 58 'Se miró las uñas ensangrentadas. No sabía por qué. Pero estaba contenta.'

p. 59 '. . . en el lugar donde nació Sor Juana: Nepantla, la tierra de en medio, el lugar de la falta de ubicación. Hasta ahora ese grupo, demasiado reducido aún, de mujeres profesionistas tiende a considerarse como integrado por criaturas mutantes.'

p. 59 '. . . construir la imagen propia, autorretratarse'.

p. 60 '. . . no tenían mucha honra que perder y ningún apellido que salvaguardar'.

p. 60 'Pero era flexible y vigoroso. Apenas suelto volvió a su posición natural.'

p. 61 '¡Has deshonrado tu apellido! ¡Y con un cualquiera! ¡Con un extranjero aprovechado!'

p. 64 'El campeón desaparece trás el halo de gloria y el mérito se reparte entre todos sus compatriotas.'

p. 64 'No hay puesto que se considere inaccesible para una mujer.'

p. 64 '. . . no hacer ningún alarde ni adopta ninguna actitud desafiante'.

p. 64 '¡Pero ese método es el de nuestras abuelas! El disimulo, el fingimiento. ¡Que originalidad!'

p. 65 '. . . trás una máscara que amplifica mi voz'.

p. 65 'En México las alternativas y las circunstancias de las mujeres son muy limitadas y muy precisas. La que quiere ser algo más o algo menos que hija, esposa y madre, puede escoger entre convertirse en una oveja negra o en un chivo expiatorio.'

p. 66 '. . . las olas se deteníanen ese límite en el que ¿por qué? abandonaban su fuerza para comenzar a retroceder, como arrepentidas del ímpetu que las había llevado tan lejos, sólo para arrepentirse de su arrepentimiento y volver a comenzar'.

p. 66 'Cuando pasó la conmoción de su muerte y se relean sus libros, se verá que nadie entre nosotros tuvo en su momento una conciencia tan clara de lo que significa la doble condición de mujer y de mexicana ni hizo de esta conciencia la materia misma de su obra, la linea central de su trabajo. Naturalmente no supimos leerla.'

# Notes

## Texts

*Ciudad Real*. Mexico: Organización Editorial Novaro, 1974 (2nd edn)
*Los convidados de agosto*. México: Ediciones Era, 1968 (2nd edn)
*Álbum de familia*. México: Serie del Volador, Joaquín Mortiz, 1975 (2nd edn)

1. Before the dictator Porfiro Díaz was overthrown in 1910, 1 per cent of the population owned 97 per cent of arable land, and 96 per cent of the population owned 2 per cent of land. During the six years of Cardenas's presidency (1934–40), over 20 million hectares of land were redistributed to 775,000 people. And more land was distributed between 1935–40 than under all previous administrations put together from 1916. Details in B. Braulio Muñoz, *Sons of the Wind: The search for identity in Spanish American Indian literature*, New Jersey: Rutgers University Press, 1982, p. 224.

2. For details of Mexico's 'official *indigenismo*' see David A. Brading, 'Manuel Gamio and Official Indigenismo in Mexico', *Bulletin of Latin American Research*, vol. 7, no. 1, 1988, p. 86. Castellanos was involved in the creation of Teatro Guinol Petul, whose chief aims were to create didactic puppet shows that would educate the Indians into the mores of the dominant culture. Castellanos described the puppet Petul as 'a man of reason ... open to the news that his white and mestizo friends brought, thanks to whom their intervention always brought the triumph of intelligence over superstitions, of progress over tradition, and of civilization over barbarism'. Quoted in Mary Seale Vásquez, 'Rosario Castellanos, Image and Idea', in Maureen Ahern and Mary Seale Vásquez, (eds.), *Homenaje a Rosario Castellanos*, Valencia: Albatros Hispanofila, 1980, p. 23. Castellanos also said, 'It is necessary that they [i.e. the Indians] understand that ... they are cells of a society, of a State, of a nation.' Quoted in Perla Shwartz, *Rosario Castellanos: mujer que supo latín*, Mexico: Editorial Katún, 1984, p. 85.

3. *Balún Canán*, translated by Irene Nicholson as *The Nine Guardians*, New York: Vanguard Press, 1970.

4. Amado Mejías Alonso, 'La narrativa de Rosario Castellanos y el indigenismo', *Cuadernos Americanos*, vol. 260, part 3, pp. 205–6.

5. '[Power] weighs as pitilessly on those who command as on those who obey ... [creating a vicious circle in which] the master produces fear in the slave, by the very fact that he is afraid of him, and vice versa' (Simone Weil). Quoted in Cynthia Steele, 'The fiction of national formation: the *indigenista* novels of James Fenimore Cooper and Rosario Castellanos', in Bell Gayle Chevigny and Gari Laguardia, (eds.), *Reinventing the Americas: Comparative studies of literature of the United States and Spanish America*, Cambridge: Cambridge University Press, 1986, p. 64.

6. Rosario Castellanos, 'La novela mexicana y su valor testimonial', *Juicios sumarios I*, Mexico City: Biblioteca Joven, 1984, p. 122.

7. Edward Said, 'Orientalism', *Race and Class* vol. XXVII, no. 2, autumn 1985, p. 4.

8. Regina Harrison Macdonald, 'Rosario Castellanos: on language', in Seale Vásquez and Ahern, p. 54–5.

9. Toril Moi, 'Language, Femininity, Revolution: Julia Kristeva and Anglo-American Feminist Linguistics', unpublished lecture, 1983, p. 23. Cited in Deborah Cameron, *Feminism and Linguistic Theory*, New York: St Martin's Press, 1985, p. 127.

10. Roland Barthes, 'Myth Today', in *Barthes: Selected writings*, Oxford: Fontana Paperbacks, 1983, p. 145.

11. Octavio Paz, *The Labyrinth of Solitude*, (translated by Lysander Kemp), New York: Grove Press, 1961, p. 31.

12. *ibid.*, p. 38.

13. *ibid.*, p. 38.

14. Barthes, pp. 147–9.

15. Her long essays 'La participación de la mujer mexicana en la educatión formal' and 'La mujer y su imagen' in *Mujer que sabe latín*, Mexico: Sepsetentas Secretaria de Educacion Publica, 1973, pp. 21–41 and pp. 7–21 respectively and 'Otra vez Sor Juana', in *Juicios sumarios I*, pp. 22–7 deal with the Mexican myths of femininity.

16. A translation of 'La muerte del tigre' ('Death of the Tiger') by Alberto Manguel appears in A. Manguel (ed.), *Other Fires: Stories from the women of Latin America*, London: Pan Books, 1986, pp. 207–17. All page references in this study refer to this translation.

17. For a good account of the Conquest, see Tzvetan Todorov, *The Conquest of America* (translated by Richard Howard), New York: Harper & Row, 1984.

18. J. Sommers, 'The Indian-Oriented Novel in Latin America', *Journal of Inter-American Studies*, vol. 6, part 2, 1964, p. 262. In reference to Castellanos's depiction of a brutal Indian

rebellion in her novel *Oficio de tinieblas*, Jean Franco criticizes Castellanos because she 'tacitly acquiesces in the view of the literal-mindedness of the indigenous population propagated by positivism' (J. Franco, *Plotting Women*, London: Verso, 1989, p. 141).

19. 'It is common practice for a prudent middle-class mestizo mother of a pubescent boy to hire a young female servant for general housework "and other duties", the latter expression being a euphemism for initiating the boy into adult heterosexual experience', (Evelyn P. Stevens, 'Marianismo: the other face of machismo', in Anne Pescatello (ed.), *Female and Male in Latin America*, Pennsylvania: University of Pittsburgh Press, 1973, p. 97).

20. 'Hay oficios . . . en los que el despojo aparece como una forma lícita de comercio. El oficio de *atajadora*, por exemplo,' ('There are jobs . . . in which plundering appears as a licit form of commerce. The job of *atajadora*, for example.') From 'El idioma en San Cristóbal de las Casas' in R. Castellanos, *Juicios sumarios I*, pp. 130–1.

21. '. . . it is possible to parallel racialized and gendered divisions in the sense that the possibilities of amelioration through legislation appear to be equally ineffectual in both cases. . . . the construction of such parallels is fruitless and often proves to be little more than an academic exercise. . . . The experience of black women does not enter the parameters of parallelism. The fact that black women are subject to the *simultaneous* oppression of patriarchy, class and "race" is the prime reason for not employing parallels that render their position and experience not only marginal but also invisible' (Hazel Carby, 'Schooling in Babylon', in Centre for Contemporary Cultural Studies, *The Empire Strikes Back*, London: Hutchinson, 1982, pp. 212–13).

22. See Castellanos's essays, 'La participación de la mujer mexicana en la educación formal', 'La mujer y su imagen', and 'Otra vez Sor Juana'.

23. J. Kristeva, 'Women's Time', in T. Moi (ed.), *The Kristeva Reader*, Oxford: Basil Blackwell, 1986, p. 193.

24. For example, see Mary Evans' critique of the outcome of Simone de Beauvoir's *The Second Sex*, in M. Evans, *Simone de Beauvoir*, London: Tavistock Publications, 1985, especially pp. 57–68.

25. Despite the prominent participation of women in the 'public' side of the revolution – as *soldaderas*, doctors, journalists, nurses, campaigners – women didn't get the national vote until 1953. This delay is largely attributed to the conspicuous participation of some conservative middle- and upper-class women in the counter-revolutionary Cristero Revolt (1926–9) led by clerics. Relevant historical articles on Mexican women are as follows:
Beth Miller, 'Women and Revolution: the *Brigadas Femeninas* and the Mexican Cristero rebellion, 1926–29', in S. McGee (ed.), *Women and Politics in 20th Century Latin America*, Studies in Third World Societies 8, no. 15, March 1981, pp. 57–64; Anna Macías, 'Women and the Mexican Revolution 1910–20', in *Americas*, 37, no. 1, 1981, p. 53–82; Anna Macías, *Against All Odds: The feminist movement in Mexico to 1940*, London and Westport: Greenwood Press, 1982; Jane Nash, 'The Aztecs and the Ideology of Male Dominance', *Signs* 4, no. 1, winter 1978, pp. 349–58; Frederick Turner, 'Los efectos de la participación femenina en la Revolución de 1910', *Historia Mexicana* 16, nos. 61-4, 1966–7, pp. 603–17.

26. Castellanos includes an essay on Friedan in *Mujer que sabe latín*, pp. 120–5.

27. R. Castellanos, 'La participación', pp. 37–8.

28. Aurora Ocampo, 'Debe haber otro modo de ser humano y libre: Rosario Castellanos', *Cuadernos Americanos*, vol. 250(5), 1983, p. 210.

29. Paz, pp. 47–64.

30. 'Leccion de cocina', translated by Maureen Ahern as 'Cooking Lesson' in Doris Meyer and Margarite Fernández Olmos (eds.), *Contemporary Women Authors of Latin America: New translations*, New York: Brooklyn College Press, 1983.

31. 'Cookery books are delightful to read. . . . A charming directness stamps them, with their imperative "Take an uncooked fowl and split its skin from end to end" and their massive commonsense which stares frivolity out of countenance' (Virginia Woolf, review entitled "The Cookery Book of Lady Clark of Tillypronie', in the *Times Literary Supplement*, 25 November 1909. In A. McNeillie (ed.), *The Essays of Virginia Woolf, vol. 1: 1904–1912*,

London: Hogarth Press, 1986, p. 301).

32. Roger Fowler (ed.), *A Dictionary of Modern Critical Terms*, London, Henley and Boston: Routledge and Kegan Paul, 1973, p. 101.

33. 'In showing us how literary fiction creates its imaginary worlds, metafiction helps us to understand how the reality we live day by day is similarly constructed, similarly "written"' (Patricia Waugh, *Metafiction*, London and New York: Methuen, 1984, p. 18).

34. Kathleen O'Quinn, '"Tablero de damas" and "Álbum de familia": farces on women writers' in Ahern and Seale Vásquez, p. 100.

35. Beth Miller, 'Female Characterization and Contexts in Rosario Castellanos' *Álbum de familia, The American Hispanist*, vol. 4, Jan–Feb 1979, p. 27.

36. Mary Eagleton, Introduction to 'Women and Literary Production', in Mary Eagleton (ed.), *Feminist Literary Theory, A Reader*, Oxford: Basil Blackwell, 1986, p. 40. 'Outwardly, what is simpler than to write books? Outwardly, what obstacles are there for a woman rather than for a man? Inwardly, I think, the case is very different; she has still many ghosts to fight, many prejudices to overcome. Indeed it will be a long time still, I think, before a woman can sit down to write a book without finding a phantom to be slain, a rock to be dashed against. And if this is so in literature, the freest of all professions for women, how is it in the new professions which you are now for the first time entering?' (Virginia Woolf, 'Professions for Women', excerpt quoted in Eagleton, p. 53.)

37. Mary Eagleton discusses the phenomenon of 'literary wives' – in many cases (she cites Dorothy Wordsworth, Zelda Fitzgerald, Alice James as examples), they were 'the power behind the throne' (Eagleton, p. 44). However, the relationship between Matilde and Victoria is more on a par with those discussed in Gillian Hanscombe and Virginia Smyers in *Writing for their Lives*, London: Women's Press, 1987. Their relationship is comparable to, say, the real-life one between Gertrude Stein and Alice B. Tolkas.

38. Beth Miller refers to Borges's essay-fiction when discussing Matilde's dilemma (Miller, 'Female Characterization', p. 28). Borges's essay can be found in English in *Labyrinths: Selected stories and other writings*, London: Penguin, 1982.

39. Virginia Woolf, 'Professions for Women', in *The Death of the Moth and Other Essays*, London: Hogarth Press, 1942, p. 149, quoted by Castellanos in 'Virginia Woolf o la literatura como ejercicio de la libertad', *Juicios sumarios I*, p. 126.

40. José Emilio Pacheco, 'Rosario Castellanos o la literatura como ejercicio de la libertad', *Diorama de la cultura*, supplement of *Excelsior*, 11 August 1974, p. 16, quoted in Ahern and Seale Vásquez, p. 16.

41. 'Si en sus poemas Rosario da amarga cuenta de su fracaso matrimonial – en su prosa, no hay más que leer la ironía en torno a su luna de miel en el cuento "Lección de cocina"...' In Elena Poniatowska, *¡Ay vida, no me mereces! Carlos Fuentes, Rosario Castellanos, Juan Rulfo, la literatura de la Onda*, México: Editoria Joaquín Mortiz, 1985, p. 63.

Two other studies that explicitly make their project the life of Castellanos are: Perla Shwartz, *Rosario Castellanos mujer que supo latín*, México: Editorial Katun, 1984; and Estela Franco, *Rosario Castellanos: semblanza psicoanalítica*, México: Plaza y Janes, 1984, in which the author makes clear her belief that through Castellanos's fiction, she would be able to 'conocerla más fondo' (p. 7). Franco also states, '... los textos sirvieron para formular y reforzar atisbos de la dinámica de la personalidad de R.C.... Se orientó exclusivamente a trazar una semblanza de la escritora sobre lineamientos psicoanalíticos a partir de su obra' (pp. 8 and 11).

42. *ibid.*, p. 91. Castellanos is said to have overheard her mother say '¿Por qué murió el varón y no la mujercita?' ('Why did the boy have to die and not the little girl?')

43. See Kate Fullbrook, *Katherine Mansfield*, Brighton: Harvester Press, 1987, p. 5.

44. Bell Gayle Chevigny, 'Introduction to the Lives and Fictions of American women', in Bell Gayle Chevigny and Gari Laguardia, p. 152.

45. Elena Poniatowska, quoted in Mary Seale Vásquez, 'Rosario Castellanos', p. 21.

46. *El eterno femenino*, Mexico: Fondo de Cultura Económica, 1975.

47. 'La novela mexicana y su valor testimonial', in *Juicios sumarios I*, p. 130. This

translation is taken from Beth Miller, 'Rosario Castellanos' *Guests in August*: critical realism and the provincial middle class', *Latin American Literary Review*, vol. VII, Spring–Summer 1979, no. 14, p. 18.

48. Dan Bell also notes this irony in 'A Woman Who Knew Latin', *The Nation*, 26 June 1989, p. 891.


# Bibliography

## Texts by Rosario Castellanos
*Ciudad Real*. México: Organización Editorial Novaro, 1974 (2nd edn).
*Los convidados de agosto*. México: Ediciones Era, 1968 (2nd edn).
*Álbum de familia*. México: Serie del Volador, Joaquín Mortiz, 1975 (2nd edn).
*Balún Canán*. Mexico: Fondo de Cultura Económica, Col. Letras Mexicanas 36, 1957, translated by Irene Nicholson as *The Nine Guardians*, New York: Vanguard Press, 1959.
*Oficio de tinieblas*. Mexico, D. F.: Joaquín Mortiz, 1962.
*El eterno femenino*. Mexico: Fondo de Cultura Económica, 1975.
*Juicios sumarios I*. Mexico City: Biblioteca Joven, 1984.
*Mujer que sabe latin*. Mexico: Sepsetentas Secretaria de Educacion Publica, 1973.


## Secondary sources
Ahern, Maureen (ed.), *A Rosario Castellanos Reader: An anthology of her poetry, short fiction, essays and drama*, Austin: University of Texas Press, 1988.
Ahern, Maureen and Mary Seale Vásquez (eds.), *Homenaje a Rosario Castellanos*, Valencia: Albatros Hispanofila, 1980.
Barthes, Roland, 'Myth Today', in *Barthes: Selected writings*, Oxford: Fontana Paperbacks, 1983.
Bellm, Dan, 'A Woman Who Knew Latin', *The Nation*, 26 June 1989, pp. 891–3.
Brading, David A. 'Manuel Gamio and Official Indigenismo in Mexico', *Bulletin of Latin American Research*, vol. 7, no. 1, 1988, pp. 75–89.
Braulio Muñoz, B. *Sons of the Wind: The search for identity in Spanish American Indian literature*, New Jersey: Rutgers University Press, 1982.
Carby, Hazel, 'Schooling in Babylon' in Centre for Contemporary Cultural Studies, *The Empire Strikes Back*, London: Hutchinson, 1982.
Eagleton, Mary (ed.), *Feminist Literary Theory, A Reader*, Oxford: Basil Blackwell, 1986.
Evans, Mary, *Simone de Beauvoir*, London: Tavistock Publications, 1985.
Franco, Estela, *Rosario Castellanos: semblanza psicoanalítica*, México: Plaza y Janes, 1984.
Franco, Jean, *Plotting Women*, London: Verso, 1989.
Fullbrook, Kate, *Katherine Mansfield*, Brighton: Harvester Press, 1987.
Hanscombe, Gillian and Virginia Smyers, *Writing for their Lives*, London: Women's Press, 1987.
Macías, Anna, 'Women and the Mexican Revolution 1910–20', in *Americas*, 37, no. 1, 1981, pp. 53–82.
Macías, Anna, *Against All Odds: The feminist movement in Mexico to 1940*, London and Westport: Greenwood Press, 1982.

McNeillie, A. (ed.), *The Essays of Virginia Woolf, vol. 1: 1904–1912*, London: Hogarth Press, 1986.

Mejías Alonso, Amado, 'La narrativa de Rosario Castellanos y el indigenismo', *Cuadernos Americanos*, vol. 260, part 3, pp. 204–17.

Meyer, Doris and Margarite Fernández Olmos (eds.), *Contemporary Women Authors of Latin America: New translations*, New York: Brooklyn College Press, 1983.

Miller, Beth, 'Female Characterization and Contexts in Rosario Castellanos' "Álbum de familia"', *The American Hispanist*, vol. 4, Jan–Feb, 1979, pp. 26–30.

Miller, Beth, 'Rosario Castellanos' *Guests in August*: critical realism and the provincial middle class', *Latin American Literary Review*, vol. VII, Spring–Summer 1979, no. 14, pp.5–19.

Miller, Beth, 'Women and Revolution: The *Brigadas Femeninas* and the Mexican Cristero rebellion, 1926–29', in S. McGee (ed.), *Women and Politics in 20th Century Latin America*, Studies in Third World Societies 8, no. 15, March 1981, pp. 57–64.

Moi, T., 'Language, Femininity, Revolution: Julia Kristeva and Anglo-American feminist linguistics', unpublished lecture, 1983, p. 23. Cited in Deborah Cameron, *Feminism and Linguistic Theory*, New York: St Martin's Press, 1985.

Moi, T. (ed.), *The Kristeva Reader*, Oxford: Basil Blackwell, 1986.

Nash, Jane, 'The Aztecs and the Ideology of Male Dominance', *Signs* 4, no. 1, winter 1978, pp. 349–58.

Ocampo, Aurora, 'Debe haber otro modo de ser humano y libre: Rosario Castellanos', *Cuadernos Americanos*, vol. 250(5), 1983, pp. 199–212.

Paz, Octavio, *The Labyrinth of Solitude* (translated by Lysander Kemp), New York: Grove Press, 1961.

Poniatowska, Elena, ¡*Ay vida, no me mereces! Carlos Fuentes, Rosario Castellanos, Juan Rulfo, La literatura de la Onda*, México: Editorial Joaquín Mortiz, 1985.

Rodriguez-Peralta, Phyllis, 'Images of Women in Rosario Castellanos' Prose', *Latin American Literary Review*, no. 11, 1977, pp. 68–80.

Said, Edward, 'Orientalism', *Race and Class* XXVII, no. 2, autumn 1985, pp. 1–15.

Shwartz, Perla, *Rosario Castellanos: mujer que supo latín*, Mexico: Editorial Katún, 1984.

Sommers, Joseph, 'The Indian-oriented novel in Latin America', *Journal of Inter-American Studies*, vol. 6, part 2, 1964, pp. 249–65.

Steele, Cynthia, 'The Fiction of National Formation: The *indigenista* novels of James Fenimore Cooper and Rosario Castellanos', in Bell Gayle Chevigny and Gari Laguardia (eds.), *Reinventing the Americas: Comparative studies of literature of the United States and Spanish America*, Cambridge: Cambridge University Press, 1986.

Stevens, Evelyn P., 'Marianismo: The other face of machismo', in Anne Pescatello (ed.), *Female and Male in Latin America*, Pennsylvania: University of Pittsburgh Press, 1973.

Todorov, Tzvetan, *The Conquest of America* (translated by Richard Howard), New York: Harper & Row, 1984.

Turner, Frederick, 'Los efectos de la participación femenina en la Revolución de 1910', *Historia Mexicana* 16, nos. 61–4, 1966–67, pp. 603–20.

Waugh, Patricia, *Metafiction*, London and New York: Methuen, 1984.

Woolf, Virginia, *The Death of the Moth and Other Essays*, London: Hogarth Press, 1942.

# 5. Clarice Lispector: An intuitive approach to fiction
## Giovanni Pontiero

Clarice Lispector once remarked, 'If I were to become famous my privacy would be invaded and I should no longer be able to write. Every author should be wary of becoming popular for success can be destructive.' In her case, such fears were groundless. When she died of cancer in 1977, her reputation was firmly established in literary circles but the introspective nature of her writing ruled out popularity in terms of commercial success.

Lispector published her first novel *Near to the Wild Heart*[1] at the age of nineteen. Several influential critics were immediately struck by the extraordinary insights and haunting lyricism of this unknown writer. As a study of marriage and infidelity, this first novel marked a new departure in Brazilian literature and already embodied all the salient qualities of Lispector's subsequent narratives. Structure is imposed by the inner thoughts and alternating moods of the main character Joana. The crucial moments which shape Joana's destiny are less important than the repercussions they provoke. The author cautiously probes the nature and integrity of human relationships as Joana struggles with an encroaching sense of unreality, which is exacerbated by emotional stress and a dispiriting awareness of her own inadequacy. Poetry and meditation combine in the novel's interior monologues. There is an almost unbearable pathos when Joana comes to terms with the vulnerability of human existence and the clouded vision of her own identity.

The much-acclaimed stories of *Family Ties*[2] published some fourteen years later show a marked development in Lispector's sensibility and technique. The dangers of existence are further explored in contrasting situations. Anguished confrontations with nothingness, failure and absurdity engulf her characters, irrespective of class, sex or age. Particularly memorable are the narratives dealing with women at various stages of life: the poignant studies of adolescence in 'Preciousness' and 'Mystery in São Cristóvão'; the exploratory musings of rebellious housewives in 'The Daydreams of a Drunk Woman' and 'Family Ties'; the irreversible crises provoked by self-recognition in 'The Buffalo', 'Love' and 'The Imitation of the Rose'; and finally the cynical musings of the outraged old woman in

'Happy Birthday'. In these powerful stories, the characters discover that they are free to conform or rebel, but all the options are hazardous.

Lispector's characters are uncomfortably alert and dangerously aware. They are seized by contradictory emotions: 'horrible ecstasy' and 'atrocious delight'. The ebb and flow of human passions when contrasted with the primordial existence of plant and animal tend to reveal less consistency or harmony in human beings. Animals appear to possess greater ontological integrity. Yet human frailty exudes its own strange pathos and as Lispector observes, 'Sometimes it is our very vices that save our soul.'

Her existential preoccupations are enhanced by a quasi-mystical aura. The philosophical quest expands into a dialogue with the soul. The battle with self is explicit. All her women characters share her vulnerability: she confides, 'Everything affects me. I see too much, I hear too much, everything exacts too much from me. . . . I make such efforts to be myself. I struggle against the tide of myself.' She frequently ponders the tortuous conflict between spirit and flesh: 'Desires and passions die once they are satisfied. The will is immortal. I understand the body and its cruel demands. I have always known the body: darkness with sudden stars. One plunges into darkness – and carries away a trickling handful of liquid mirrors.' The persistent sense of weariness voiced by her characters, notably Ana in 'Love' and Laura in 'The Imitation of the Rose' betrays the intensity of this self-questioning. The dilemma of those women mirrors Lispector's own frustration where she confesses, 'I have spent my life trying to correct the mistakes I have made in my anxiousness to get things right. In trying to correct one mistake, I have often committed another. I am innocently guilty.' Haunted by a sense of incompleteness, Lispector admits to exploiting her own being as a form of knowing. The discovery of her own weakness is painful, but somehow essential. She asks:

> Only my needs justify me. What would become of me if I were to have no needs? What would become of my body if I were to feel no hunger? What would become of me if there were no future? What would become of me if I did not need God?

Her definition of this personal God is worth noting: 'God means the perfecting of a dream, signifies a person's ability to get rid of the burden of self.' Elsewhere she discourages any notion of an orthodox faith.

> Only by deceiving myself that God exists can I hope to live. Were it not for my inexplicable faith in the Unknown, despair would destroy me. I pretend that God exists in order to withstand the inexplicable by means of the inexplicable.

The ambiguities of existence inevitably lead to ambivalent responses. In describing herself as someone who feels timid yet undaunted in the face of life's terrors, she realizes that once having grown accustomed to the difficulty of accepting life, an easy existence would disorientate her, that only by accepting human misery can she hope to ascend. As the intimate jottings in her most private book, *The Foreign Legion*,[3] reveal, solitude and silence played an important part in the conception and actual writing of her narratives. She frequently counselled others, 'Remain alone from time to time, otherwise you will become submerged. Even the excessive love of others can submerge a human being.' Human love was something she mistrusted. In many of her narratives there is a lingering fear that what humans call love or friendship might suddenly turn into emotional blackmail or even dangerous possession.

The obsessive questioning and subverting of reality in Clarice Lispector's fiction have prompted critics to compare her with existentialist writers in Europe. Such comparisons are valid and useful, but in the final analysis, her conclusions about the human condition tend to be even more complex and pessimistic than those of Sartre and his followers. The very fabric of life disintegrates before Lispector's gaze.

The depth and subtlety of her portraits of women, rich and poor, young and old, have made her the 'new prophet of the female world' among the French proponents/exponents of feminine writing. The critic Clare Hanson, in a recent article entitled 'Clarice Lispector: a new Eve' in *PN Review*,[4] persuasively argues that Lispector concentrates on the third stage of feminist awareness. Hanson defines the first stage as a demand for equality, the second stage as the extolling of feminine virtues and the third stage as a rejection of the polarities of masculine and feminine. This theory is certainly applicable to Lispector's last novel *The Hour of the Star*,[5] where the conflict between male and female attitudes in Latin America is at its most naked in the dialogues between the self-effacing Macabea and the bullying Olímpico: 'Macabea who exists in an impersonal limbo', whose 'existence is sparse' and Olímpico who gauges his *machismo* in terms of wanton cruelty, theft and murder. Yet ironically, Lispector deliberately opts for a male narrator to guide the reader through one of her most searching and ambivalent accounts of sexual mores and attitudes among the underprivileged.

The importance of Lispector's contribution to contemporary fiction in Brazil had already been acknowledged by the late 1960s. Her plotless narratives and linguistic innovations betrayed certain affinities with the experimental prose of Brazilian writers like Antônio Callado, José Condé, Lúcio Cardoso and Osman Lins, who had helped to steer Brazilian fiction away from regionalism and biased propaganda to a deeper exploration of human experience. Predictably her impact on a younger generation of women writers was considerable and is still in evidence today. More women writers have come to the fore in Brazil within the last ten years than in the previous fifty. Some have started to have their work translated and published abroad. Lispector, however, remains unrivalled in terms of creative genius.

Her working habits were idiosyncratic but effective. She annotated constantly as ideas came to her and jotted down dialogue as she listened to the conversations of others. A single word could inspire a flood of sentences, a solitary image could lead to the conception of a whole narrative. She invariably typed out her stories with the assistance of random notes. Then she would cut or add to the text but never rewrite it. In later years, as she became increasingly ill, she found the problem of structuring her material much more difficult. She suffered from insomnia and would spend her sleepless hours either meditating or writing, as she listened to classical music. She recognized that writing was a solitary act but 'solitary in a way that is different from solitude' and in no sense remote from the real world. She explained: 'The writer is not a passive being who limits himself to gathering facts culled from reality. He must be in the world as an active presence in communication with everything around him.' She described her approach to writing as being largely intuitive: 'I have never really had what can be truly defined as an intellectual life. Even when writing, I use my intuition rather than my intelligence. One writes as one loves. No one knows why they love just as they do not know why they write.' And it was the only feasible approach for a writer who was drawn to things fragmentary and incomplete. She wrote: 'I have a real affection for things which are incomplete or badly finished, for things which awkwardly try to take flight only to fall clumsily to the ground.' She clarified her intuitions by transposing them into words, a process which made her apprehensive lest she should falsify her emotions in the telling. This cautious probing for an exact correspondence between image and emotion is clearly illustrated by a fragment in *The Foreign Legion* entitled 'Body and Soul':

In Italy, *il miracolo* is night fishing. Mortally wounded by the harpoon, the fish releases its crimson blood into the sea. The fisherman unloading his catch before sunrise, his face livid with guilt, knows that the great burden of miraculous fishing he is dragging over the sands – is love. *Milagre* is the tear of the leaf which trembles, escapes and falls: behold thousands of miraculous tears glistening on the ground. The *miracle* has the sharp points of stars and much splintered silver. To pass from the word to its meaning is to reduce it to splinters just as the firework remains a dull object until it becomes a brilliant flare in the sky and achieves its own death. (In its passage from the body to the senses, anger reveals the same supreme achievement – by dying.) *Le miracle* is a glass octagon which can be turned slowly in the palm of the hand. It remains in the hand but only for gazing at. It can be viewed from all angles . . . very slowly . . . and on each side there is revealed a glass octagon. Until suddenly – threatened and turning quite pale with emotion – the person understands: in the palm of his hand he no longer holds an octagon but a miracle. From this moment onwards, he no longer sees anything. He possesses it.

For Lispector, as for the existentialists, the clouded frontiers of human experience are reflected in the writer's struggle with words. Language remains as mysterious as life itself. Her various statements about writing explain how she succeeded in saying the unsayable by paradoxical means. 'What cannot be expressed only comes to me through the breakdown of language. Only when the structure breaks down do I succeed in achieving what the structure failed to achieve.'

Recurring stylistic features of her prose, such as stream-of-consciousness, interior monologue, paronomasia, oxymoron and antithesis have been widely discussed by the critics. Less easy to analyse is Lispector's unorthodox use of syntax and punctuation. These are subordinated to the demands of her fleeting perceptions, her own idiosyncratic rhythms, the subtle patterns of sound that have become the hallmark of her prose. Even the pauses create what Benedito Nunes has defined as an 'awesome silence' – the refuge of a writer who sees and knows too much.

The depth and intensity of Lispector's meditations might suggest a tragic muse. That is merely one facet of this complex and versatile writer. The misfortunes of Macabea, for example, in *The Hour of the Star*, are painfully moving, yet Macabea's encounter first with the poor man's doctor who bemoans his fate, and then with the loquacious whore-turned-fortuneteller Madame Carlota, have all the wit and innuendo of a Feydeau farce. And the humour is positively savage in chronicles such as 'An Angel's Disquiet'[6] and 'A Spanish Gentleman',[7] where a day spent with 'Pepe – *The* Guide of Cordoba' proves to be a scarring experience. In both chronicles, emotional blackmail (Lispector's *bête noire*) rears its ugly head.

Woman, mother, writer, critic, artist, mystic, Lispector cast her own unmistakable spell on every literary genre she practised. The briefest character sketch or travel note elicits fresh insights; for example, her description of an Italian village:[8]

> The men have crimson lips and produce offspring. The women become deformed from breastfeeding. As for the elderly, the elderly do not betray any emotion. The work is strenuous. The night, silent. There are no cinemas. On the threshold, the beauty of a young woman is to remain there standing in the dark. Life is sad and abundant as one would expect life to be in the mountains.

And her transcendental vision of the new capital Brasilia:[9]

> Brasilia is the image of my insomnia. . . . In Brasilia there is no place where one may enter, no place where one may leave. . . . Brasilia is asexual. . . . In Brasilia you find the craters of the Moon. The beauty of Brasilia is to be found in those invisible statues.

Her dialogues with children, whether mental or voiced, are unparalleled in Brazilian literature, and her essays on the visual arts and music are as individual as they are thought-provoking. Her frequent aphorisms and startling declarations invariably carry a sting in the tail:

Just to have been born has ruined my health.[10]

After I discovered in my own mind how people think, I was no longer able to believe in the thoughts of others.[11]

To err is a much more serious matter among intelligent people: for they have all the arguments to prove their point.[12]

Hers is clearly a talent to amuse and wound. Yet in the final analysis, human frailty is exposed with pathos rather than malice. The understanding she craved for herself, she also extends to her readers. She feared *counterfeit* emotions and *creative* lies and once declared with utter sincerity, 'If I had to give a title to my life, it would be the following: "In search of my own thing".' A truly worthwhile search, which her readers are privileged to share.

## Notes

1. *Perto do coração selvagem* [Near to the Wild Heart – a phrase taken from James Joyce's novel *Portrait of the Artist as a Young Man*], Rio de Janeiro: A Noite, 1944.
2. *Laços de família*, Rio de Janeiro: Francisco Alves, 1960.
3. *A Legião Estrangeira*, Rio de Janeiro: Editôra do Autor, 1964.
4. *PN Review* 52, vol. 13, no. 2, 1986, pp. 69–71.
5. *A hora da estrela*, Rio de Janeiro: José Olympio, 1977.
6. 'Mal-estar de um anjo', (in *A Legião Estrangeira*, pp. 152–7).
7. 'Um homem espanhol', (in *A Legião Estrangeira*, pp. 240–4).
8. 'Aldeia italiana', (in *A Legião Estrangeira*, p. 160).
9. 'Brasília: cinco dias', (in *A Legião Estrangeira*, pp. 162–7).
10. 'Avareza', (in *A Legião Estrangeira*, p. 198).
11. 'As negociatas', (in *A Legião Estrangeira*, p. 198).
12. 'Mas é que o êrro...', (in *A Legião Estrangeira*, p. 139).

## Clarice Lispector: select bibliography

### Primary sources

*1 Novels*
*Perto do coração selvagem*, Rio de Janeiro: A Noite, 1944.
*O lustre*, Rio de Janeiro: Editôra Agir, 1946.
*A cidade sitiada*, Rio de Janeiro: A Noite, 1949.
*A maçã no escuro*, Rio de Janeiro: Francisco Alves, 1961.

*A paixão segundo G. H.*, Rio de Janeiro: Editôra do Autor, 1964.
*Uma aprendizagem ou o livro dos prazeres*, Rio de Janeiro: Editôra Sabiá, 1969.
*Água viva*, Rio de Janeiro: Artenova, 1973.
*A hora da estrela*, Rio de Janeiro: José Olympio, 1977.
*Um sopro de vida: pulsações*, Rio de Janeiro: Nova Fronteira, 1978.

## 2   Stories
*Alguns contos*, Rio de Janeiro: Ministério de Educação e Saúde, 1952.
*Laços de família*, Rio de Janeiro: Francisco Alves, 1960.
*A Legião Estrangeira*, Rio de Janeiro: Editôra do Autor, 1964.
*Felicidade clandestina*, Rio de Janeiro: Sabiá, 1971.
*A imitação da rosa* (a collection of previously published stories), Rio de Janeiro:
    Artenova, 1973.
*Onde estivestes de noite*, Rio de Janeiro: Artenova, 1974.
*A via crucis do corpo*, Rio de Janeiro: Artenova, 1974.
*A bela e a fera*, Rio de Janeiro: Nova Fronteira, 1979

## 3   Children's literature
*O mistério do coelho pensante*, Rio de Janeiro: José Álvaro, 1967.
*A mulher que matou os peixes*, Rio de Janeiro: Sabiá, 1968.
*A vida íntima de Laura*, Rio de Janeiro: José Olympio, 1974.
*Quase de verdade*, Rio de Janeiro: Editôra Rocco, 1978.

## 4   Translations by Clarice Lispector
*O retrato de Dorian Gray* (Portuguese translation of Oscar Wilde's *The Picture of
    Dorian Gray*), Rio de Janeiro: Edições de Ouro, 1974.

## 5   Translations into English of works by Clarice Lispector (novels, portions of novels, and short-story anthologies)
(*Água viva*) *Stream of Life* (translated by Elizabeth Lowe and Earl Fitz). Minnesota:
    University of Minnesota Press, 1984.
(*Uma aprendizagem ou o livro dos prazeres*) *An Apprenticeship or The Book of
    Delights* (translated by Richard A. Mazzara and Lorri A. Parris). Austin:
    University of Texas Press, 1987.
(*A Hora da Estrela*) *The Hour of the Star* (translated with an Afterword by Giovanni
    Pontiero). Manchester: Carcanet Press, 1986; London: Grafton, 1987.
(*Laços de família*) *Family Ties* (translated with an Afterword by Giovanni
    Pontiero). Austin: University of Texas Press, 1972, Manchester: Carcanet Press,
    1984.
(*A Legião Estrangeira*: extracts) *The Foreign Legion* (translated by Giovanni
    Pontiero). *Review* 24, 37–43. New York: Center for Inter-American Relations,
    1979.
(*A Legião Estrangeira*) *The Foreign Legion: Stories and chronicles* (translated with an
    Afterword by Giovanni Pontiero). Manchester: Carcanet Press, 1986; New
    York: Carcanet Press, 1987
(*A maçã no escuro*) *The Apple in the Dark* (translated by Gregory Rabassa). New
    York: Knopf, 1967; London: Virago, 1985.
(*A mulher que matou os peixes*) *The Woman Who Killed the Fish* (translated by Earl E.
    Fitz). *Latin American Literary Review* no. 32, July–December 1988.

(*A paixão segundo G.H.*) *The Passion According to G.H.* (a portion of the novel translated by Jack E. Tomlins). In *Borzoi Anthology of Latin American Literature*, New York: Knopf, 1977.

(*A paixão segundo G.H.*) *The Passion According to G.H.* (translated by Ronald W. Sousa). Minneapolis: University of Minnesota Press, 1989.

(*Perto do coração selvagem*) *Near to the Wild Heart* (translated with an Afterword by Giovanni Pontiero). Manchester: Carcanet Press, 1989.

## 6 Stories translated and published separately

'Marmosets' (translated by Elizabeth Bishop). In *The Eye of the Heart*, New York: Bard/Avon, 1973.

'Better Than to Burn'. In Anne Fremantle (ed.), *Latin American Literature Today* (translated by Alexis Levitin). New York: New American Library, 1977.

'The Man Who Appeared' (translated by Alexis Levitin). In Anne Fremantle (ed.), *Latin American Literature Today*, New York: New American Library, 1977.

'Pig Latin' (translated by Alexis Levitin). *Ms.* 13, no. 1, July 1984, pp. 68–9.

'The Smallest Woman in the World' (translated by Elizabeth Bishop). In *The Eye of the Heart*, New York: Avon, 1973.

'The Solution' (translated by Elizabeth Lowe). *Fiction 3*, winter 1974, p. 24.

'Temptation' (translated by Elizabeth Lowe). *Inter-Muse 1*, no. 1, Michigan State University, 1976. 'Sofia's Disasters' (translated by Elizabeth Lowe). Review 24, New York: The Center for Inter-American Relations, June 1979.

'Love' (translated by Giovanni Pontiero). In *New Directions 25*, New York: New Directions, 1972.

'Daydreams of a Drunk Woman' (translated by Giovanni Pontiero). In *Women and Men Together*, Boston: Houghton Mifflin, 1978.

'The Smallest Woman in the World' (translated by Giovanni Pontiero). In *Foreign Fictions*, New York: Vintage Books, 1978.

'The Imitation of the Rose' (translated by Giovanni Pontiero). In *Short Story International 21*, New York: International Cultural Exchange, 1980.

'Love' and 'The Chicken' (translated by Giovanni Pontiero). In *An Anthology of Latin American Jewish Writings*, Marblehead, Massachusetts, 1980.

'Mineirinho' (translated by Giovanni Pontiero). In *PN Review* 52, no. 2, vol. 13, Manchester: Poetry Nation Review, 1986.

'Journey to Petrópolis', (translated by Giovanni Pontiero). In *PN Review* 51, no. 1, vol. 13, Manchester: Poetry Nation Review, 1986.

'The Imitation of the Rose' (translated by Giovanni Pontiero). In *Other Fires*, New York: Clarkson N. Potter, Inc., 1986; and London: Picador Books, 1986.

'Since One Feels Obliged to Write . . .' (translated by Giovanni Pontiero). In Doris Meyer (ed.), *Lives On the Line*, Berkeley: University of California Press, 1988.

'The Fifth Story' (translated by Giovanni Pontiero). In Robert Shapard and James Thomas (eds.), *World Sudden Fiction*, New York: W. W. Norton and Co., 1989.

## 7 Selected and collected writings

*A imitação da rosa* (a selection of Lispector's best stories). Rio de Janeiro: Artenova, 1973.

*Para não esquecer* (a selection of some of Lispector's chronicles and essays). São Paulo: Atica, 1978.

*Seleta de Clarice Lispector* (edited by R. C. Gomes and A. G. Hill). Brasília: Instituto Nacional do Livro, 1975.

## Secondary sources

### 1 Bibliographies
Fitz, Earl E. 'Uma bibliografia de e sôbre Clarice Lispector'. *Revista Iberoamericana* 50, no. 126 (January–March 1984), pp. 293–304. Includes articles, books, parts of books, book reviews and newspaper articles published through 1984. Not annotated.

### 2 Books
Borelli, Olga, *Clarice Lispector: um esboço para um possível retrato*, Rio de Janeiro: Nova Fronteira, 1981.
Brasil, Assis, *Clarice Lispector*, Rio de Janeiro: Editôra Organização Simões, 1969.
Campedelli, S. Y., and Abdala, B., Jr, *Clarice Lispector*, São Paulo: Literatura Comentada, 1981.
Fitz, Earl E., *Clarice Lispector*, Boston: Twayne Publishers, 1985.
Nunes, Benedito, *O mundo de Clarice Lispector*, Manaus: Edições Governo do Estado do Amazonas, 1966.
Nunes, Benedito, *Leitura de Clarice Lispector*, São Paulo: Editôra Quirón, 1973.
Pereira, Teresinha Alves, *Estudo sôbre Clarice Lispector*, Coimbra: Edições Nova Era, 1975.
Sá, Olga de, *A escritura de Clarice Lispector*, Petrópolis: Vozes, 1979.

### 3 Parts of books
Amora, Antônio Soares, *História de literatura brasileira* (7th edn), São Paulo: Edição Saraiva, 1968, pp. 163–74.
Cândido, Antônio, 'No raiar de Clarice Lispector', in *Vários escritos*, São Paulo: Livraria Duas Cidades, 1970, pp. 125–31.
Castro, Silvio, *A revolução de palavra*, Petrópolis: Editôra Vozes, 1976, pp. 263–7.
Coutinho, Afrânio, *An introduction to Literature in Brazil* (translated by Gregory Rabassa), New York: Columbia University Press, 1960, p. 249.
Coutinho, Afrânio, *A literatura no Brasil* (2nd edn), vol. 5: *Modernismo*, 1959, pp. 449–72.
Filho, Adonias, *Modernos ficcionistas brasileiros* (2nd series), Rio de Janeiro: Edições Tempo Brasileiro, 1965, pp. 81–3.
Jozef, Bella, *O jogo mágico*, Rio de Janeiro: Livraria José Olympio, 1980, pp. 32–40, 75, 122.
Lins, Ávaro, *Os mortos de sobrecasaca*, Rio de Janeiro: Editôra Civilização Brasileira, 1963, pp. 186–93.
Lowe, Elizabeth, *The City in Brazilian Literature*, Rutherford: Farleigh Dickinson University Press, 1982.
Moisés, Massaud, 'Clarice Lispector Contista', in *Temas brasileiros*, São Paulo: Conselho Estadual de Cultura, 1964, pp. 119–24.
Monegal, Emir Rodríguez, *El boom de la novela latinoamericana*, Caracas: Editoria Tiempo Nuevo, 1972, pp. 27 and 93.
Monegal, Emir Rodríguez, *The Borzoi Anthology of Latin American Literature*, New York: Knopf, 1977, pp. 779–92.
Monegal, Emir Rodríguez, 'The Contemporary Brazilian Novel' in Henri Peyre (ed.), *Fiction in Several Languages*, Boston: Houghton Mifflin, 1968, pp. 1–18.
Nunes, Benedito, 'O mundo imaginário de Clarice Lispector', in *O dorso do tigre*,

São Paulo: Editôra Perspectiva, 1969, pp. 93–139.

Olinto, Antônio, *A verdade da ficção*, Rio de Janeiro: Companhia Brasileira de Artes Gráficas, 1966, pp. 62, 100, 110, 142, 144, 213–16, 226, 227.

Patai, Daphne, *Myth and Ideology in Contemporary Brazilian Fiction*, Cranbury, N.J.: Fairleigh Dickinson University Press, 1983.

Perez, Renard, *Escritores brasileiros contemporâneos* (2nd series), Rio de Janeiro: Editôra Civilização Brasileira, 1964, pp. 69–80.

Silverman, Malcolm, *Moderna ficção brasileira* (translated into Portuguese by João Guilherme Linke), Brasilia: Civilização Brasileira, 1978, pp. 70–84.

## 4 Articles

Araújo, Laís Corrêa de, 'Texto/improviso', *Minas Gerais Suplemento Literário*, no. 392, (2 March 1974), p. 9.

Bruno, Haroldo, 'A presença renovadora de Clarice Lispector,' *Minas Gerais Suplemento Literário*, 14 July 1979, pp. 6–7.

Bryan, C. D. B., 'Afraid to be Afraid', *New York Times Book Review*, 3 September 1967, pp. 22–3.

Cook, Bruce, 'Women in the Web', *Review* 73, spring 1973, pp. 65–6.

Fitz, Earl E., 'Clarice Lispector and the Lyrical Novel: a re-examination of *A maçã no escuro*', *Luso-Brazilian Review* 14, no. 2, winter 1977, pp. 153–60.

Fitz, Earl E., 'Clarice Lispector's *Um sopra de vida*: the novel as confession,' *Hispania* (forthcoming).

Fitz, Earl E., 'The Leitmotif of Darkness in Seven Novels by Clarice Lispector', *Chasqui: Revista de Literatura Latinoamericana* 7, no. 2, February 1978, pp. 18–28.

Fitz, Earl E., 'The Rise of the New Novel in Latin America: a lyrical aesthetic,' *Inter-Muse* 2, 1979, pp. 17–27.

Fitz, Earl E., 'Freedom and Self-Realization: feminist characterization in the fiction of Clarice Lispector', *Modern Language Studies* 10, no. 3, 1980, pp. 51–6.

Fitz, Earl E., 'Point of View in Clarice Lispector's *A hora da estrela*', *Luso-Brazilian Review* 19, no. 2, winter 1982, pp. 195–208.

Foster, David William and Foster, Virginia Ramos (eds.), *Modern Latin American Literature*, New York: Frederick Ungar, 1975, pp. 484–91.

Garcia, Frederick C. H., 'Os livros infantis de Clarice Lispector', *Minas Gerais Suplemento Literário*, 10 February 1979, pp. 4–5.

Goldman, Richard Franko, 'The Apple in the Dark', *Saturday Review*, 19 August 1967, pp. 33, 48.

Hamilton, D. Lee, 'Some Recent Brazilian Literature', *Modern Language Journal* 32, no. 7, November 1948, pp. 504–7.

Hanson, Clare, 'Clarice Lispector: a new Eve?', *PN Review* 52, vol. 13, no. 2, 1986, pp. 43–5.

Herman, Rita, 'Existence in *Laços de família*', *Luso-Brazilian Review* 4, no. 1, June 1967, pp. 69–71.

Howlett, Jacques, 'Pour que l'horreur devienne lumière', *Quinzaine Littéraire*, no. 293, 1–15 January 1979, pp. 11–12.

Jozef, Bella, 'Chronology: Clarice Lispector' (translated by Elizabeth Lowe), *Review* 24, June 1979, pp. 24–6.

Jozef, Bella, 'Clarice Lispector: um sopro de plenitude', *Minas Gerais Suplemento Literário*, no. 688, 8 December 1979, p. 4.

Jozef, Bella, 'Clarice Lispector: la recuperación de la palabra poética', *Revista*

*Iberoamericana* 50, no. 126, January–March 1984, pp. 239–57.

Jozef, Bella, Review of *Onde estivestes de noite, Revista Iberoamericana* 50, no. 126, January–March 1984, pp. 317–18.

Jozef, Bella, Review of *Um sopro de vida, Revista Iberoamericana* 50, no. 126, January–March 1984, pp. 314–17.

Lindstrom, Naomi, 'Clarice Lispector: articulating women's experience', *Chasqui* 8, no. 1, 1978, pp. 43–52.

Lindstrom, Naomi, 'A Discourse Analysis of 'Preciosidade' by Clarice Lispector', *Luso-Brazilian Review* 19, no. 2, winter 1982, pp. 187–94.

Lowe, Elizabeth, 'The Passion According to C. L.' (interview with Clarice Lispector), *Review* 24, June 1979, pp. 34–7.

Lucas, Fábio, 'Aspectos de la ficción brasileña contemporánea'. *Nueva Narrativa Latinoamericana* 3, no. 1, January 1973, pp. 113–23.

Martins, Wilson, 'O novo romance brasileiro contemporáneo', *Inti*, no. 111, April 1976, pp. 27–36.

Moisés, Massaud, 'Clarice Lispector: fiction and cosmic vision' (translated by Sara M. McCabe), *Studies in Short Fiction* 8, no. 1, winter 1971, pp. 268–81.

Monegal, Emir Rodríguez, 'Clarice Lispector en sus libros y en mi recuerdo', *Revista Iberoamericana* 50, no. 126, January–March 1984, pp. 231–8.

Nunes, Benedito, 'Dos narradores brasileños', *Revista de Cultura* 9, no. 29, December 1969, pp. 187–204.

Nunes, Maria Luisa, 'Narrative Modes in Clarice Lispector's *Laços de família*: the rendering of consciousness', *Luso-Brazilian Review* 14, no. 2, winter 1977, pp. 174–84.

Nunes, Maria Luisa, 'Clarice Lispector: artista andrógina ou escritora?' *Revista Iberoamericana* 50, no. 126, January–March 1984, pp. 281–9.

Oswaldo Cruz, Gilda, 'Clarice Lispector cerca de su corazón salvaje', *Quimera*, no. 80, Barcelona, 1988, pp. 12–18.

Patai, Daphne, 'Clarice Lispector and the Clamor of the Ineffable', *Kentucky Romance Quarterly* 27, 1980, pp. 133–49.

Pereira, Teresinha Alves, 'Coincidéncia de la técnica narrativa de Julio Cortázar y Clarice Lispector', *Nueva Narrativa Hispanoamericana* 3, no. 1, January 1973, pp. 103–11.

Pontiero, G., 'The Drama of Existence in *Laços de família*', *Studies in Short Fiction* 8, no. 1, winter 1977, pp. 256–67.

Pontiero, G., 'Estranhos itinerários: Julio Cortázar and Clarice Lispector', *Suplemento Cultural (O Estado de São Paulo)*, November 1978.

Pontiero, G., 'Excerpts From the *Chronicles of the Foreign Legion*', *Review* 24, 1980, pp. 37–43.

Pontiero, G., 'Testament of Experience: some reflections on Clarice Lispector's last narrative *A hora da estrela*', *Ibero-Amerikanisches Archiv*, no. 10, vol. 1, 1984, pp. 13–22.

Pontiero, G., 'O canto do cisne de uma escritora', *Cultura (O Estado de São Paulo)*, December 1987, pp. 1–3.

Rabassa, Gregory, *Encyclopedia of World Literature in the Twentieth Century*, New York: Frederick Ungar, 1975, vol. 4, pp. 220–3.

Reis, Fernando G., 'Quem tem mêdo de Clarice Lispector', *Revista Civilização Brasileira*, no. 17 January and February 1968, pp. 225–34.

Reis, Roberto, 'Além do humano', *Minas Gerais Suplemento Literário*, 5 December 1981, pp. 6–7.

Rocha, Diva Vasconcelos, '*Laços de família* ou a enunciação do humor', *Minas Gerais Suplemento Literário*, 25 May 1974, p. 3.

Rocha, Diva Vasconcelos, 'Paixão e morte do narrador segundo o narrador', *Minas Gerais Suplemento Literário*, 22 November 1980, p. 2; 29 November 1980, p. 4.

Rossi, Maria Helena, 'Os sucessivos e rodondos vácuos', *Minas Gerais Suplemento Literário*, no. 779–80, 12 September 1981, pp. 14–15.

Sá, Olga de, 'Clarice Lispector: processos criativos', *Revista Iberoamericana* 50, no. 126, January–March 1984, pp. 259–80.

Seniff, Dennis, 'Self-Doubt in Clarice's *Laços de família*', *Luso-Brazilian Review* 14, no. 2, winter 1977, pp. 199–208.

Senna, Marta de, 'Clarice Lispector's *A Imitacão da Rosa*: an interpretation', *Portuguese Studies*, vol. 2, 1986, pp. 159–65.

Severino, Alexandrino E., 'Major Trends in the Development of the Brazilian Short Story', *Studies in Short Fiction* 8, no. 1 (winter 1971), pp. 199–208.

Szklo, Gilda Salem, 'O conto "O búfalo" de *Laços de família* e a questão da escrita em Clarice Lispector', *Minas Gerais Suplemento Literário*, 31 March 1979, p. 5.

# 6.   'I will be a scandal in your boat': Women poets and the tradition
## *Myriam Díaz-Diocaretz*

## Our founding discourses

'It is hard to imagine what it means to be a woman and a poet in Latin America,' an American translator said recently.[1] Perhaps the greatest problem to imagine lies in what the very *idea* of Latin America may represent and what it might mean as a continent with so many economic, political and historical contradictions and diversities, with so many geographic, ethnic and linguistic differences, extending from the Caribbean and the Mexican plateau to the Andean *altiplano* and the Strait of Magellan. Yes, it is hard to image what it means to be a woman and a poet in a world which began to be named by *the other* five centuries ago. Since that time, the first impulse has been to see what we lacked, what we did not have. As Eduardo Galeano puts it:

> [N]one of the native cultures knew iron or the plow, or glass, or gunpowder, or used the wheel except on their votive carts. The civilization from across the ocean that descended upon these lands was undergoing the creative explosion of the Renaissance: Latin America seemed like another invention to be incorporated, along with gunpowder, printing, paper, and the compass, in the bubbling birth of the Modern Age.[2]

The notion of 'invention' is not new, of course: it was introduced when Columbus was termed 'the inventor of the Indies'.[3] The defeat of the native civilizations still goes on, so does the Latin American 'invention'. Yet the New World began its course in an intricate and conflicting interaction between the *emerging* and *emergent* cultural spheres, which were heterogeneous since their origin and have remained so in spite of the apparent homogeneity of the notion of a 'Latin American' world. True, there was no iron, no printing, but there was poetry. Aztec poetry, for example, had a very elaborate aesthetic, and consisted of theories of musical composition which preceded the arrival of the Conquerors; its ancient tradition of verbal and musical art was conceived within a rich mythological and religious order.[4] Gradually, after the Conquest, we started speaking Spanish, now our 'common' language, although many other languages and cultures still struggle to survive and prevail in the daily existence of their peoples. On the other hand, from colonial times we had to reinvent our language, appropriating it to take it away from the Conquerors. Even if some may claim the Spanish literary tradition as their central ancestry, the oral tradition of pre-Columbian poetry, although unknown to most, is evident in many corners of Latin America, echoing what seem to be vestiges, shadows of the distant past; and yet its spirit is renewed with the changes required by our own century. The Chilean Violeta Parra's 'sung poetry' is true evidence of the continued practice of the oral tradition.

Both as a poet and a singer Violeta Parra, celebrating or condemning life as a kind of metaphysical revenge (for example in 'Here's to Life' and 'God Damn the Empty Sky'), criticizing society from the viewpoint of 'the people' with an authentic working-class concern, or scanning the triumphs and defeats in her own life (in her 'Décimas'), represents a significant part of our collective unconscious 'return' to the origins of our culture. And somehow she embodies part of the twentieth-century 'social imagery'[5] of the Latin American woman poet. Other dimensions of this social imagery are still be to explored, particularly in connection with the aesthetic and artistic movements of the turn of the century within the process of 'Americanization' and of wilful disengagement from Europe, at a time when Latin American writers were not at all indifferent to European trends.[6]

To be a poet, man or woman, in Latin America, also implies that at some point we come to the awareness that writing is not to be kept behind closed doors – unless the ruling political system gives us no choice – that poetry is not the exclusive art by and for an élite, but that the poet is part of the world, and that world belongs in our vision.

The women poets whose work for years remained unacknowledged are just beginning to be discovered. Those whose verse did gain some recognition at certain periods of our history since Colonial times were nuns (for example, Leonor de Ovando, Santo Domingo, c. 1609; Santa Rosa de Lima, Peru, 1586–1617; Madre Josefa del Castillo y Guevara, known as la Madre Castillo, Colombia, 1671–1742; in addition to the greatest of all, Sor Juana Inés de la Cruz, Mexico, 1651–95); they were nuns because that was the only way for a woman to receive instruction in matters that were exclusively reserved for men; others were artists, critics. They have belonged to all echelons of society; the Latin American woman poet has also been a teacher (for example, Gabriela Mistral, Rosario Castellanos), or has participated in a revolution and has sung to it, or has rejected imperialism and has denounced in her poetry the intervention of foreign powers in Latin America. From another perspective, poetry by women has been produced by presses with government consent, or has been self-published (a common practice in Latin America for those who can afford it, and sometimes the only possibility of seeing the poems in print) or printed clandestinely, overcoming external censorship but complicated by the inner struggle of self-censorship; or else the poet has been an *emigrée*, an exile.

The situation of the Latin American woman poet before the turn of the twentieth century needs to be re-examined – though briefly – in the context of the previously existing discourses in the Hispanic culture at large. Feminist studies in the last decades have shown how women have been absent and *mis*-represented in the state constitutions of each Latin American nation and how we have been severely confined by laws that rule marriage and the structure of the family; more and more we have become aware of the ways in which we have been socialized and institutionalized within the confines of the patriarchal order through systematic decisions to exclude women from different areas of action in society. No doubt the limited access to education available to women was frequently concealed by the numerous exceptions and prominent intellectual women in our history. The patriarchal paradigms of women's 'inferiority' and their subsequent exclusion have been applied – with the same ideological intention – to the cultural expressions produced by women, namely literature, and particularly poetry.[7] In the literary domain, too, the term 'feminine' has been a synonym of 'not so good', and 'proper to her sex'.

The socio-historical origins of Hispanic culture result from the coexistence of Muslim, Christian and Jewish cultures in medieval Spain. The women poets that existed at that time were very few and, since they were from Andalucía, wrote mostly in Arabic. Among them were Wallada (fifth century), Maria Alphaizuli, known as the Arab Sappho (Sevilla, eighth century), Maria Abi Jacobi Alfarsuli (Seville, eleventh century), Aisha (Cordoba, twelfth century), and Labana (Cordoba, tenth century). The first social function of women in written culture was as translator and transcriber of manuscripts. While in the world of letters women did not have a major role, they had many active roles in their communities. In the thirteenth century, the institutional conjunction between the civil power and ecclesiastical doctrine deprived women of the few rights they enjoyed during the Middle Ages. The Council of Trent (1545–63) reinforced this deterioration of woman's position in society.[8] Likewise, the religious and authoritarian monosemic readings of the Bible by the Catholic Church disseminate two distinct ideologies for women: what I call *the trope of the angel*, often referred to as Marianism – the cult of the Virgin Mary – which creates the moral and social paradigms shaping the image of the virtuous woman, the one to be admired, a type which includes the representation of women in courtly love, and goes further to the images of the ideal woman in literature and popular patriarchally dominated culture; and *the trope of evil*, or what I have called elsewhere *Evephobia*, the image of the woman as temptress and bound to sin. These two tropes later proliferated in all forms of social discourse throughout the centuries; nowadays, women have to tiptoe or tapdance between those tropes and stereotypes which are so ingrained in Hispanic culture that these ideologies are taken as facts.

In a world in which for centuries we have been educated to be dutiful daughters under the Catholic ideology of Marianism, to be a writer and poet is indeed more than an intellectual task. The internalization of man's authority over women still has not been fully unravelled from within, much less eradicated. This is true both in the world of written discourse and in the world of life. Men's roles and authorities having been reinforced in the social system and in culture since the fifteenth century, women's exclusion from these cultural formations coincides with the propagation of derogatory representations of women and the 'feminine'. The male-identified and male-oriented ideologies in colonial America were not different from the Spanish belief systems brought to the New World; in fact, if anything they were even more male-dominated, since the number of women who migrated from Spain was very limited, and the mixture of Spanish with Indian in no way meant an exchange of power relations. Thus, for centuries women have been passive receptors of patriarchally identified and oriented discourses; this is particularly evident in the discourses of normative and prescriptive literature, which neither attacks woman nor defends her, which treats her as if she were an infant devoid of consciousness and will.

It is against the background of the medieval texts against women and those in her defence, as well as of the above-mentioned prescriptive texts that the woman's voice began to emerge in written discourse in convents. An outline of the discursive formations and textual practices about women that form the context for any discourse written by a woman in the Hispanic world from medieval times to the turn of the twentieth century contains the following types of discourse:

1. Written by a man in favour of men and at the same time against women (for example, medieval misogynous texts).
2. Written by a man in defence of women (in reply to the misogynous writings).
3. Written by a woman, criticizing men (for example, Sor Juana Inés de la Cruz's poem 'Arguye de inconsecuentes el gusto y la censura de los hombres que en las mujeres acusan lo que causan' [She demonstrates the inconsistency of men's wishes in blaming women for what they themselves have caused]).[9]
4. Written by a woman in defence of herself (as individual and as woman). Sor Juana's 'Respuesta de la poetisa a la muy ilustre Sor Filotea de la Cruz' [Reply to Sor Philotea] is an example.
5. Written by a woman in favour of women (as a collective) and of women's condition.
6. Written by a woman in favour of women and criticizing men. Margarita Hickey's poems in eighteenth-century Spain, and Adela Zamudio (1824–1928) of Cochabamba, Bolivia, with her poem 'Nacer hombre' are examples of this type of discourse.

It is not an exaggeration to state that for women in the Hispanic culture, besides the representation of women through the trope of the angel and the trope of evil, the *given* is imbedded with a collective cultural muteness as far as women's active role as producers of discourses is concerned. Even if we isolate the question of a 'feminist' discourse, the reality is loud and clear: if by feminist we take a primary requirement that a text be in favour of women, or defending women *vis-à-vis* men, we find that the first texts of this kind were written by men. For example, these texts include, in medieval times, part of Hernan Mejía's *Dictado en vituperio de las malas mujeres y alabanzas de las buenas*, and Don Alvaro de Luna's *Libro de las virtuosas e claras mujeres*; Bernat Metge and Francisco Eiximenes, *Libro de les Dones*; during the Enlightenment, Padre Feijóo, in his *Teatro Crítico Universal* and his *Cartas eruditas*, and Juan Bautista Cubié with his *Las mujeres vindicadas de las calumnias de los hombres*; in the eighteenth century, Gaspar de Jovellanos and many others. All these texts were also part of the origins of the discursive practices in the colonial texts of the New World.

It is evident that the *given*, for women writers, exists as an already organized culture, and is sustained by a dual orientation, first, as *social discourse*, and, second, as *the discourse of patriarchy*.[10] With a few exceptions such as Sor Juana Inés de la Cruz, it is only in the nineteenth century that women begin to create their own discursive fields in literary discourses, particularly in essays and fiction.[11]

The event of the life of the text, that is, its true essence, always develops on the boundary between two consciousnesses, two subjects, as the philosopher of culture M. Bakhtin has stated.[12] The discursive formations of the Latin American text, therefore, as a reflection of all texts of literary production, have functioned primarily in an interplay between a patriarchally identified collective subject and an equally patriarchally oriented consciousness towards which understanding and response are directed.

In the twentieth century a few women poets begin to have some prominence, during the development of *modernismo* and later of *post-modernismo*, and to generate many varieties of lyric discourse, from traditional and post-romantic, to surrealist, erotic, revolutionary, and feminist writing. Writing in the Castilian inherited from her region and education, each poet offers her angle(s) of view(s) from which culture, history, the world, and her own existence are observed and from which these acquire a particular meaning.

A woman who is a poet in the Hispanic world sooner or later has to come to terms with her own position(s) in her community and society, and with what her communities expect from her, both in her life and her aesthetics. This unavoidable problem may provoke radical decisions, and often involves a challenge which must be confronted, through the very selection of themes, metaphors, figures of speech, poetic forms, through the implicit or explicit discursive polemics. The textualization or verbal expression of this challenge is by no means a direct transposition of experience into the text. The ground rules of life are transposed to the fieldwork of language as the site for the forces contending within, and as the territory to assess the values inherited and the values chosen – a situation of 'take it or leave it', so to speak.

As we read the work of those who have paved the way for contemporary poetry the question of the poet's subject positions reveals the core of what we might identify as a 'woman's voice'. This is a distinctive set of discursive strategies rather than any biologically determined characteristic. I am proposing that the subject position in the poetics of the lyric by women is a conjunction of the speaker(s) and the world vision(s) in complex webs of overt or covert relationships in which the poet is evaluating the world of reality which has formed her and which she chooses to represent textually.[13] The Latin American tradition, as *the given,* appears in the absence or presence of the features of literary movements, of co-participation with poetic practices inherited from the work of the preceding generations; it may also appear through her contribution to the innovations produced by a given contemporary group or artistic phenomenon; it may be concomitant with the socio-political, the historical, the philosophical contexts, or with particular sets of images and metaphors, or poetic forms which she is expected or supposed to practice (which would be proper or appropriate), such as the sonnet. The texts of culture, as *the given*, constitute the texts which 'are not her own', which are alien to her.

The relationship between the woman poet and the patriarchal or non-patriarchal 'alien text' can be studied in its intertextual rapports. Significantly, the primary alien text with which a poet with a consciousness of being a woman in the patriarchal world has to contend is the whole ensemble of texts in which women are subjected, defined, addressed, erased, since all forms of discourses and ideologies, as we saw briefly above, were produced by *male* ideologies. The interaction between the woman poet and the patriarchal or non-patriarchal alien text can be studied through these rapports.

Central to the writing of contemporary Latin American women poets is the *strategic discursive consciousness* which seeks to speak through a woman's voice. As we approach such practices in Latin America – within its pluralities – we must remember the precursors, whose 'feminist' practice goes back to Hispanic modernism, in its second phase, after 1910. The power of such discourse emerges very specifically in four geographical locations, Argentina, Uruguay, Chile and Cuba, in what we can call the matriheritage of 'founding discourses' in contemporary poetry written by women: Delmira Agustini (Uruguay, 1886–1914), Alfonsina Storni (Argentina, 1892–1938), Gabriela Mistral (Chile, 1889–1957), Juana de Ibarborou (Uruguay, 1895–1979), Dulce María Loynaz (Cuba, b. 1902), and later Julia de Burgos (Puerto Rico, 1918–53). Their poetic practice coincides with the peak of *modernismo*, with Pablo Neruda, Leopoldo Lugones, and the avant-gardism of Vicente Huidobro, César Vallejo, Jorge Luis Borges and Nicolás Guillén, who represent the canonical and legitimating poetical texts or 'master codes' of Latin America.

In Agustini's poetry, we have one of the first examples of an erotic language that does not follow the tradition; significantly, her style has been consistently described using lexicon of excess, for example as 'too sensual', 'too passionate'.[14] The 'feminine' eroticism of her poems has been discussed in direct connection – one might even say fusion – with her physical beauty and her personal life as an over-protected woman, and her tragic end at the hands of her husband. By contrast, Storni has been labelled as a poet whose hard life was the cause for her embittered opinions about marriage, men and love; she is considered the most rebellious. Mistral, the most widely known of all, has been stereotyped as the 'most universal' of all because 'she transcends' individual concerns – namely, womanhood.

The founding discourses of the modernist and post-modernist women poets is a social practice of adjustment, of non-acceptance of what was already there as prevalent social discourse in the culture's texts. Of importance here are the gendered constructions and the hierarchies between masculine and feminine, male/female, constructions that are directly related to the semiotic constraints of speech within the cultural hegemony. At the same time, however, even if structured against the background of modernist normative literary language within the expected literary horizon, every utterance is set against that system *dialogically*; the woman's strategic consciousness and world view are opposed to patriarchal paradigms, one evaluation responding to another, one accent and one register interacting with another. If they come to be in opposition, it is in a dialogic tension between specific evaluations and belief systems. Woman's authorial intention is a presence at every point of the poem. This great change can be synthesized as the new formation of the woman's voice as collective and individual speaking subject, as discursive production, to challenge the sovereignty of androcentrism.

The poetical practice of these 'founding discourses' questions history, the ancestral fate of women and their situation in human social formations, and explores the contradictory nature of the concrete world of everyday social life. Style and writing practice are to poets generally the medium for producing knowledge. But in the case of the women poets of the 1970s and 1980s, their textual practice is more clearly accompanied by a recognition of the need for effective political and aesthetic strategies of resistance. It is well known that the notion of the 'feminine' is determinant and already available to the phallocentric tradition(s); some women writers question many of these assumptions and formulate relationships between women and a structurally imposed silence, between women and power, women and representation, women and the intertextual, and women as subject (self). These founding discourses – different as they are – reveal how a voice not only inscribes itself as a woman's but also names the world from the strategic consciousness of a woman-oriented position. From the poem the speaker(s) situates herself and others in the world perceived and represented in its gendered condition, thus creating a discursive field in which to ground a *situation* and a *viewpoint* for the text. Following this framework, I present below a condensed reading of Alfonsina Storni, Julia de Burgos, and Rosaria Castellanos, three major poets.

Alfonsina Storni's first book, *La inquietud de rosal* [The Restlessness of the Rosebush] was published in 1916. Influenced by the turn-of-the-century French Symbolists and the Modernistas, especially by Rubén Darío, Storni begins her writing submerged in her literary tradition. Storni does not accept the world as it is given, with male/female hierarchies of gender working at all levels. To label Storni a *feminist* poet would be misleading, but several significant features constitute an underlying or manifest *feminist discourse* in her poetry. These are developed in several ways. Her individual style evolves in a double orientation, where the first dimension is the various interrelations within her work with the literary texts that predominate during the period in which she writes, and the horizon of evaluations of her 'potential' audience – regardless of whether she was aware of this or not. Her second orientation involves both her own acceptance of traditional values and topics in her poems about love, and her own aesthetics rejecting those values (and constructing a woman-identified addressee), which is reflected in the selection of particular images and themes about women, and the point of view from which her topics are presented. Storni's 'voice' is a result of her strategic discursive consciousness in which these two apparently contradictory discusive orientations occur. It is on the question of her 'voice' that her aesthetics (the compositional arrangement of the poetic world, and the poem as literary text) and her ethics arc bound by the speaking subject–author.

Among her recurrent themes, love is presented in some poems in accordance with the ideas of her time and of the Hispanic lyric tradition. In this context, the woman who speaks is a *specular subject*:[15] her poetic voice reflects her acceptance of patriarchy. She responds to the expectations and the ideological environment of the masculinist idea of woman. This reinforcement of the patriarchal mode will, however, become a covert equation in the reading of the more overtly feminist poems, one that will displace the question of the speaker's acceptance of formal constraints and expectations. This equation by contrast appears, for example, if we read the well-known 'Tú me quieres blanca' [You want me white].[16] Here Storni, in her *postmodernista* mode, parodies the notion of the idealized woman, the one who is perfect, free from sin, faultless in moral excellence and propriety of behaviour, pure, a virgin. While the poem speaks of different kinds of sexual self-restraint she is also, but purposely, restraining herself from speaking in what would be her own register, one that would pronounce those falsifying expectations directly, as she does in other poems. The self-restraint in her discourse is indeed a strategy in which she takes the tropes of *modernismo* commonly used and over-used by her immediate male predecessors and her contemporaries: she chooses to represent the ideal woman in the codes of her implied addressee, men, in *modernismo*.

When she wishes to use her own idiolect she is not shy, and it is this characteristic which gained her the reputation of being a 'rebellious' voice. To her, man is a 'little, little' man, in 'Hombre pequeñito' because 'you do not understand me, nor you will ever do' (p. 66). The poet's rapport with the models of the given tradition actually constitutes her 'voice', the foregrounding of the major paradigms of her speaking subject – as a woman – in connection with some topics that are not part of the given, which therefore form her own inner speech of the 'created'. Not only does Storni choose some topics that are specifically about women,[17] but also she articulates a woman-identified world vision. Equally important, other poems speak of a sense of a collective identity that is gendered: an implicit and explicit 'we' which stands for *we women* (for example, 'Capricho'). She travels beyond the boundaries of tradition. The effect within her own poetry is that the woman-identified, woman-oriented voice interacts and contests internally her own voice in the more traditional poems. The different speaking subjects – either accepting traditional evaluations of women or refuting them – intersect.

The work of Julia de Burgos (Puerto Rico, 1914–53) reveals a project of self-definition as a Puerto Rican, as a woman, and as a poet, all forms of being which were in constant transformation in her poetic world. She once described her existence, in a letter sent from New York, her city of exile, to Puerto Rico, as 'this life split in two which I'm living, between essence and form'.[18] The poetics of the self and of 'form' have at least three major movements in her work. First, a sense of isolation from the world, in the loss of connection with others. Second, the world itself, separated from the speaker, becomes divided. Third, there emerges with remarkable intensity and lucidity, a relationship of the speaker with herself. By objectifying herself, two forms of being emerge, as a heroic alienation and self-alienation. Neither self can eliminate or ignore the other, yet one is constantly refuting, looking to annul the other; both are the sources for all other forms of being she discovers. With this ambivalence expressed as an inner rivalry Burgos creates an authentic dialogic relation with herself. This crucial splitting of the subject culminates in the poet's awareness and her desire to pursue self-analysis and self-reflection as a means of searching for the fundamental 'forms'. From her first poems (1938) the self in its plurality is central, as her representation of the two Julias, the I and the other in 'A Julia de Burgos' shows.[19] It is important to note that this is not an incidental theme in one poem only, but a wide network of images and a central preoccupation in her work. In this poem, the self as essential being and the self as poet are split in opposite realities. The poem is a step-by-step correspondence and contrast of the two selves, one of which is assumed to be the enemy of the other. It begins with the poet's intent to uncover the 'lie' that the Julia who writes poetry is the enemy. The assumption with which the poem begins to quarrel is opposed image after image, and the arguments are not directed at showing that such separation does not exist –between the poet and the one who 'is' – but to show that the other, the

Julia of the social world is the enemy of the poet. The initial motif of the supposed 'lie' is reinforced by the repetition of '*mienten*', making the tone of intensity more salient. Significantly, the poem itself provides a description of what a woman is, in Burgos's terms. The two sets of images refer to the selves of the poet, the one independent, only ruled by her heart, the 'flower of the people', owing nothing to anyone, the number one in the social '*dividor*', and the other the woman who is the colonial subject, restricted and bounded, without freedom. The imminent triumph of the speaker (poet) over the other is one of the ways in which the split self appears as a recurrent major metaphor in Burgos's work; that imminent triumph is only a half triumph, for the defeat of the other is also a defeat within. The inner struggle of the self is an impossible contest where there is no real winner or loser. 'Intima' (1938) develops the image of the self splitting within as a journey: 'A pilgrim in myself, I walked a long while [. . .] and I arrived at myself, intimate.' But this pilgrimage is not a vicious circle, because the end of the road is a new awareness of divisions: 'I continue being a message far from the word', an essence far from the form.

'Pentacromía' (1938) is another significant poem, which shows Burgos's open awareness of the double standard for men and for women. The tone of irony is sustained until the penultimate line. The leading argument here is the speaker's deepest desire ('*deliro el afán*') to be a series of admirable figures in Hispanic culture: Don Quixote, Don Juan, a bandit, a worker, or a great military man. Except for the first stanza, all the others reiterate the sentence: 'Today, I want to be a man.' The articulation of the gendered world is made more complex in the very last line, which shifts the tone from pure parody and suspends all stereotypes to converge on the effects of being a woman on the one hand, and on yet a new meaning in the theme of the split self in her poetry: the speaker wants 'to abduct Sor Carmen and Sor Josefina/to make them surrender, and Julia de Burgos to rape'.[20] The sharp criticism of male heroes and of what is celebrated in them is set in the context of at least two interwoven subjects, of Burgos's idea of men and of the man–woman relationship in the social world (what is virile and manly and socially acceptable) and her relationship with her own self. There is an implicitly tragic sense in the self-reflective act of the poem's closure. Julia de Burgos continually wrote of the ever-changing nature of the self, including the imagined, and premonitory, passage to death. Several of her last poems are also poems of self-love, and of the realization that only when she lost her essence, the source of all forms, would the end come.

Rosario Castellanos (Mexico, 1925–72) recognized from the start her inheritance from what I have called the founding discourses (Storni, Mistral, Ibarborou). Her voices are filled with intensity, and a very profound irony through which a major critique of patriarchal structures is achieved. Her reflections express non-forgiveness of injustice and the cruelties of life. From her early poems in *Apuntes para una declaración de fe* (1948) to her last book, *Materia memorable* (1969), the world is in constant re-definition through the 'gift of the word', 'a gift you receive/and which you no longer return'.[21] This is true, the poems suggest, not just in the world of conventions but also in the world of the given in general: her poems offer intertextual transformations of biblical stories and motifs, of philosophical propositions, popular axioms, and of myths.

*Apuntes para una declaración de fe* is a critique of the dream of endless innovation and is set against the myth of the modern as perpetual progress and happiness. In *Trayectoria del polvo* (1948), the poet begins to mediate all experiences through the speaking subject in the feminine. This is achieved by emphasizing the woman's world view and situating the self in the textual world in a more explicit way than a poet would in the male lyric tradition. The act of naming herself is as crucial for the speaker as the naming of the world: it is an act to be done over and over, as a way to respond and not to accept what has been given. In 'El resplandor del ser' (pp. 88–98), a philosophical poem on the joys of being from *El rescate del mundo*, the immanent 'bliss' of the word and the resistance to be its mere instrument are articulated as the 'joy of being two', a way of being richer, of experiencing doubly. Next to the immanence of language that must be confronted, two major ideas dominate Castellanos's poetics. The first one is the idea that nature is 'like toys in a child's hands'. Another fundamental assumption, contradicted by the texts, is the conviction that like nature, woman is but a toy, without control over her destiny. It is in this context that 'being two' also means being a woman in the world as it is perceived (a view which excludes woman), and being a woman in the world as it might or could be apprehended (including woman). Her poetry is relentlessly faithful to this idea, in affirming the woman's (other) selves as subjects rather than objects. This is in crucial contradistinction to the male lyric tradition. She makes this affirmation first of all by a systematic exploration of woman-related themes presented from the woman's perspective: loneliness, the assigned functions of motherhood and maternity.

Castellanos seeks to overcome the feared self-centredness of the 'I' through the objectification of her self and through a search for referentiality that originates in other women, which allow her to view the world differently. She rewrites the world in such a way that a woman's perception can make a difference. Her woman-identified lyric 'I' looks for connections with other women. The crucible between the rejection of self-centredness and the constant exploration of existence through the self is made more complex by the search for solidarity and the belief in the fundamental isolation of the individual, especially the woman. This complexity results in an attempt to find what women signify as a collective, a task which is not without difficulty. It seems possible, for the individual woman, only through an articulation of the questions of womanhood's self-definition and self-affirmation (for example 'Monólogo de la extranjera', pp. 112–14). The traditional images of women, particularly of their 'passivity' and 'submission', are filtered through the poet's deep conviction that these are only a mask, and because they are a mask accepted by women they become a paradox, which causes a constant tension between pessimism and rebellion. The poems that reflect on this phenomenon are among the most interesting written in the 1960s in Latin America and the most influential – as feminist texts – for the subsequent generation of women poets. Being an unmarried woman, and the themes of sterility, being alone, being 'fruitless', join visions of the other side of femaleness, motherhood, in a polemic with Mistral's related texts. Likewise, the difficulty of talking about being a mother, about being born, is overcome by the speaker by means of a surpassing directness and poetic boldness comparable to the syntax, forms of dialogues and tones of Sylvia Plath and Ann Sexton.[22] Likewise, texts about domestic interiors and the woman as housewife immersed in her tasks question a woman's fate and her social conditioning with a feminist depth and vision comparable with Adrienne Rich's poetry of the 1960s.

Irony used as a medium to achieve depth of vision, to express a thought that will not be relinquished, singles Castellanos out among Latin American women poets. It should be noted that the effect of this irony, used to show the patriarchal precedents for women's fate and for social structures constraining a woman's existence, is that of a profoundly feminist critique. The represented world in Castellanos is not only the mythic world, or daily life. Literary figures, characters in male literature and women as creators are the evoked subtexts structuring 'Meditacion en el umbral' (p. 326). The polemical/ironic mode is no doubt a distinctive strategy of Castellanos's feminist discourse. An intertextual polemic factor appears in 'Malinche', where Castellanos identifies the negative mythical figure of Malinche (who sold Mexico to Cortés) with Electra, the wanderer, through ample dramatic monologues and dialogues which stress a sort of 'everywoman's death'. The deictic (lyrical 'I') is collective; the play of voices is formed with the shifting positions of Malinche/Electra/ mother/'I'. These positions are not necessarily actualized as those of a personified speaker: hers is a discourse which stresses the *act of speech* and speaking itself.

Castellanos frequently reveals the tensions of the decentred woman's subject; a subjectivity driven by the split in its condition, and the imaginary construction of woman's socialization, which is reinforced by traditions and customs that support passivity. The ironic twist is to be heard in the following quotation:

> Mi madre en vez de leche
> me dio el sometimiento

('Instead of milk, my mother gave me subjugation' [p. 126]). If Castellanos champions an avant-garde textuality, it is posed as the emblem of a linguistic and political feminist resistance that helps disturb identities, stereotypes, systems and orders. Her essays and narratives also feature this communicative reconstruction of subjected voices, breaking limits, fixed positions and rules. The woman's situation in the poems – in a general sense – is torn between her own awareness of constraints, the expressed realization of this as an act of consciousness, and the dilemma of being caught between acceptance – albeit reluctant – and rejection of patriarchal paradigms.

In Castellanos's world, woman exists as a private being, but outside that world lies tradition, the family, and traditional roles and mutual expectations. Yet woman's truest being is the outcome of her own constructions:

> I am a daughter of myself.
> From my dream I was born.
> My dream sustains me. (p. 46)

Such is the strategy in 'Autorretrato', in which the poet emphasizes the image in simultaneity with the counter-image (revealing interesting parallels and differences with Julia de Burgos). The 'I' that speaks is the organizing subject of the fictionality in the imaginary construction of the self reproduced by society, in the same way that the speaking subject is the poet's work. The assumption left for the reader is that the human agent (the woman) can create her own story and her own history, which are dynamic interactions of changing subject positions.

There is in Rosario Castellanos a voice that questions the act of being and the subject of being, and this voice imprints the poet's meditation about existence. That being is a woman who knows herself in a world of men, who knows that she is not defenceless, powerless or weak, but who knows that she has been profoundly conditioned, rigidly framed since she was born. From that generic essence, the woman's voice makes her journey and from time to time she veers towards the woman's world, exploring it, expressing visions of experiences which are unique yet recognizable to other women. These experiences may either be the speaker's own, or those of the characters and symbols of the inherited, given culture. Thus this culture is the link that communicates the speaker to the others, it is what is shared by men and women, and the rest seems an illusion. Culture in Castellanos's poetry functions as mediator of experiences and emotions. Through the emotions mediated in this way, the intimate, private being can be reached. Castellanos makes it clear that a woman's passivity is not restful, that her silence is not empty, that the stronger the social expectations and pressures, the deeper the strength that gives birth to her rebellion.

## Our contemporaries

In the work of Alfonsina Storni, one of the first contributors to our Latin American founding discourses for contemporary women poets, we can delineate the presence of the 'social text' of *modernismo*. The work of Julia de Burgos is linked to the Hispanic lyric tradition, and closer to that of Gabriela Mistral, but develops in isolation from most trends prevalent in her time. Rosario Castellanos emerges from the tradition of the founding discourses, rewrites their codes with more emphasis on the woman's perspective from an anti-traditional stand, and inscribes a more clearly defined and systematic poetics of feminist discourse.

A close reading of these forerunners, different as they are, reveals the use of specific aspects of the social text, for example, the presence of the alien texts of patriarchy. It shows how woman's voice names the world, and how women situate themselves and others in the gendered and represented world to create a viewpoint from which to speak. Alfonsina Storni's poem 'Hombre pequeñito' ('Little man') is representative:

> Estuve en tu jaula, hombre pequeñito,
> hombre pequeñito que jaula me das.

'I was in your cage, little man,/little man who hands me a cage'. Juana de Ibarbourou is, perhaps, the most polemical and anti-traditional. Her intertextual bonds are mostly transgressions against mythology, teleology and the canonical tropes of Western discourse. Such is the thrust of the poem 'Charon: I will be a scandal in your boat' ('*Caronte, yo seré un escándalo en tu barca*'). Agustini, Storni, Ibarbourou and Loynaz speak from the viewpoint of a woman subject who reclaims the right for self-representation. This is distinct from Mistral, who uses the female speaking subject to project the social texts of women as they are represented in traditional discourse.

The poems published by Mistral during her lifetime[23] that transgress these norms are neutralized by a discursive displacement within the traditional male lyric tradition. Thus, the woman-identified and -oriented structures of address in the poem 'Miedo' (p. 262) are shifted by the poem's rhyming patterns and intonation, as well as by the use of the codes of the fairy tales to suggest a mother's fear of losing her little daughter, to a context of a lyric text for children. The poem begins:

> I do not want my little girl
> to be made into a swallow

A variant of this couplet starts the second stanza:

> I do not wish my little girl
> to be made into a princess

The fear of separation from the loved one can also be read as a type of homo-social discourse.

Julia de Burgos creates a world view not only as a woman but within an anti-colonial affirmation of 'otherness' and heterogeneity. Burgos textualizes the emancipatory struggle through tropes and myths (the river, the sea) and she legitimates the revolutionary subject through the personal and the political, in collective projections of desire for independence. The split subject of colonization is further signified in her poem 'To Julia de Burgos'; her body and her name are tropologically figural in the multiple and variable limits within which relations of power and knowledge are produced: institutions, the private, the public, racism, class.

The explicitness of these women poets recodes and re-territorializes themes, lexical material and a repertoire of metaphors from their speaking subjects' position in the world, and with an awareness of both the constraints of the patriarchal interlocutor(s) as horizon of reception and of their circumscription in gendered oppositions. All these women poets, in varying degrees, develop and potentialize what could be called a woman's *register*,[24] against the *modality* of the practice of writing and the semantic domain of hegemonic and patriarchal subject matters. Inscribing this register in the structure of the lyrical genre, they articulate the formerly repressed position whose status of non-subject has been concealed by the (pseudo) universality of dominant registers of male lyric tradition, and of modernism and postmodernism. Poetry allows them to subvert the canonized modes of authority (institutional, sexual, political), through a rejection of *appropriate* and *assigned* positions, and a refusal to collaborate in the unequal distribution of social and cultural capital. If, as Benveniste argues, subjectivity is founded on the linguistic category of person (a structural category with purely linguistic reference), these founding poetical texts indicate the different degrees of *subjectivity* and *subjection* articulated within the contextual norms of discourse. As subjects of discourse, poets and speaking subjects take over the structures of meaning which are presupposed in the structure of the lyric poetic genre. From the 'given' patriarchal and monologic tradition and language, they 'create' a new discourse through re-appropriation from the hegemony of the male gender in textual production.

All the formulations the discourse in question offers are a possible object of a future discourse for poets of the 1960s and the 1980s. These founding modernist and postmodernist poetic texts have developed in accordance with social and discursive determinations. The decisive question is to differentiate the forms of temporality they reveal: whether after these 'founding texts' there is an ongoing repetition, internal to a literary series, or at a specific time; what events initiate a new pattern of repetitions or deflect existing patterns into new orientations. To a certain extent one could say that in contrast with the *moments* of canonization of modernism and avant-garde poetical texts written by men, women's founding texts have still not been sanctioned by the institutions governing literary production – even if Ibarborou was acclaimed as 'Juana de América', Mistral received a Nobel Prize and the lesser known Loynaz is recognized in the Caribbean as one of Latin America's great poets.

An important framework with which to approach these poets is the notion of the articulation of the poetic world through and within strategies and dominances which refer to representation in poetry and the problematized notion of intertextuality. Such bridging indicates the relationship between the woman poet and the patriarchal or non-patriarchal 'alien' text.

New semiotic modes of artistic production as a direct result of the extension of the communicative network are to be found in the more recent, post-1960s, and contemporary discourses by women. A *mise-en-abîme* of the canons can be found in the dialogue and the intersections of the textual surfaces. The 'other' structure, the intertextual, is not only the dominant literary canon, but the signifier or representing subject of the dominant cultural text.

Within an ample spectrum of voices in Latin America, I will refer – even if only by way of suggesting the richness of sources to read – to a few whose registers draw from other realms, and to those who transgress stylistic decorum and tend to subvert the authority of the dominant discourses and the official values: Alejandra Pizarnik (Argentina), Delia Domínguez (Chile); Cristina Peri-Rossi (Uruguay); Nancy Morejón and Belkis Cuza Male (Cuba); Gioconda Belli, Yolanda Blanco, Rosario Murillo and Daisy Zamora (Nicaragua); Diana Morán (Panamá); Iris M. Zavala, Rosario Ferré (Puerto Rico); Claribel Alegría (San Salvador), and Jean Aristigueta (Venezuela). These last poets, all from the Caribbean and Central American region, have all taken on insurgent and revolutionary avant-garde projects, in solidarity with the social destinies of each country and of Latin America.

The emancipatory project is a vast polemic against colonialism, and the traditional position of woman, as well as a rejection of the corresponding myths and mythologizations. The writers all share a critical view towards authority; while Castellanos re-territorialized the Indian, Morejón speaks from a black emancipatory perspective.

From a younger generation (poets born between 1950 and 1965), such writers as Etnairis Rivera speak from the Puerto Rican ghettoes of New York; Sandra María Esteves and Luz María Umpierre speak from the bilingual and bicultural New York experience, often in 'Spanglish' as Nuyoricans.[25] The Chilean women poets of the most recent generation (for example, Cecilia Vicuña, Marjorie Agosín) write from a feminist position.[26] In all these cases, the lyric voice is not only on the woman's side but speaking from the woman's perspective. Using the linguistic and expressive codes of her culture, each poet generates a mimetic displacement in which what appear to be society's norms and universal discursive functions are replaced. In the work of some, such as Castellanos, they are named as men's norms. Women's strategic consciousness delimits, confines, frames the dominant world, reducing the notions of general and common knowledge to a recognizable set of male-dominating structures. The *sociolect* – as a set of represented ideologies of a given society and a culture's beliefs – is displaced to become frequently a *patriarchal sociolect*.

Bakhtin's proposition that 'a word is apprehended through the voice of another which will remain forever embedded with it',[27] proves valid considering that a text written from woman's strategic consciousness is an ensemble of verbal signs that foreground a gendered sociality that a text written from woman's strategicin discourse. This occurs not only at the level of representation but also with the dynamics of discourse itself, since the world is already inhabited by another context when it achieves a new one.[28] Writing by women, in the terms I have described, is the site of an implied dialogue with the areas of a culture dominated by patriarchy – a domination which preceded the utterance in question.

This dialogic and gendered dimension may be suggested by means of an intertextual trace either in the represented world, or through the form of the poem. Frequently, the poem's metamessage refers to the existence of all discourses in the woman's culture, the poet's, which, as abstract systems, become fragments of social pragmatic action. The world is shown in its unequal dichotomy, from the woman's perspective. That is the stress and function of the founding discourses of the modernist and postmodernist technique; the empirical subject (the woman writer) and the speaking subject converge in one voice, which may also be split (Burgos, Castellanos, Pizarnik). The poem may also become woman-identified (for example, in the work of Diana Morán, Rosario Ferré); the social uses of language gendering lyric discourse are questioned. As a result, the project of the textual world (which may be woman-identified) may be correlated, through a set of strategies, with the ideology shaping such a world. Content (subject matter, myth, stereotype) includes the system of beliefs acceptable or in polemic as well as different discursive practices predominant in each historical context (and each culture). The very fact that the female speaking subject is addressing a given theme may indicate that the woman writer is re-territorializing discursive practices for herself. Examples are the rewriting of the swan myth carried out by Ibarborou, and more recently Morejón's reading of Rubén Darío.

In feminist poetic writing in Latin America from the 1960s to the present, the intertextual factor is clearly determined as one of the dominant strategies. In some of this writing, the poet's design is to deprivilege the authoritative word, and to unveil female passivity and complicity. Alejandra Pizarnik (1936–72) was a privileged writer of the avant-garde in Argentina, and was originally connected with the parasurrealists as well as with the younger intellectuals around *Sur* (the journal owned and directed by Victoria Ocampo). Pizarnik's poetic strategies include onyric metaphors, self-irony and self-parody, normally expressed through ironical nouns and pronouns. Her early 'Solo un nombre' [Just a name] (1956) introduces negativity in the actual internal construction of the subject.

> alejandra alejandra
> debajo estoy yo
> alejandra[29]

The subject of the utterance can never stand in the place of the other, except by the illusion of language. The split subjectivity tries to maintain the coherence and supposed unity of a subject where the 'I' (name) is elided. Critics have successfully proved that Pizarnik's main concern is language: one could carry this insight further, and read her 'autobiographical' strategies as what de Man[30] called 'de-facement': the poem is a cognitive artifact which is submitted to tropological runarounds with no certainty. Under Alejandra there is always another Alejandra, like the Chinese Box or like Borges's Aleph. Absent receding mirrors constitute self-reflection, and the autobiographical is impossibility, uncertainty, undecidability. The enunciating gap is never closed:

> la lengua natal castra
> la lengua es un órgano de conocimiento
> del fracaso de todo poema
> castrado por su propia lengua
> que es el órgano de la re-creación
> del re-conocimiento
> pero no el de la resurrección
> de algo a modo de negación
> de mi horizonte de maldoror con su perro.[31]

Pizarnik's speaking subject adopts a critical view towards authority, in multiple intertextual rapports, but this polemic does not necessarily distinguish the text as woman-oriented. Her texts may be outlined, however, from a reading of the paradigmatic strategy of the gendered voice in the terms suggested above.

Such paradigmatic strategy is also present in Iris M. Zavala's poetry, which is a poetics of resistance against imposed representations, more specifically, against the representation of the colonized. To challenge structures of power is a basic impetus she shares with the contemporary Central American women poets mentioned. The resistance takes place within a social context that has already construed subject positions for the human agent. The site of that resistance is to be glimpsed in the interstices of those positions, through polemical intertextual bindings with authoritative language. Zavala's intertextuality is also made *interdiscursive*, thus making it *heteroglossic*,[32] as she lets a variety of languages intervene (Latin, French, Italian, English, German), to project a *revolutionary* subject, and an intended effect of closing down the enunciatory gap through a new definition of language as communication and collectivity.

> Sentado entre tú
> y yo
> el lenguaje;
> un lenguaje
> el único abecedario espacial

(rebelde)
arma
hermandad
fusil
lucha
libertad[33]

Zavala's polemic is also against the stability of creeds, doctrines and values. Their immobility is generated through the paradoxical, the only kind of linguistic and political dissidence possible in relation to the reappropriation of political revolutionary representation. If Zavala questions language through heteroglossia, she also questions the negative values imposed on different ethnicities through the inscription of Third World subjectivities (black, Indian, Asian). Poetry is to her the communication of truths, and the project of a revolutionary subjectivity, through a questioning of language and form. This is more evident in the transformation of themes that function in her novels, where poetry, prose, documents and visual arts, present as an intersemiotic mixture, are metacommentaries and meta-narratives of the speaking subject's resistance to constraint. This remark-able aesthetic feature is also found in the work of the Jamaican writer Michelle Cliff in English. Both these Caribbean writers are liable to be misunderstood if critical interpretation categorizes them as either poetry or prose.[34] My perspective is intended to view these texts without that kind of categorization, since the latter only incorporates canonical works into the tradition.

In spite of the diversity of strategies in poetic discourse, the gendered voice and perspective are common denominators in most Latin American poets mentioned in this chapter. Ethnic experience and its corresponding identity (see the work of Nancy Morejón), and their subsequent textual-ization need to be analysed as a starting point of divergence among women poets in general, and as important in the making of an individual poet's artistic and ideological world. Ethnicity is disclosed in stylistic and structural elements (similarly for Afro-American poets, Native Indian Americans, Asian Americans, Hispanics in the USA such as Chicanas, women of colour). The black Latin American poet creates a congenial dialogue with the past and with a number of aspects of contemporary empirical reality through a variety of modes of expression, which I have elsewhere called (in the case of black American poets) 'social texts'[35] and which are inscribed to bring into poetic discourse the language of the city as messages or parts of messages from the social world. These texts seek to make explicit a correlation between the poetic model of the world and the world of reality. Such is 'Mujer negra' [Black woman] by Nancy Morejón. The speaker is the black woman, who undergoes slavery and emancipation. The poem crosses time, and comes to the present, to modern Cuba:

Nada nos es ajeno.
Nuestra la tierra
Nuestros el mar y el cielo.
Nuestras la magia y la quimera.
Iguales míos, aquí los veo bailar
alrededor del árbol que plantamos para el comunismo.
Su prodiga madera ya resuena.[36]

G. Aristigueta stresses the Indian heritage and representations. She establishes dialogues with a Latin American history disinhabited by the Indian as a sociocultural sign in diachronic muteness, and with patriarchal history as social texts. More recently, with wars of national liberation, bilingualism is a norm in the practice of many Central American writers who stress the ethnic and linguistic wealth of their roots. Daisy Zamora, for example, interpellates Miskito in the bilingual poem aimed at joining Indians and Sandinistas against a common enemy: '*Wan Luphia Al Kra Nani Ba Ti/Kai Sa*' ['Death to the assassins of our children/their mothers shouted']. Other poets write in Mayan or Cakchikel as a move to communicate and legitimate the linguistic and cultural plurality of their countries and, of course, to resist a monolithic and hegemonic Hispanization.

Murillo and Zamora, as well as most contemporary Central American poets, are overtly feminist, and they link central women's concerns to the projects of the revolution. This exploration of the questions of woman, language and nation in their gendered voice and perspective is revealing of the work produced during the 1980s. The inclusion of colloquial and dialectal forms of natural language to subvert lexical repertoire have become consciously verbalized social forms (quite evident among Hispanics and women of colour in the USA). Moreover, in contemporary work by writers who belong to an ethnic group that is not only Spanish but also is under Hispanic domination, writers who also identify with the dominated and resisting cultural sphere, the intention clearly exists to de-territorialize the hegemonic standards of the Spanish (Peninsular) authoritative world views. In this context, poetry and prose are culturally determined discursive practices.

## Conclusion

I have proposed some readings in which we do not assume that all women poets resist patriarchy, but in which we can read a shared continuity in texts by women from the founding discourses (what I have called elsewhere the 'matriheritage of the sociotext') to the present. This is an alternative to the notion of an 'independent female tradition', proposed by some feminist critics. My notions of the intertextual factor in feminist discourse, of the poetics of the social text, of the re-territorialization of language in writing by women is not based on a static structure, nor on concepts of tradition and culture understood as fixed phenomena.

I conclude by suggesting that we need to rethink the role of the woman as writer, as language user, as practitioner of literary conventions, as subject of her own historical and artistic project, within her corresponding sociocultural codes (empirically and textually given). Such a poetics of the social text, of subject positions can lead us to map a diachronic development of the Latin American woman poet's artistic attitude towards the discursive practices of society and the authoritative languages of the social, and to explore how woman's perception of everyday life is transmuted into a poetic context. It can also show us how textuality is often posed as the emblem of linguistic and political dissidence, and how discursive practices are resistance, a resistance which is the source of writing.

## Notes

1. Joanna Bankier, Preface to Mary Crow (ed.), *Woman Who Has Sprouted Wings: Poems by contemporary Latin American women poets*, Pittsburgh: Latin American Literary Review Press, 1984, p. 10.

2. Eduardo Galeano, *Open Veins of Latin America: Five centuries of the pillage of a continent* (translated by Cedric Belfrage), New York: Monthly Review Press, 1973, p. 26.

3. The historian Andrés Bernáldez, 'Historia de los Reyes don Fernando y doña Isabel', p. 679, quoted in José Antonio Maravall, *Estudios de historia del pensamiento español. La época del Renacimiento*, Madrid: Cultura Hispánica, 1984, 2, p. 1984.

4. John Bierhorst, 'On the Nature of Aztec Poetry', *Review* 29, 1981, pp. 69–71.

5. On the 'social imaginary' in this context, see Iris M. Zavala, 'The Social Imaginary: the cultural sign of Hispanic modernism', *Critical Studies* vol. 1, no. 1, 1989, pp. 23–41.

6. Max Henríquez Ureña, *Breve historia del Modernismo,* México: Fondo de Cultura Económica, 1954; Enrique Amberson Imbert, *Historia de la literatura hispanoamericana*, México: Fondo de Cultura Económica, 1954; Emir Rodríguez Monegal, *Narradores de esta América*, vol. I, Montevideo: Alfa, 1969; Jean Franco, *Historia de la literatura hispanoamericana*, Barcelona: Ariel, 1980.

7. See the essays in Beth Miller (ed.), *Women in Hispanic Literature: Icons and fallen dolls*, Berkeley: icons University of California Press, 1983. It is also important to remember that most of the anthologies of Latin American poets edited by men have systematically excluded women poets. See, for example, José Olivio Jiménez (ed.), *Antología de la poesía hispanoamericana contemporánea: 1914–1987*, Madrid: Alianza editorial, 1971. The only women poets included are Gabriela Mistral and Sara de Ibáñez.

8. A useful study on this aspect is Anabel González *et al.*, *Los orígenes del feminismo en España*, Madrid: Zero, 1980.

9. For the title in English, I rely on the translation by Alan S. Trueblood, in *A Sor Juana Anthology*, Cambridge, Mass.: Harvard University Press, 1988, pp. 111–13.

10. I have explored these two discursive formations of the Hispanic world in 'Estrategias textuales: del discurso femenino al discurso feminista', *Molinos, La mujer en cambio*, March 1986, pp. 38–48; in connection with the theories of M. Bakhtin, on contemporary American

poetry by women in *The Transforming Power of Language: The poetry of Adrienne Rich*, Utrecht: Hes, 1984, especially pp. 31–50; 'Sieving the Matriheritage of the Sociotext', in Elizabeth Meese and Alice Parker (eds.), *The Difference Within: Feminism and critical theory*, Amsterdam: John Benjamins, 1989, pp. 115–47; *Per una poetica della differenza. Il testo sociale nella scrittura delle donne*, Firenze: Estro editrice, 1989.

11. The essays that predominate are on education; unfortunately this area has been better studied in Peninsular than Latin American literature. Writing by nuns in Colonial Latin America presents a different problematic; on this topic see Jean Franco, *Plotting Women: Gender and authority in Mexico: 1650–1970*, New York: Columbia University Press, 1989.

12. M. M. Bakhtin, 'The Problem of the Text', in *Speech Genres and Other Late Essays*, translated by Vern W. McGee and edited by Caryl Emerson and Michael Holquist, Austin: University of Texas Press, 1986, p. 106.

13. I explored this problem in *Translating Poetic Discourse: Questions on feminist strategies in Adrienne Rich*, Amsterdam: John Benjamins, 1985.

14. For example, Dolores Koch, 'Delmira, Alfonsina, Juana y Gabriela', *Revista Iberoamericana*, nos. 132–3 (July–December 1985), *Número especial dedicado a las escritoras de la América Hispánica*, pp. 723–9. By contrast, two important studies on this poet are Emir Rodríguez Monegal, *Sexo y poesía en el 900 uruguayo*, Montevideo: Alfa, 1969, pp. 35–43; Sylvia Molloy, 'Dos lecturas del cisne: Rubén Darío y Delmira Agustini' in Patricia Elena González and Eliana Ortega (eds.), *La sartén por el mango*, Puerto Rico: Ediciones Huracán, 1984, pp. 57–69. On the question of *modernismo* and women poets, see Sidonia Carmen Rosenbaum, *Modern Women Poets of Spanish America: The precursors Delmira Agustini, Gabriela Mistral, Alfonsina Storni, Juana de Ibarbourou*, New York: Hispanic Institute, 1945. Nancy Saporta Sternbach, 'The Death of a Beautiful Woman: modernismo, the woman writer and the pornographic imagination', *Ideologies and Literature*, Spring 1988, vol. 3, no. 1, pp. 35–59, offers an interesting analysis of the polemics around the definition of *modernismo*, and the exclusionary assumptions of male critics in relation to the concepts of *poeta* and *poetisa*.

15. 'Specular' is used here in a restricted sense within the boundaries of the dialogics and other theories from the Bakhtin Circle, and not in its psychoanalytical resonations.

16. Alfonsina Storni, 'Nocturno', *Antología Poética*, p. 55. All subsequent references to this poet will be to this edition, and page numbers will be indicated in the text.

17. See especially 'Fecundidad', p. 31, a modern ode to the triumph of woman's ovum; 'Peso ancestral', p. 66; 'El siglo XX', p. 87, and 'Van pasando mujeres', p. 83.

18. Quoted in Yvette Jiménez de Báez, *Julia de Burgos: Vida y poesía*, San Juan de Puerto Rico: Editorial Coquí, 1966, p. 10.

19. Julia de Burgos, *Obra poética* (edited by Consuelo Burgos and Juan Bautista Pagán), San Juan de Puerto Rico: Instituto de Cultura Puertorriqueña, 1961, p. 65–6. This poem has appeared in English, but only its first part was included as if it were the poem itself, in Joanna Bankier (ed.) *The Other Voice: Twentieth-century women's poetry in translation*, New York: W. W. Norton, 1976, p. 15. The poem suffered the same fate in Alfredo Matilla and Iván Silén (eds.), *The Puerto Rican Poets: Los poetas puertorriqueños*, New York: Bantam Books, 1972, pp. 60–1.

20. *ibid.*, p. 81.

21. Rosario Castellanos, *Poesía no eres tú: obra poetica 1948–1971*, México: Fondo de Cultura Económica, 1972, p. 92. All subsequent references to this poet's work will be from this edition, page numbers will be indicated in the text.

22. This applies especially to 'Jornada de la soltera', p. 175, and 'Entrevista de prensa', pp. 303–4. The comparison I suggest deserves a detailed discussion. From a different perspective, Beth Miller, *Rosario Castellanos: una conciencia feminista en México*, Chiapas: UNACH, 1983, pp. 17–38, is one of the earliest studies of feminist themes in Castellanos's poetry.

23. I make the distinction between what Mistral published and what has been found after her death. The differences between what she allowed for publication and the texts she kept for herself have important textual and interpretative implications which I will develop elsewhere. An example of the 'official' Gabriela Mistral is *Gabriela Mistral: poesías completas*, Madrid: Aguilar, 1958. The poem mentioned in this paragraph is from this edition.

24. 'Register' in the sense given to this concept by M. A. K. Halliday, *Language as Social Semiotic*, Edward Arnold: London, 1978. It refers to the semantic potential of how what is said is said in multiple convergent planes.

25. On Esteves's 'anxiety of influence' in relation to Julia de Burgos, see Luz María Umpierre Herrera, 'La ansiedad de la influencia en Sandra María Esteves', *Nuevas aproximaciones críticas a la literatura puertorriqueña contemporánea*, Río Piedras: Editorial Cultural, 1983, pp. 115–27.

26. A selection of the work by the new generation of women poets can be found in Juan Villegas (ed.), *Antología de la nueva poesía femenina chilena*, Santiago: Editorial La Noria, 1985.

27. Mikhail Bakhtin, *Problems of Dostoevsky's Poetics* (edited and translated by Caryl Emerson), Manchester: Manchester University Press, 1984.

28. I follow Bakhtin's theory of discourse, understood in terms of *the dialogic*, but have integrated the intervention of gender into the sociality of the subject and of discourse. See notes 10 and 16 above.

29. Alejandra Pizarnik, from *La última inocencia* (1956), included in *El deseo de la palabra*, Barcelona: Ocnos, 1975, p. 27.

> alejandra alejandra
> I stand below
> alejandra

30. Paul de Man, 'Autobiography as De-Facement', *Modern Language Notes* 94, 1979, pp. 920–30.

31. Pizarnik, *El deseo de la palabra*, p. 101.

> a mother tongue castrates
> the tongue is an organ that understands
> the breakdown of the whole poem
> castrated by its own tongue
> which is the organ for re-creation
> for re-cognition
> but not the one that can resurrect
> any of the negativity
> of the outcast and his dog on my horizon.

32. I use the concept of heteroglossia in the sense given in Michael Holquist (ed.), *The Dialogic Imagination: Four essays by M. M. Bakhtin*, Austin and London: University of Texas Press, 1981.

33. Iris M. Zavala, *Escritura desatada*, Santurce: Ediciones Puerto, 1973, p. 47.

> Sitting between you
> and me
> is language;
> one language
> the sole spatial alphabet
> (in revolt)
> weapon
> brotherhood
> rifle
> struggle
> freedom

34. The comparison I suggest includes I. M. Zavala's *Chiliagony* (translated by Susan Pensak), Bloomington, Indiana: Third Woman Press, 1984, and her *Nocturna más no funesta*, Barcelona: Montesinos, 1987, with Michelle Cliff's *Claiming an Identity They Taught Me to Despise*, Watertown, Mass.: Persephone Press, 1980, and *Abeng*, New York: Crossing Press, 1984.

35. See my study 'Black North-American Women Poets in the Semiotics of Culture', in Myriam Díaz-Diocaretz and Iris M. Zavala (eds.), *Women, Feminist Identity and Society in the 1980s: Selected papers*, Amsterdam: John Benjamins, 1985, pp. 37–60.

36. Nancy Morejón, 'Mujer negra', in *Poesía feminista del mundo hispánico (desde la edad*

*media hasta la actualidad). Antología crítica*, México: Siglo Veintiuno Editores, pp. 257–9.

Nothing is foreign to us.
The earth is ours
The sea and sky are ours.
Magic and mystery are ours.
Here I can watch people like myself dancing
around the tree we planted to communism.
Its amazing wood has taken up the dream.

# 7. Images of women in Cuba's post-revolutionary narrative
## Nissa Torrents

The Cuban revolution of 1959 not only freed the country from oppression and colonialism but, in the words of Castro, it aimed for a revolution within the revolution: the liberation of Cuban women and the eradication of *machismo* at all levels, a task which was codified in the admirable Family Code of 1975 which legally declared the equal status of the sexes. The literacy campaign of 1961 had given women – they constituted the large majority of the illiterate – access to culture; other campaigns that followed stressed the importance of education. The growth of the amateur movement in the arts and the opening of sport to all, as well as the gradual breaking of genre taboos in sport, were major breakthroughs.

The revolution itself, as had been the case in Mexico, became the central theme of Cuban literature. It had been a revolution made by the young and it was the very young who benefited the most: the children who went to school, drank milk and had their health monitored from before birth.

Revolutions tend to create epic and romantic imagery and Cuba's was no exception. Made by handsome young men and women, though men were in the majority, their apparently impossible task captured the imagination of the world. The overthrow of the tyrant, a great theme of Romantic literature, necessitated extreme individual and collective courage and for a time the domestic and the private, traditionally women's terrain, was pushed into the background. In the familiar images of the Sierra, men held guns and engaged in battle while women nursed, collected funds or liaised between the different groups, fulfilling a traditional and, of course, secondary role. The literature of the revolution follows this model and seems to forget (unlike the cinema) the revolution within the revolution that Castro had declared.

In this literature, no specific women's needs are recognized beyond those that concern motherhood. Voluntarily unmarried women are considered an aberration and are not the centre of a writer's interest. In real life, equality is reduced to performing jobs and undertaking duties that used to be exclusively masculine, but without relinquishing the feminine. Public work is added to private work and women's role as reproducer of the labour force stays as it was, in spite of legislation. Posters and photos show women truck drivers, cane cutters or doctors but invariably with a touch of the 'feminine': the handkerchief hiding the curlers, the painted nails.

The exemplary woman, according to the revolutionary images still proposed in the island's women's magazines, is a model worker who belongs to social and defence organisations, studies at night, acts in some amateur group, cooks, sews and educates her children properly in sound Marxist principles. A triple or quadruple shift! She is also a woman without a private life and without conflicts or tensions, even though Cuba has the highest divorce rate in Latin America. Adultery is unknown or only committed by men and the family is the pillar of the socialist state.

Today there are many women poets and short-story writers but women novelists are thin on the ground. The novel requires time, continuity and that famous 'room of one's own' that is harder to arrive at than a mirage in the island's crowded spaces. Although one of the great writers of nineteenth-century Cuba was a woman, Gertrudis Gómez de Avellaneda, who excelled in all genres, and the twentieth century has produced one great literary critic, Mirta Aguirre, enormously influential from her chair at Havana University, only Dora Alonso, born in 1910, has had a continuous literary career as novelist, short-story and children's book writer. More significantly, that admirable though overworked New Woman hardly appears in the novel of the revolution (written by men) and it could be easily inferred by a reader ignorant of the momentous changes that have taken place in the island since 1959, that women in Cuba continue in the traditional roles of mother/whore, voluntarily subject to the male, and that if they ever do appear as revolutionaries it is because of love for a man.

Cinema has tackled the issue of women's rights since ICAIC, the Cuban organisation responsible for all aspects of film production and distribution, was founded in 1960 but although most films and documentaries on the subject are undoubtedly progressive, they are directed by men. Women film-makers continue to be very rare and mostly limited to documentaries dealing with 'female' subjects: children, education and the arts.

An examination of the public language of the Revolution confirms that the category 'man' still includes woman as it did at the beginning when the country was undertaking the creation of the New Man, and as it did, of course, prior to 1959. An examination of executive positions shows that although women constitute almost half the labour force and are a majority in traditionally 'female' professions such as teaching and medicine, this is not reflected in the power hierarchy, in spite of public speeches, timid initiatives and the existence of excellent pre-school care. The centrality of the family, renamed as 'socialist', and the paucity of household appliances (attributable not only to the blockade but also to the fact that those who decide economic priorities are men), mean that a woman's day is so full that there is little time to prepare for power or for writing and both continue to be almost exclusively male prerogatives.

UNEAC (Union of Writers and Artists of Cuba) decides whose book will be published and when, and although the leadership has changed much since January 1988, when a new, more open group took over, it still consists of middle-aged men. In the lovely house of El Vedado, women remain in their usual posts of secretaries, telephone operators and cleaners.

If we examine some of the novels that have as a theme the revolution or the defence of the island, we see that women are portrayed as appendages to men; even when they are allowed sexual desire, their sexuality is a natural force which they cannot control and usually leads to their downfall and, occasionally, to that of the male also. Decision-taking is a male preserve and women are what they are. No change is allowed. We are born mothers or whores or the new revolutionary version of the former: 'exemplary workers'.

Noel Navarro in *Los caminos de la noche* [Night Paths] (1967), has as a protagonist an 'exemplary' woman, a prostitute whom the revolution has transformed into a militia soldier, a desirable change that does not extend to the language used in the torrid erotic scenes that pepper the novel:

> From above, an impetuous vertical force, capable of tearing, was looking for depths while, underneath, the conquered matter heaved up and down with a violence that backed the uncontrolled violence from above, joining two realities, whose physicality came together in one desire; that of possessing and being possessed.

Miguel Cossío Woodward, who in *Sacchario* (1970) seemed to be looking for a new revolutionary morality, went back in *Brumario* (1980) to a more traditional view of gender. His male protagonist likes as companion an equally revolutionary girl but, we are told, will not hestitate to leave her behind when the defence of the motherland needs him. Elena, pregnant as melodramatic convention demands, will wait for her man to return from the front where he went to repel imperialist threats. Egotistically (one-parent families are acceptable if the man is bettering himself or fighting other people's wars) she will stop her man going abroad to study, thus curtailing his chances (although she studies medicine, nothing is made of her career) in a society that gives enormous importance to qualifications. Monogamous marriage, which had been rejected in the previous novel, is exalted as the necessary step towards the founding of the communist family; the exemplary couple state that they will never get tired of each other because they 'will know how to take care of the small details, how to understand and back each other up, in order to take care of their relationship which is the most important thing that has ever happened'.

Manuel Cofiño in *La última mujer y el próximo combate* [The Last Woman and the Next Fight] (1971), proposes a humanist communism, one that wants to persuade and not to force. He writes about the difficult task of convincing the backward and suspicious peasantry of the advantages of the revolution. Two couples are offered for comparison: Bruno–Mercedes and Siaco–Nati. Bruno is a leader and Mercedes a worker active in the local co-op. Siaco is a loafer who will end up as a counter-revolutionary and Nati is that typical male fantasy product: the woman who is all sex and whose presence disturbs the male and stops him working. Although not counter-revolutionary herself, she follows the male because her sexuality is her only guiding force. Black-haired and olive-skinned, she has something of the witch in her. Thunder does not frighten her and she loves walking naked in the rain, unconsciously looking for its cleansing power, because her sexual appetite makes her feel guilty and gives her nightmares. She was raped at the age of twelve by the local boss, a scene told in a lurid passage in which the child is described as enjoying the experience. The author shows no pity or even understanding for Nati, a woman with 'frightened and wet eyes' that contrast with those of Mercedes, 'transparent like water drops'. Mercedes with the beautiful, holy name of Our Lady of Mercy, the freer of slaves; Mercedes with her white skin and blonde hair, who blushes on seeing Bruno and keeps her hair demurely covered, whilst Nati appears naked even when dressed. It is not difficult to discover Mary under the blond curls of Mercedes and Eve the temptress under the passionate body of Nati, which is constantly being described in terms of wriggling, mud and sex. The relationship between the couples is as different as the women: white, asexual, reminiscent of that of Mary and Joseph in the case of the earnest revolutionaries, and ruled by primeval sexuality in the case of the traitor Siaco and sexy Nati.

In Cofiño's *Cuando la sangre se parece al fuego* [When Blood Looks Like Fire] (1977), a male protagonist overcomes his marginality and becomes a revolutionary against a gallery of women characters where appearances punctuate his progress. There are respected and respectable mothers and grandmothers, raped young women, sad schoolteachers and assorted whores but the question of how and why women become whores or why rape seems to be the common form of sexual initiation for poor girls is never addressed. One of the characters is Laura, who belongs to an urban guerrilla group because her husband belongs to it. She is dismissed as a meddling busybody who thinks the revolution is about getting a house in a better district, changing cars yearly and shopping in Miami. Although she is blonde, we are told that she has slit eyes and a fringe! Another wife, Azelma, is approved by the narrator because of her sobriety in dress and because of her silence. After his triumph our lumpen hero – rescued through work and revolutionary action – finds Gloria in the office where he works. She is the secretary of the head of department, thus fulfilling all requirements: she plays a secondary role but with the top notch. Gloria types the forms but takes them to the men to fill in, has pink silky skin, always smells fresh and laughs frankly. She lowers her eyelashes demurely and likes 'being looked at'. The narrator protagonist further tells the reader that Gloria had a 'flat life compared with mine. She had had a boyfriend. Nothing really, just that bad memory that all girls must have.'

Questions of race and gender arise for 'revolutionary' writers from the persistence of a colonised female image as the desirable model. These questions have not been addressed by writers or critics in the new Cuba. The ideal women continue to be distinguished, white-skinned blondes who know their place, a place that the revolution has only cosmetically altered.

In these novels sex appears as a flaw overcome by the strong, and destructive for the weak. Bourgeois and counter-revolutionary men succumb to sex but the New Man successfully rejects it or channels it into monogamous marriage. Catholic morality and its insistence on sexual sin still dictate public morality, at least so far as the novelists are concerned.

## Select bibliography

Calderón, Rogelio Rodriguez, *Novela de la Revolución y otros temas*, Havana: Editorial Letras Cubanas, 1983.

Desnoes, Edmundo, *Los Dispositivos en la Flor*, Hanover (USA): Ediciones del Norte, 1981.

Lemoins, Maurice, (ed), *Cuba, 30 ans de revolution*, Paris: Autremont, 1989.

# 8. Subverting the dominant text: Elena Poniatowska's *Querido Diego* Juan Bruce-Novoa

*(for Ana Bundgaard and Aralia López-González)*

Since Rosario Castellanos's death in 1974, the title of leading female author in Mexican letters has passed to Elena Poniatowska.[1] Through her work as a journalist and the author of documentary narratives, Poniatowska, who was born in 1933, has taken a clear position regarding literature and its social function: since the oppressed of society are doubly victimized through a marginalization process in which they are rendered invisible and unheard, authors who have access to publishers must bring to the reading public's attention what the oppressed have not been allowed to express in print. Within the Latin American tradition of social protest literature, this may not sound unusual; in truth, Poniatowska can be placed squarely in that tradition. But as I argued in a study of Poniatowska's first book, her work adds a corollary: when a dominant rhetorical code – political, literary, religious, patriarchal, etc. – arrogates the theme and images of people excluded from the power structure in which that same code functions as a means of representation and propaganda, the disenfranchised often pass from the state of being ignored to that of being falsely represented and even exploited. In popular media and politics, as well as in art and academia, both well- and ill-intentioned people tend to simplify, when they portray them, the images of marginalized peoples. In Poniatowska's specific national context of Mexico, cynical populism is the institutionalized rhetoric of a highly class-conscious society and a ruling political party which claims to carry out a perpetual revolution for the disadvantaged.

Poniatowska endeavours to avoid misrepresenting the voices she documents by making of her writing not the original personal statement so prized in literary circles but rather a reportage-style medium for the promulgation of materials, such as oral history and political opposition, which are normally omitted from social and literary discourse. Hence her similarity to the Oscar Lewis school of anthropological witnessing and narrative documentation. Yet her open manipulation of materials, according to aesthetic principles, to create what must be considered fiction rather than supposedly objective and unmediated recording of testimonials brings her more in line with the practitioners of the 'new journalism'. Without opening up here the thorny question of the fictionality of all representational rhetorics, even those like history which, as Hayden White has admirably pointed out, so desire to retain their status as objective science, we should pursue Poniatowska's point concerning the difficulty of presenting the voice of the oppressed, since it is a key to her literary project.

Accepting what has been said about the co-opting capacity of the mediators of marginalized testimonies, one might be tempted to propose that anyone sincerely desiring to open the print media to the oppressed should limit themselves to transcribing that testimony verbatim. Yet this, of course, falls back into the naïve privileging of orality that Derrida and his followers have spent so much effort debunking. No linguistic formulation can be free of the rhetorical strategies ingrained in language itself, strategies which accurately, although not always obviously, reflect the ideological discourse at play in a given field. We can accept this in reference to spokespersons for dominant groups, but we would like those from marginal groups, when they speak their vision, to also bespeak that of their group, which we assume should be radically different from the dominant discourse. Yet this is not always true. Even when the testimony comes directly from the oppressed, the language and forms through which they express themselves often derive from the dominant sector. More than a problem of surface language, this situation reflects an often deep-seated interiorization of the dominant, repressive ideology on the part of the oppressed. Thus even when they speak in their own voice, there is no guarantee that the recorded text will be clearly in opposition to the status quo as maintained by the dominant classes; quite the opposite can be true: the text may well meet the expectations of the dominant classes in either or both expression and/or content. This is especially clear in the case of those sectors of society which have appropriated the language of the middle class, either through their own efforts or as a result of indoctrination. For feminists like Poniatowska, determined to open the print media to female expression, as well as to rescue the suppressed writing of their predecessors, this is a fundamental dilemma.

Approaches to this problem vary. Nicos Poulantzas suggests that

> every social formation or historically existing society has in fact consisted in the overlay and structural coexistence of several modes of production all at once, including vestiges and survivals of older modes of production, now relegated to structurally dependent positions within the new, as well as anticipatory tendencies which are potentially inconsistent with the existing system but have not yet generated an autonomous space of their own. (Jameson, p. 95).

Jameson goes beyond Poulantzas to aver that the ultimate level of critical concern is the 'ideology of form' in which works will be seen as 'the determinate contradiction of the specific messages emitted by the varied sign systems which coexist in a given artistic process as well as in its general formation' (*ibid.*, pp. 98–9). Mikhail Bakhtin insisted that all cultural production be seen as dialogical, with continual struggle among competing voices. Harold Bloom argues for literature as the dialogical attempt to devour influential masters through deliberate misreadings. Berndt Ostendorf, in his studies of black writing, describes a similar tradition of dialogical devouring of white masters, which he calls minstrelsey.

With very little anxiety about Bloom's heavy influence on them, Sandra M. Gilbert and Susan Gubar choose to emphasize a consciously manipulative rhetoric in their interpretation of women's writing. They suggest that women practise palimpsestic strategies intended to 'both express and camouflage' (Gilbert and Gubar, p. 81), strategies in which 'surface designs conceal or obscure deeper, less accessible (and less socially acceptable) levels of meaning' (*ibid.*, p. 73). The implication here is that female authors, like Ostendorf's blacks in blackface make-up, know the possibilities of combining two codes, which they have such mastery over that they can carry out such a balancing act to their advantage. Gilbert and Gubar's, and Ostendorf's foregrounding of the power freely to manipulate oppositional codes could be seen as rhetorically utopian in itself, creating as it does the impression that authors control the palimpsestic game. Other critics are less optimistic.

More in line with Lenin's 'two culture' theory, Sigrid Weigel sees the situation of women not as one of freedom, but one of limiting and limited necessity.

> Women are always defined according to male criteria as regards their characteristics, behaviour, etc. Woman within the male order has learnt to see herself as inferior, inauthentic and incomplete. As the cultural order is ruled by men but women still belong to it, women also use the norms of which they themselves are the object. That is, woman in the male order is at once *involved and excluded*. This means for woman's self-awareness that she sees herself by seeing *that* and *how* she is seen. She sees the world through male spectacles. (The metaphor 'spectacles' implies the utopia of a liberated, unhindered gaze.) She is fixated on the self-observation refracted in the critical gaze of man, having left observation of the external world to his wide-ranging gaze. Thus her self-portrait originates in the distorting patriarchal mirror. In order to find her own image she must liberate the mirror of *images of woman* painted on it by the male hand. (Weigel, p. 61)

Weigel's metaphor is a *de facto* palimsest of images over images, but it differs from Gilbert and Gubar's in that it underscores the extreme difficulty faced by women in attempting to express themselves.

In my study of *Lilus Kikus*, Poniatowska's first novel, I explained how the apparently innocent, traditional text of social indoctrination, in which a young girl is schooled out of her intuitive, free-spirited childhood state and into a controlled and directed adulthood, can be read through a subversive subtext if we approach it with an eye attuned to palimpsestic overlays. This approach reveals the ironic tone of the third-person narrator. Poniatowska uses the apparently trivial subject of a playful little girl to mask her feminist critique of repressive patriarchal social norms. The hope is that the protagonist, Lilus, will have learned to feign acceptance of society's dictates while, like the author, actually putting into practice both defensive and offensive palimpsestic manoeuvres. When, in her effort to minimize her mediating presence, Poniatowska shifts to first-person narratives in which women speak directly, the problem shifts as well: one must distinguish between the apparently sincere text of the narrator, who to some extent incarnates the ideologemes of the dominant culture, and the ironic subtext of the feminist author, who infiltrates the character's monologue to subvert it and, in the end, transform it into a dialogical space. I will reserve the analysis of Poniatowska's best-known book, *Hasta no verte Jesus mío* for another time, and concentrate here on *Querido Diego, te abraza Quiela*.

This small book – barely 72 pages – has been the object of little critical attention. The attitudes of Carlos Monsivais or Marta Robles are typical: in major essays on Poniatowska they both mention *Querido Diego* in passing, as if only to assure the reader that they have covered all the published titles, but give relatively little analysis. One suspects that the book's subject matter has as much to do with the critics' negative posture as the brevity of the text. *Querido Diego* is comprised of twelve fictitious letters from the Russian painter Angelina Beloff to her lover for ten years and father of her dead child, Diego Rivera. Beloff, a member of the pre-Revolutionary Russian upper class, lived and worked among the avant-garde artists of Paris shortly after the turn of the century, so for writers like Monsivais and Robles, who assume a position of leftist progressiveness, she seems the epitome of bourgeois decadence, hardly a desirable image worthy of perpetuation. They prefer Jesusa, the lower-class Mexican mestiza protagonist of *Hasta no verte, Jesús mío*, who is capable of personifying the national infrahistory from a popular and semi-subversive stance. Poniatowska's fascination with Beloff, and her recreation of her letters, have even been implicitly seen as a nostalgic remnant of Poniatowska's own elitism. Similar opinions once relegated *Lilus Kikus* to the status of children's literature, blinding readers to its feminist subtext. With that precedent in mind, we should avoid naïve one-to-one correlations that might lead us to dismiss *Querido Diego* as the repressed sign of bad consciousness, and practise instead a dialogical, palimpsestic reading.

The Angelina Beloff recreated by Poniatowska strikes one on first reading as a stereotypical woman. That is, her characterization satisfies expectations firmly codified in Occidental patriarchal culture. She is motherly: she calls Rivera *chatito* and adds, 'me gusta mucho llamarte chatito, me hace pensar en tus padres, siento que soy de la familia' ('I like to call you little pug-nose, it makes me think of your parents, I feel like part of the family') (p. 20).[2] Elsewhere she asks him why children are always *chatitos* (p. 38). She is passive and even though she confesses to be madly jealous, she is understanding and forgiving: she implores him to tell her if he has a new woman adding, 'Si así fuera Diego, dímelo, yo sabría comprenderlo, ¿acaso no he sabido comprender todo?' ('If this is the case Diego, tell me, I'll understand, haven't I managed to understand everything?') (p. 32). She is emotionally malleable, existing only for and through her lover, to the extent that her value is predicated entirely on him, and he even dictates her own self-image:

> después de todo, sin ti, soy bien poca cosa, mi valor lo determina el amor que me tengas y existo para los demás en la medida en que tú me quieras. Si dejas de hacerlo, ni yo ni los demás podremos quererme...
> [... after all, without you I'm almost nothing, my value is determined by the love you have for me and I exist for others to the extent that you love me. If you stop loving me, neither I nor anyone else can love me...]
> (p. 17)

Beloff portrays herself as Rivera's creation, from whom she has learnt even her career skills:

> ... hice un apunte, de ti he aprendido a tomar notas, a expresarme en vez de rumiar en secreto, a moverme, a dibujar todos los días, a hacer, a decir en vez de meditar, a no disimular la conmoción y me siento fuerte por esta abundancia de actividad, este sentimiento de expansión y de plenitud...
> [I drew a sketch, from you I have learned to take notes, to express myself instead of ruminating in secret, to move, to draw every day, to act, to speak instead of thinking, not to hide my emotions and this wealth of activity, this sensation of growth and fullness makes me feel strong...]
> (p. 30).

She goes further, creating synonymy between her two passions: Rivera *is* painting. She goes to the Louvre and is transported by a sudden epiphany of comprehension, which she relates by saying, '*sentí* Diego y esto me dio una gran felicidad' [I *felt* Diego and this made me very happy] (p. 20). In the same letter she goes on to say 'estoy llena de ti, es decir de pintura' ['I am full of you, that is to say, of painting'] (p. 21). In Rivera's absence, she maintains a semblance of his presence through the dual synonymy: painting is Rivera; she is Rivera through her participation in painting. So she paints frantically, and attributes her actions to his influence. The following passage is long, but necessary to my analysis.

> Me levanté a las cuatro de la mañana como tú lo hacías y traté de organizar la composición ... y continué hasta la noche.... Pensé que tu espíritu se había posesionado de mí, que eras tú y no yo el que estaba

dentro de mí, que este deseo febril de pintar provenía de ti y no quise perder un segundo de tu posesión. Me volví hasta gorda Diego, me desbordaba... era alta como tú, combatía en contra de los epíritus – tú me dijiste alguna vez que tenías tratos con el diablo – y lo recordé en ese momento porque mi caja torácica se expandió a tal grado que los pechos se me hincharon, los cachetes, la papada; era yo una sola llanta, busqué un espejo y en efecto, allí estaba mi cara abotagada y ancha, palpitante como si la soplaran con un fuelle desde adentro ¡cómo me latían las sienes! ¡Y los ojos! ¡que enrojecidos! Sólo entonces me... di cuenta de que tenía fiebre ¡bendita fiebre! ... te sentí sobre mí, Diego, eran tus manos y no las mías las que se movían. Después no supe lo que pasó, debo haber perdido el conocimiento porque amanecí tirada junto al caballete con un frío tremendo. La ventana estaba abierta. Seguramente la abrí en la noche como tú solías hacerlo cuando sentías que tu cuerpo se agigantaba hasta cubrir paredes, rincones, abarcaba una mayor extensión sobre la tierra, iba más allá de sus límites, los rompía. Naturalmente pesqué una angina de pecho y si no es por la solicitud de la *concierge*, sus *bouillons de poule* diarios, ahora mismo estarías despidiéntote de tu Quiela. Me he debilitado mucho.

[I got up at four that morning like you used to and tried to plan the composition... and continued into the night.... I thought your spirit had possessed me, that you and not I was inside me, that this feverish desire to paint came from you and I didn't want to lose a moment of your possession. I grew fat, Diego, I overflowed... I was tall like you, battling the spirits – you once told me that you had dealings with the devil – and I remembered it then because my thorax expanded so much that my breast, cheeks and double chin swelled; one huge tyre, I looked for a mirror and in reality my face showed blotchy and puffy, pulsing as if blown by bellows from within; how my temples pounded! And my eyes! How red! Only then did I... notice that I had a fever, blessed fever!... I felt you over me, Diego, they were your hands and not mine moving. Later I don't know what happened, I must have passed out, because I awoke next to the easel very cold. The window was open. Surely I opened it during the night like you used to do when you felt your body expand until it covered the walls, corners, embracing a larger expanse of the earth, going beyond its limits, breaking then. Naturally, I caught a chest cold and if not for the attentions of the *concierge*, her daily *bouillons de poule*, this very moment you would be saying goodbye to your Quiela. I have grown very weak. (p. 23–4)

This extended re-creation of mystic union in terms of the physical possession of Angelina by Diego is the ultimate and logical result of her interiorization of the cultural norm of male-centredness. If she can have value only in and through him, then in his absence she somehow must invoke his presence to fill the void. The letters themselves are one strategy: they re-create or re-present a conversation at a distance, they establish the deferred relationship of reading, and they allow her to focus on him as the centre to which she directs herself. Yet his silence threatens her: 'mientras no tenga noticias tuyas estoy paralizada' ['until I receive word from you I am paralysed'] (p. 32); that is, his silence holds her in a state of suspended life. To respond to the perceived threat, she must go beyond representation. Her problem is essentially that of the mystic: with travel to God only possible if He calls one to His presence through death, how can one encounter Him physically here and now? She must make of her body the material vessel for his spirit. The goal would be to fuse two spirits in one body. But as students of mysticism know, this means the preliminary elimination of one's self through asceticism and prayer to, and meditation on, the Godhead. From the beginning of the text, Angelina displays the capacity for self-annihiliation: 'Yo podría borrarme con facilidad' ['I could rub myself out easily'] (p. 9).

All of this can be accepted from the perspective of patriarchal cultural norms. Angelina's behaviour resembles the process of grieving or the hysterical response to divorce. Society accepts, even expects, women to enact such behaviour when they 'lose their man'. After all, he is their societal touchstone, their world centre, their god. Angelina Beloff's actions are not strange to us; that she goes on to re-create her suffering and actions in writing so as to offer them as simultaneously a sign of enduring love and a *de facto* prolongation of a waning relationship does not strike us as unusual. She is following an established cultural pattern.

Poniatowska's re-creation and publication of the letters can be seen, then, as an ambiguous act of opening the print media to the voice of a wronged woman who seems to prove the stereotypical rule about female behaviour. And to some extent this is true. Poniatowska does not deny that women react this way. In fact, her text re-creates successfully the process of grieving for a lost love. Yet this type of limited interpretation is possible only if we read with those patriarchal expectations, as Bertram D. Wolfe read and re-created Beloff in his biography of Rivera. His explanation of their ill-fated relationship is that while Rivera's life was quite literally painting, hers was love, with painting only a pastime to fill the empty moments – a chauvinistically stereotypical view of sex roles in which man is his work, while woman is her relationship with a man. Unfortunately, as Poniatowska demonstrates, Beloff was not immune to this patriarchal ideology.

Perhaps the ease with which one interiorizes these societal prejudices, even with respect to a woman as educated and talented as Angelina Beloff, explains why Poniatowska recreated and fictionalized Beloff's correspondence, instead of simply gathering and publishing it. It was necessary to go beyond the mere revelation of the existence of the texts – which might easily lend themselves to misreading – to infuse them with a feminist dialectic. In so doing, Poniatowska actually engages in dialogue, not only with Beloff but with Bertram Wolfe. After all, it was the reading of Wolfe's book, in which she read one actual letter, that catalysed the writing of

*Querido Diego.*[3] Poniatowska carefully refutes his re-creation of Beloff, which was a pro-Rivera reading of her into patriarchial stereotypes.

Poniatowska's strategy is to create a text and simultaneously undermine it with contradictions that her character Beloff lives, expresses within her written communiqués, but does not consciously confront. For instance, while she claims to have learned to take notes and sketches from Rivera, in another place she recalls that already before meeting Rivera she carried her notebook everywhere, making so many sketches that 'parecía yo un fotógrafo con lápiz en vez de cámara' ['I was like a photographer with a pencil instead of a camera'] (p. 36). That she imitates his painting habits and routine is similarly refuted when we learn that she used to paint sixteen hours a day before meeting Rivera, and that at times she would be so engrossed in her work that she would ignore friends and relatives, and even spend the night working. She gives the following explanation for her life then:

> Yo creo que la pintura es así, se le olvida a uno todo, pierde uno la noción del tiempo, de los demás, de las obligaciones, de la vida diaria que gira en torno a uno sin advertirla siquiera...
> [I think painting is like that, one forgets everything, loses sense of time, of others, of obligations, of daily life moving all around without one even noticing...] (p. 37)

In answer to Wolfe's accusation that art was not her life, Poniatowska has Beloff remember:

> ¿Y si de pronto fuera yo a perder esta facilidad? ¿Si de pronto me estancara consciente de que no sé nada? ¿Si de pronto me paralizara la autocrítica o llegara al agotamiento de mi facilidad? Sería tanto como perder mi alma, Diego, porque yo no vivía sino en función de la pintura; todo lo veía como un dibujo en prospecto...
> [And if I were to suddenly lose this facility? If suddenly I stagnated, knowing that I know nothing? If suddenly self-criticism paralysed me or this facility of mine ran out? It would be like losing my soul, Diego, because I lived only in relation to painting; I saw everything as if in the perspective of a drawing...] (p. 38)

But although it is clear to readers that Beloff, like Rivera, initially is totally centred on painting, she herself admits:

> Ahora todo ha cambiado.... No sólo he perdido a mi hijo, he perdido también mi posibilidad creadora; ya no sé pintar, ya no quiero pintar...
> [Now everything has changed.... Not only have I lost my son, I have lost my creative possibilities as well; I no longer know how to paint, I no longer want to paint...] (p. 39)

To ask what happened to Beloff is a rhetorical question, for the facts are available and undeniable. More pertinent would be to question through which rhetorical code are we going to respond to the obvious. Bertram Wolfe's response was that Beloff, being a woman, logically fell victim to a woman's typical prioritization of life: love is more important than art. Poniatowska's text might take us to the same conclusion, because Angelina herself seems to have internalized those norms. Yet we could read it and Beloff from the perspective of a feminist rhetoric: she tried to become the typical woman, and when that failed she blamed herself instead of the patriarchal system.

According to this reading, when she met Rivera, he absorbed her into his conversation and then brought her into his circle of activity and friends, but only under the guise of female passivity, which he admired and praised. In other words, she repressed herself into a stereotypical role at their first meeting, found that it pleased him, and then imposed it upon herself out of fear of losing him:

> Yo te escuchaba quemándome por dentro, las manos ardientes sobre mis muslos, no podía pasar saliva y sin embargo parecía tranquila y tú lo comentabas: '¿Qué sedante eres Angelina, qué remanso, qué bien te sienta tu nombre, oigo un levísimo rumor de alas!
> [I listened to you burning up inside, my hands scorching my thighs, I could swallow and yet I appeared calm and you commented: 'How sedate you are, Angelina, what a still pool, how well your name suits you, I hear the lightest rustle of wings.] (pp. 44–5)

Her reaction was significant: 'Yo estaba como drogada, ocupabas todos mis pensamientos, tenía un miedo espantoso de defraudarte . . .' [I was like a woman drugged, you filled all my thoughts; I was afraid of disappointing you] (p. 45). Although she plans to reveal her true self, she remains silent. When he persists in seeking her out, she continues to act the passive role so as not to alter whatever attraction he feels for her. That she felt drugged should have warned her that she was entering upon a self-destructive experience that would alter her perception of the world and eventually distance her from painting.

Rivera achieves this displacement in Beloff by producing an effect literally quite similar to that of drugs. He interrupts her sense perceptions by reorienting her away from direct experience of outer stimuli to a state in which she receives all stimuli solely in a mediated form, already encoded by a pre-empting receptor/interpreter: Rivera. As a result, she is reduced to a state of being unable to perceive the world except through him, cut off from her own perception and her own source of direct inspiration. We understand this when Beloff recalls her epiphany at the Louvre, explained above. Yet, while in her effort to evoke and recentre Rivera in her life, she sincerely attributes her experience in the Louvre to him, Poniatowska deconstructs the event subtly by revealing the negative effects Rivera's presence produces. Beloff comes to a revelation about art only in Rivera's absence, because when she went with him, he dominated the experience by talking. After meeting Rivera, her perception becomes centred, fixated not on art as its own presentation, but on Rivera's verbal representation of his experience of the art. She shares his passion to the exclusion of her own. Her fixation shifts from art to Rivera as a spokesman for art, and thus her need to 're-speak' the experience of art in her own terms, as the act of painting, is suppressed, just as the mere possibility of an action as simple as hand movements had been suppressed when they first met. After all, as quoted above, she had not wanted to disappoint him with either physical or mental actions. It was much safer to listen and not speak, watch him act from the stillness of the stereotype. From this we can extrapolate that it was much safer to stop painting in his presence, for painting is the painter's true synthesis of speaking and acting.

Surely Beloff allowed herself to be silenced, accepting the role of passive listener, because that was the social role of the woman. Only when Rivera has abandoned her can she feel herself to be once more the centre of perception and experience life directly. Having internalized male-centred-ness, she can only explain her sensations by saying that she feels them through him, as if she were he: 'Sentí Diego.' Yet, we know that before meeting Rivera she was well on her way to this epiphany. It was Rivera who distracted her, ruling, in the grand patriarchal style, all of her emotions and sensations.

We should be careful with terminology, however, for Poniatowska takes pains to distinguish between caring fathers – Beloff's and Rivera's – and a self-centred, debilitating *macho* husband. So we should really aim our attack at the *machista* system in which the man does not want to be a parenting father at all, but rather the sole male in the woman's life: husband, father, son and lover. While Beloff's father demanded that she prepare herself for life by learning to work and then allowed her to move into the world on her own, Rivera absorbed her completely. Her father led her to develop her choice of the manner in which she would interact with the world, and then freed her to follow that choice. Rivera truncated her freedom, perverting her attraction for him as an artist and man into service for his own sake, turning her away from the world and focusing all her attention strictly on him. Like an evil father who enslaves his child in the name of love in order to retain control and reap the benefits of the offspring's productivity, Rivera used Beloff for his egotistical ends.

Under Rivera's influence, Beloff's function in the economy of human interaction is reduced from primary producer to that of servant of a producer. In a word, she is colonized. Her role is to serve Rivera; passively by listening to him when he is not painting, actively by taking care of him when he is working and keeping him connected with the outer world in those necessary areas of life that insure basic health and order. By so doing, she allows the artist to live free of the bothersome demands of everyday existence. Another way of putting it comes from one of those details Poniatowska creates to undermine the surface text. Beloff's real significance for Rivera is that she serves as his *concierge*, but then perhaps *concierge* and *mother* are largely synonymous for men. Revealing one of the few cracks in her exterior role of the accepting woman, Beloff comments:

> Sonreí para mi misma al pensar que ojalá y hubiera una Angelina que cuidara de mí y me rogara interrumpir tan sólo un momento para comer un poco . . .
> [I smiled to myself when I wished there could be an Angelina to care for me and beg me to stop just a moment to eat a little something . . .] (p. 22)

When she is alone and ill, and someone does interrupt her to impose order and necessity, it is the *concierge*, yet another female in the service economy. Here Poniatowska again opposes a feminist alternative to Wolfe's interpretation of the failure of the Rivera–Beloff relationship. It was the latter's abandonment of her real centre and function, painting, which allowed Rivera to remain faithful to his.

Her acceptance of this relationship should be read through its metaphorical reproduction in the mystical transport scene quoted above. She surrenders herself to a diabolical spirit who, while pretending to lead her to her goal – painting – actually detours her towards the role of mother, which is subsequently also frustrated. She is left, then, having reached neither goal, only near the material support of painting, the easel, half dead and alone through the effort, much weaker than when she began and with no accomplished work to show for the experience. Worse still, in the end she must struggle with the emptiness of having once been capable of creating – both as artist and mother – and now being barren. She was fooled into thinking that she was giving herself to a god, but delivered herself instead to a demonic incubus in a union that took her to the brink of insanity and death.

Beloff did not get Rivera back, nor was she ever recognized as a significant painter, nor does Poniatowska's text attempt to alter these historical facts by flights into fantasy. Once again, however, she imposes a rereading, this time of the end. Bertram Wolfe would want us to see Beloff essentially unchanged years later, still dependent on Rivera for money and still speaking of him as a grown child: 'He was just a child, he is still just a grown child, she told me years later,' Wolfe writes (p. 142). This reading reduces Beloff to a deluded, fixated, possessive ex-lover who would like to have continued being Rivera's mother figure, and in so doing vindicates Rivera: who can blame a child for leaving his mother to find a mate, or a man from abandoning a possessive woman who treated him like a child? While acknowledging these tendencies in Beloff – recall her use of the word *chatito* – Poniatowska also attacks Wolfe's position directly when she creates the possibility of reading the letters as a recuperative healing process. Let me explain.

In 'Die sich selbst verdoppelnde Frau', Elisabeth Lenk states:

> Woman often believes when she enters into this relationship to herself
> for the first time, when she first reflects herself [sees her own reflection in
> the mirror], that she has gone mad. But this apparent madness is no
> madness; it is the first step toward sanity. (Lenk, p. 57)

Beloff begins to encounter herself only when Rivera abandons her. In spite
of her struggle to keep Rivera as her centre, she is forced to function on her
own, rediscovering herself. Yet what she has become is something other
than what she was, or is at least an Angelina Beloff trying to be something
or someone else. Her encounter with her mirror image happens during the
mystical possession scene when, realizing she is ill, she seeks her image in
the mirror. It is his she sees reflected there, grotesquely superimposed on
her own, turning her into a monster. That hideous image accurately
captures what she has become under Rivera's influence in the sense that
– like Beloff herself *vis-à-vis* external stimuli in the Louvre scene – the
reflection filters sense perception through the mediating, distorting
presence of Rivera. In the mirror scene Rivera interposes himself – or
perhaps Beloff projects her internalized state – between Beloff and her
self-image, a metaphoric depiction of Lenk's description of a first reflective
encounter. She sees the hellish situation into which she has descended only
when Rivera is no longer there to interpret it into something else and
distract her gaze away from herself. Alone, she is led back to herself, only to
discover '*that* and *how* she is seen' 'in the distorting patriarchal mirror' of a
man. As Sigrid Weigel says, this is the initial step in self-awareness that then
leads to the liberation of 'the mirror from the *images of woman* painted on it
by the male hand' (Weigel, p. 61), another metaphor for the healing
process.

At another level, that of metonymic and synecdochtal allusions, her
'self-portrait as Rivera' recalls another in the text, that of her dying son,
Dieguito, yet one more reproduction of Rivera and very possibly also a
victim of his neglect and egotism. Poniatowska has Beloff remember that
her son's head expanded horrendously, becoming a 'cráneo inflado como
globo a punto de estallar' [a skull inflated like a balloon about to burst'] (p.
17). Her image in the mirror, six pages later, is quite similar: 'mi cara
abotagada y ancha, palpitante como si la soplaran con un fuelle desde
adentro' [my face blotchy and puffy, pulsing as if blown by bellows from
within'] (p. 23). Significantly, this synonymy with the dead son, more than
that with the living husband, imposes itself as Beloff's true image. Both
Dieguito and Beloff are striken by an illness that distorts and consumes
them, a malady that turns the victim into a monster repulsive to Rivera,
who wants nothing to do with either one. Horrified at what his creations
(Beloff and Dieguito) have become, he refuses to acknowledge nor even
look at them. And when they have been eliminated from his sphere of
movement, he will not allow them to come back into existence in a renewed

form. Even before Dieguito's birth, Rivera had proclaimed that if the child bothered him he would throw it out the window. After Dieguito was born, he had to be taken care of outside the home because his crying grated on Rivera, who wanted his child to be as passive and quiet as his wife. Is it any wonder then that he should avoid her letters, refuse to respond and metaphorically toss her out when she dares to complain?

Beloff can only grasp these revelations through the writing of the letters, because only then is her life, her self-image, set outside her as if seen in a mirror positioned to reflect her. In this sense the letters are part of the encountering of her objectified self for the first time, and thus can function in a healing mode. Significantly, Poniatowska has created a writing scene within the insanity episode. We should recall that no mention is made of what work was achieved after the mystical union scene (Letter 4). It is only some time later (Letter 8), that reference appears to some notes written on a sheet of paper usually reserved strictly for drawing, notes that Beloff does not recall having written. They are products of a forgotten burst of revelation materialized in the space of her art. We could even stretch the symbolism to say that they constitute a message from the space of art and thus are an unsolicited reflection of the artist imposed on her by the medium itself. In those notes she thinks she is insane because Rivera is gone and will not return. When she cannot work on the etchings she is supposed to finish, she apparently releases her frustrations in an outpouring of truth:

> Hoy no quiero ser dulce, tranquila, decente, sumisa, comprensiva, resignada, las cualidades que siempre ponderan los amigos. Tampoco quiero ser maternal; Diego no es un niño grande, Diego es un hombre que no escribe porque no me quiere y me ha olvidado por completo.
> [Today I don't want to be sweet, tranquil, decent, submissive, understanding, resigned, the qualities that our friends always observe. Nor do I want to be maternal; Diego is not a large child, Diego is a man who does not write because he no longer loves me and has forgotten me completely.] (p. 42).

It is only in this burst of creative writing that the truth is fully confronted, a truth that directly contradicts Wolfe's evocation of the ageing Beloff cited above. The suddenly self-aware Beloff rejects her motherly, passive, stereotypical role, the one which allows Rivera a convenient excuse for his childish egocentrism, and she admits the truth.

Yet Beloff immediately backs away from this frank statement of her situation and emotions with a disclaimer: her conscious self, her socialized self, has no knowledge of its creation; or stated another way, the socialized self she wishes to be rejects the knowledge revealed because it undermines her self project. She must attempt to distance herself – quite literally, her self – from it in order to be able to reassume her imploring tone and rhetoric, but the crack in the mental armour can not be so easily repaired or ignored. It is at this moment that Beloff predicts that they will steadily grow more and more apart until they eventually look upon one another as strangers – a prefiguration of the ending of the book in which Poniatowska adds a note to say that exactly this happened years later in Mexico. The confrontation with herself, her monstrous reflection as the image of Rivera possessing and distorting her body, forces her to face the truth, which in turn elicits from her a prediction of her eventual return to health. The fact that she will one day be able to pass by Rivera unnoticed implies that she learns to reorient herself back upon her own self, to recentre her life.[4] That recognition comes through and in an act of writing a contradictory and too-revealing text in a space intended for another form of expression, a synecdoche of Beloff's letters, and a metaphor for Poniatowska's book.

Poniatowska has admitted that she identifies with Beloff, and that the writing of *Querido Diego* provided her with a vehicle to express her own ideas: 'It was a very personal thing, very personal and impulsive. I think that I used Angelina Beloff to say many things that I felt' ('A Feminist Affinity', p. 28). Instead of interpreting this to indicate some persistent nostalgia for the bourgeois life, it would be more logical to take it as a recognition of kindred spirits through the desperate act of writing. Beloff's unanswered letters are a metaphor for the history of women's literature in the male-dominant culture. They go either unread, or read but unacknowledged. Written expression is tantamount to confrontation, and men do not desire confrontation with women, perhaps not even communication; traditionally they prefer passive silence and appreciative listening. To write is to risk rejection. But then silence has not always guaranteed fidelity or permanence, so why should women maintain it? They are caught in a double bind. Beloff and Poniatowska both have experienced that double bind, yet something in them pushed them to choose to write, although only Poniatowska has dared to take the final step and invade the male bastion of publication as well. From her hard-won beachhead within that bastion, she then clears a small space for Beloff to reappear from the shadows of oblivion and the stereotypical representations she suffered. Most probably Poniatowska's Beloff is not as she actually was, but at least she is a more positive Beloff than the one Rivera and his cronies presented. That is because she is no longer Beloff, nor completely Poniatowska, but a combination of the two in a dialogue of transformation, liberation and female solidarity.

## Notes

1. This chapter is part of a longer chapter in a book in progress on Elena Poniatowska.
2. All English translations that follow quotations are the author's and will differ from the published version. Page numbers for the original citation will follow after each translation.
3. Poniatowska has explained that *Querido Diego* was inspired by her reading of Wolfe's *Fabulous Life of Diego Rivera*. 'I read as far as the chapter on Angelina Beloff, and there I could go no further. I so much identified with her... after reading a letter in the chapter, from Angelina to Diego, I started to write Angelina's letters to Diego, letters that were based on the historical facts that Bertram Wolfe included in this chapter' ('A Feminist Affinity', p. 28).
4. Ironically, this final encounter is another fiction invented either by Bertram Wolfe or, perhaps, Rivera himself. Poniatowska took it from the Wolfe book, but later learned that it was not true ('A Feminist Affinity', p. 29). Through the redefinition of Beloff which Poniatowska achieves in *Querido Diego*, this fictional episode can take on a different significance, one of healing and reorientation, which the real events do not support so well.

## Works cited

Bakhtin, Mikhail, *Rabelais and His World*, Cambridge, Mass.: MIT, 1968.
Bloom, Harold, *The Anxiety of Influence: A theory of poetry*, New York: Oxford University Press, 1973.
Bruce-Novoa, Juan, 'Elena Poniatowska: The feminist origins of commitment', *Women's Studies International Forum* 6, 5 (1983), pp. 509–16.
*Feminist Aesthetics* (edited by Gisela Ecker, translated by Harriet Anderson), Boston: Beacon Press, 1986.
'A Feminist Affinity', *Texas Observer*, 10 October 1986, pp. 28–9.
Gilbert, Sandra M. and Susan Gubar, *The Madwoman in the Attic: The woman writer and the nineteenth century literary imagination*, New Haven: Yale University Press, 1979.
Jameson, Fredric, *The Political Unconscious: Narrative as a socially symbolic act*, Ithaca: Cornell University Press, 1981.
Lenk, Elisabeth, 'Die sich selbst verdoppelnde Frau', translated into English as 'The Self-reflecting Woman', in *Feminist Aesthetics*, pp. 59–68.
Monsiváis, Carlos, '"Mira, para que no comas olvido..." las precisiones de Elena Poniatowska', *La Cultura en México*, 1007 (15 July 1981), pp. ii–v.
Ostendorf, Berndt, *Black Literature in White America*, Totowa, New Jersey: Barnes & Noble, 1982.
Poniatowska, Elena, *Querida Diego, te abraza Quiela*, México: ERA, 1978.
Poulantzas, Nicos, *Political Power and Social Classes*, London: New Left Books, 1973.
Robles, Marta, 'Elena Poniatowska', in *La sombra fugitiva, escritoras en la cultura nacional*, vol. 1, Mexico City: Universidad Nacional Autónoma de México, 1985, pp. 343–65.
Weigel, Sigrid, 'Der schielende Blick: Thesen zur Geschichte weiblicher Schreib-praxis', translated into English as 'Double Focus: on the history of women's writing', in *Feminist Aesthetics*, pp. 59–81.
White, Hayden, *Metahistory: The historical imagination in nineteenth-century Europe*, Baltimore: Johns Hopkins University Press, 1973.
Wolfe, Bertram, *Diego Rivera, His Life and Times*, New York: Knopf, 1939.

# Elena Poniatowska: Select Bibliography

## Works by Elena Poniatowska

### 1. Narratives
*De noches vienes.* México: Grijalbo, 1980.
*La 'Flor de Lis'.* México: Era, 1988.
*Hasta no verte Jesús mío.* México: Era, 1969.
*Lilus Kikus.* México: Los Presentes, 1954.
*Querido Diego, te abraza Quiela.* México: Era, 1978.

### 2. Works for the Theatre
*Melés y Teleo. Panoramas,* 2 (summer), 1956.

### 3. Journalism
*Domingo 7.* México: Océano, 1982.
*Fuerte es el silencio.* México: Era, 1980.
*Gaby Brimmer* (in collaboration with Gaby Brimmer). México: Grijalbo, 1979.
*Nada, nadie.* México: Era, 1988.
*La noche de Tlatelolco.* México: Era, 1971.
*Palabras cruzadas.* México: Era, 1961.
*Todo empezó en domingo.* México: Fondo de Cultura Económica, 1963.
*El último guajolote.* México: Sexretaria de Educación Pública and Martín Casillas, 1982.

### 4. Translations into English
*Dear Diego* (translation of *Querido Diego, te abraza Quiela* by Katherine Silver). New York: Pantheon Books, 1986.
*Massacre in Mexico* (translation of *La noche de Tlatelolco* by Helen R. Lane). New York: Viking Press, 1975.

## Secondary sources
Bruce-Novoa, Juan, 'Elena Poniatowska: the feminist origins of commitment', *Women's Studies International Forum* 6, 5, 1983, pp. 509–16.
Chevigny, Bell Gale, 'The Transformation of Privilege in the Work of Elena Poniatowska', *Latin American Literary Review* 13, 26, July–December 1985, pp. 49–62.
Davis, Lisa, 'An Invitation to Understanding among Poor Women of the Americas: *The Color Purple* and *Hasta no verte Jesús mío*', in Bell Gale Chevigny *et. al.* (eds.), *Reinventing the Americas: Comparative studies of literature of the United States and Spanish America*, New York: Cambridge University Press, 1986, pp. 224–41.
'A Feminist Affinity', *Texas Observer*, 10 October 1986, pp. 28–9.
Flori, Mónica, 'Visions of Women: symbolic physical portrayal as social commentary in the short fiction of Elena Poniatowska', *Third Women* 2, 2, 1988, pp. 77–83.
Hancock, Joel, 'Elena Poniatowska's *Hasta no verte Jesús mío*: the remaking of the image of women', *Hispania* 66, 3, September 1983, pp. 353–9.

Jaén, Didier T., 'La neopicaresca en México: Elena Poniatowska and Luis Zapata', *Tinta* 1, 5, spring 1987, pp. 23–9.

Jorgensen, Beth Ellen, 'Texto e ideología en la obra de Elena Poniatowska', *Dissertation Abstracts Index* 47, 4, October 1986, p. 1344a.

Kiddle, Mary Ellen, 'The *Novela Testimonial* in Contemporary Mexican Literature', *Confluencia* 1, 1, Fall 1985, pp. 82–9.

Kushigian, Julia A., 'Transgresión de la autobiografía y el Bildungsroman en *Hasta no verte Jesús mío*', *Revista Iberoamericana* 53, 140, July–September 1987, pp. 667–77.

Lemaitre, Monique J., 'Jesusa Palancares y la dialéctica de la emancipación femenina', *Hisanopamérica* 10, 30, December 1981, pp. 131–5.

Méndez-Faith, Teresa, and Elizabeth Heinicke (translator), 'Translation of an Interview with Elena Poniatowska', *Atlantis* 9, 2, spring 1984, pp. 70–5.

Monsiváis, Carlos, '"Mira, para que no comas olvido . . ." las precisiones de Elena Poniatowska', *La Cultura en México* 1007, 15 July 1981, pp. ii–v.

Pérez Pisonero, Arturo, 'Jesusa Palancares, esperpento femenino', in Aralia López-González *et al.* (eds.), *Mujer y literatura mexicana y chicana, culturas en contacto*, Tijuana: El Colegio de la Frontera Norte, 1988, pp. 221–9.

Robles, Martha, 'Elena Poniatowska', *La sombra fugitiva, escritoras en la cultura nacional*, México: Universidad Nacional Autónoma de México, 1985, pp. 343–65.

Roses, Lorraine, 'Entrevista con Elena Poniatowska', *Plaza* 5–6, Fall–Spring 1981–82, pp. 51–64.

Saltz, Joanne, '*Hasta no verte Jesús mío*: el testimonio de una mujer', in Aralia López-González *et al.* (eds.), *Mujer y literatura mexicana y chicana, culturas en contacto*, Tijuana: El Colegio de la Frontera Norte, 1988, pp. 231–8.

Shea, Maureen, 'A Growing Awareness of Sexual Oppression in the Novels of Contemporary Latin American Women Writers', *Confluencia* 4, 1, Fall 1988, pp. 53–9.

Starcevic, Elizabeth D., 'Breaking the Silence: Elena Poniatowska, a writer in transition', in Rose S. Minc (ed.), *Literatures in Transition, the Many Voices of the Caribbean Area: A Symposium*, Gaithersburg, Maryland: Hispamérica, 1982, pp. 63–8.

Starcevic, Elizabeth D., 'Elena Poniatowska: witness for the people', in Doris Meyer (ed.), *Contemporary Women Authors of Latin America: Introductory essays*, Brooklyn: Brooklyn College Press, 1983, pp. 72–7.

Steele, Cynthia, 'La creatividad y el deseo en *Querido Diego, te abraza Quiela* , de Elena Poniatowska', *Hispanoamérica* 14, 41, August 1985, pp. 17–28.

Steele, Cynthia, 'La mediación en las obras documentales de Elena Poniatowska', in Aralia López-González *et al.* (eds.), *Mujer y literatura mexicana y chicana, culturas en contacto*, Tijuana: El Colegio de la Frontera Norte, 1988, pp. 211–19.

Young, Dolly J. and William D. Young, 'The New Journalism in Mexico: two women writers', *Chasqui* 12, 2–3, February–May 1983, pp. 72–80.

# 9. One hundred years of unread writing: Soledad Acosta, Elisa Mujica and Marvel Moreno
## *Montserrat Ordóñez*

## A country without women writers?

Literary production, in Colombia, belongs traditionally to the realm of male writers, with very few significant exceptions. The reasons for the lack of participation of women in the literary production of the country are very difficult to assess – they are closely related to the history of misogyny in Colombian literature, and to the place of woman as audience, consumer and, mostly, as cultural executive and administrator. A contemptuous or paternalistic criticism has systematically undervalued her world and her subjects. She has had to write without female models and without a language of her own, in the midst of political, social and family pressures that have never supported an activity that, if done well, may turn out to be critical and subversive, though it usually remains economically unproductive, and very often ends up isolating her.

Unlike other Latin American countries, Colombia has no internationally well-known woman author, like Sor Juana Inés de la Cruz, Rosario Castellanos or Elena Poniatowska from Mexico; Gabriela Mistral, María Luisa Bombal or Isabel Allende from Chile; Victoria Ocampo, Beatriz Guido or Luisa Valenzuela from Argentina; Clarice Lispector from Brazil. On the other hand, Colombia has a long list of famous male writers who have written obsessive fictions about women, such as Jorge Isaacs's *María* (1867), José Asunción Silva's *De sobremesa* (1886–7), José Eustasio Rivera's *La vorágine* (1924), Gabriel García Márquez's *Los funerales de la Mamá Grande* (1962) and *Cien años de soledad* (1967), R. H. Moreno Durán's trilogy *Femina Suite* (1969–82). Women writers do not appear consistently throughout our literary history. If they have written, their production is still waiting to be identified and studied – Colombian literary history has systematically ignored the contribution of women's writing. We do not have the research tools to start – we have no list of women writers, no list of their works, no critical bibliography. In his book *Bibliografía de la novela en Colombia*, Ernesto Porras Collantes includes some sixty names of women writers (many of them pseudonyms), most of them unknown even to the specialists. Only nine of these writers[1] seemed, at the time the bibliography was published, to have written at least two books, or have received some critical attention. At present, to decide to work on a Colombian woman writer means, in practice, to take a chance, or to pick up one of the very few names that are getting, if not a wide reading audience, at least some critical international attention, such as Fanny Buitrago, Albalucía Angel, or María Mercedes Carranza. Although all of these deserve serious studies, they are usually chosen without an awareness of the complexities of Colombian literary history. The field of women's literature is so undefined and so closely related to the revision of our literary canon, that finding coherent lines of research means drawing the map of an unknown territory. Until now, Colombia has had a literary history coming from and geared to a world of exclusively masculine values.

The Colombian critic and fiction writer Helena Araújo explores part of the unread corpus of women's writing in her article 'Siete novelistas colombianas' [Seven Colombian Women Novelists], in which she analyses novels by Rocío Vélez de Piedrahita, Elisa Mújica, Alba Lucía Angel, Flor Romero, Fanny Buitrago, Amparo María Suárez and Marvel Moreno. In another recent article, Jacques Gilard studies four women writers from the Atlantic Coast: Amira de la Rosa, Olga Salcedo de Medina, Judith Porto de González and Marvel Moreno. With an interesting approach, he criticizes the production of the first three writers as examples of *palabra resignada* [resigned word], and validates Marvel Moreno's work as *palabra rebelde* [rebel word]. These two articles prove the need to multiply our critical readings – only by comparative analyses will this unread writing become part of our literary history and cease to be considered an anomaly or a marginal production.

As one more attempt to draw part of this map, in this chapter I present three moments of the Colombian novel written by women, through three novels belonging to very different literary periods. First, I discuss Soledad Acosta de Samper, our most prolific writer in the nineteenth century, and her novel *Dolores*, published the same year as Jorge Isaacs' *María*. Second, a short reading of Elisa Mújica's *Catalina* introduces a novel that makes a significant contribution to Colombian literature before *One Hundred Years of Solitude*. Third, Marvel Moreno's *En diciembre llegaban las brisas* represents contemporary literature, a post-garcíamárquez and postmodern writing of rupture and a total questioning of gender and history.

## Soledad Acosta de Samper: leprosy and eroticism in *Dolores*

Solitude and void have beset this writer for more than a century. She was born in 1833 in a country that was then called República de Nueva Granada and died in 1913, after have devoted most of her life to writing, in a Republic of Colombia quite different from the present one. Soledad Acosta de Samper is the most significant Colombian woman writer of the nineteenth century and one of the most outstanding in Latin America. Her contribution appears as marginal, however, in Colombian literary history. She is not considered as a person with her own identity and fulfilments; rather, she is defined as daughter and wife to two outstanding politicians and writers. Some of her works are mentioned in passing, but apart from a recent anthology of her writing she has not been re-edited regularly and is hardly read. Like her country, which changed its name five times during her lifetime and went through all the difficult processes of national formation, Soledad Acosta has been looked upon with suspicion and contempt: for having done too much, for her contradictions, for her mistakes. With critical inconsistencies that have much to do with Colombian cultural history, she has been accused of opposite sins – of copying her sources and not writing a personal novel, and of basing her writing on her own experience and using too much imagination. Her work is overwhelming for its quantity and for the difficulty of finding it – it is scattered in different publications and signed with several pseudonyms – and of classifying it. Like most of the nineteenth-century Latin American writers, she wrote without thinking of genres. Throughout her life, her work as a journalist predominated – she not only published in the press, but also founded and edited numerous journals and magazines. With the exception of poetry, she tried all the genres of the period, and integrated journalism, fiction, history and translation. Her work parallels development of the great national Latin American novels and growing awareness of the difference of the literature of the new Latin American countries.

Soledad Acosta de Samper's personal experiences placed her in a privileged situation for her task of reception and appropriation of discourses. She was an only child; her mother, Caroline Kemble, was English and her father, a patriot from the Independence wars, was a general, a politician and a historian; during her adolescence she lived for a while with her maternal grandmother, a Protestant, in Halifax (Canada) and went to school in Paris for several years. With all these experiences, she enjoyed an exceptional education for a woman of her time and had a very good knowledge of French and English, the languages of the two cultures in conflict with the Spanish inheritance during the entire nineteenth century. Her husband, José María Samper, was a prominent politician, journalist and man of letters, one of the most influential Colombian intellectuals of the last century. They had four daughters, two of whom died in an epidemic. When required, Soledad Acosta worked in commerce to sustain her family, without ever ceasing to write. Harold E. Hinds notes that there was probably not another person, man or woman, more prolific in the history of Colombian letters, with the exception of her husband. The couple seem to have operated a division of intellectual labour – he wrote poetry and social and political journalism, and she wrote history, novels and short stories, scenes of everyday life, literary criticism, translations, and articles that she considered of interest for a female audience. These articles ranged over aspects of the culture and daily life of the woman of the period, from travel to art and fashion. Her trips were not only imaginary; her travels – initially when still single, later as a married, then widowed woman – were extraordinary for the period and gave her experience of daily life in very different places, and an awareness of the diversity of oral tradition and allowed her to engage in the characteristic writing of the period (diaries and letters), and to participate in the nineteenth-century appreciation of exotic nature.

In terms of Colombian literary history, Soledad Acosta's first book was a surprise. The 438-page *Novelas y cuadros de la vida sur-americana* (1869) included narratives, and first appeared, starting in 1864, in periodical publications, mostly as *feuilletons* signed with pseudonyms. So, at 36 years of age, Soledad Acosta de Samper added a new identity to those of daughter, wife, mother, traveller and semi-anonymous writer – that of contributor to the formation of Colmbian literature. That is the way her husband expresses it, in a prologue called 'Dos palabras al lector' [Two words to the reader], in which he explains that he is solely responsible for the selection and the edition of the volume, oscillating between pride and panic:

He querido, por mi parte, que mi esposa contribuya con sus esfuerzos, siquiera sean humildes, a la obra común de la literatura que nuestra joven república está formando.
[I have wanted, on my part, for my wife to contribute with her efforts, however humble, to the common task of the literature being formed in our young republic.]

The step from publication as *feuilletons* to an edition in book form indicates a clear awareness of the value of the work and a desire for permanence. *Novellas y cuadros de la vida sur-americana*, however, is today an almost lost book, hardly read. To rediscover it means to reconsider our literary history. Not only are the texts themselves valuable and interesting, but they belong to an early date in the development of Colombian and Latin American narrative: Gertrudis Gómez de Avellaneda's *Sab* had been published in 1841, Domingo Faustino Sarmiento's *Civilización y barbarie: vida de Juan Facundo Quiroga* in 1845, Bartolomé Mitre's *Soledad* in 1847, José Mármol's *Amalia* in 1851 and Alberto Blest Gana's *Martín Rivas* in 1862. Jorge Isaacs's *María* appeared in 1867. Novels by other well-known Latin American women writers came later, among them Juana Manuela Gorriti's *El pozo de Yocci* (1876), Mercedes Cabello de Carbonera's *Blanca Sol* (1889) and Clorinda Matto de Turner's *Aves sin nido* (1889). *Novelas y cuadros de la vida sur-americana* thus belongs to a key period in the formation of a narrative tradition that had been repressed during the period of colonization and which, after Independence, resorted to all the possibilities of intertextuality and textual cannibalism, besides showing the tensions between nation and narration.[2]

According to the bibliography compiled in 1937 by Gustavo Otero

Muñoz, Soledad Acosta's fiction appeared from 1864 to 1906. He lists a total of 48 short narratives and 21 novels, a classification that, even if it should be revised, indicates the great volume of this neglected writing. From a historical and a literary perspective, to approach Soledad Acosta de Samper by reading her book *Novelas y cuadros de la vida sur-americana* seems to be the right decision. The book includes a new edition of *Dolores* (*Cuadros de la vida de una mujer*) [Scenes From the Life of a Woman]; *Teresa la limeña* (*Páginas de la vida de una peruana*) [Pages from the Life of a Peruvian Women], *El corazón de la mujer* (*Ensayos psicológicos*) [The Woman's Heart (Psychological Essays)], 'La Perla del Valle' ['The Pearl from the Valley'], 'Ilusión y realidad' ['Illusion and reality'], 'Luz y sombra (Cuadros de la vida de una coqueta)' ['Light and darkness (Scenes from the life of a coquette)'], 'Tipos sociales: la monja y mi madrina' ['Social Types: the nun and my godmother'] and 'Un crimen' ['A Crime']. Among all these texts, *Dolores, Teresa la limeña* and *El corazón de la mujer* could be considered novels – notwithstanding their unimaginative subtitles – based on their length and narrative organization, while the rest of the texts are short stories or brief narratives of very different interest and quality.

*Dolores* was published for the first time as a *feuilleton* in the journal *El mensajero* (1867). It was translated into English as *Dolores: The story of a leper.*[3] Sickness, as Susan Sontag points out, 'is the night-side of life', a dark kingdom of metaphors not necessarily linked to their referent. Tuberculosis, cancer and leprosy belong not only to real experience but to the symbolic world, and their strength as images capable of interpreting reality exceeds their historical and medical evolution. Leprosy belongs to the nocturnal kingdom of isolation and punishment. Its history and treatment have biblical roots. Whilst lunatics were abandoned in ships during the Middle Ages, lepers were sent to islands or buried in caves where they would not be able to see themselves. Leprosy means the loss of skin sensitivity and the mutilation of the body; it is related to flaying and excoriation, to the impossibility of touching another body, to physical and psychological torture. In 1880, Lewis Wallace mythified and miraculously cured leprosy in *Ben Hur*, a widely read novel which was later reinstalled in the twentieth-century imagination through its various film versions. Twenty years earlier, without any kind of concession, Soledad Acosta de Samper chooses this complex sickness for her first significant heroine, a choice that could have easily led her to a grotesque treatment of her subject. Instead, she shows the inner development of her protagonist with an amazing knowledge of the mental processes of a terminal patient. Dolores's story is told by her cousin Pedro through letters, confessions and diaries that function as vehicle of her inner life. There is clear stylistic differentiation between Pedro's paraphrases, the transcription of letters from his father and cousin, and Dolores's desperate diary, in which she understands everything and everybody, including her cousin's geographical, psychological and narrative distance. The first part of the novel takes place in an idyllic world of religious and popular feasts, of flowers and tropical birds, in which the love between Dolores and Antonio (Pedro's close friend) arises. Predictions of sickness and future unhappiness appear frequently, implicitly via the book's title but also through the name of the heroine and recurrent references to the exaggerated whiteness and beauty of Dorores's skin and dress. The second part of the novel is built around a melodramatic narration that includes hereditary sickness, a meeting with the self-denying and loving father, a duel between Pedro and Antonio, and her fantasies of suicide. Dolores feels harassed, like a wild animal, and suffers the torment of knowing the horror she inspires. Pedro's short goodbye visit, before his trip to Europe as a doctor, reminds readers of a character in another novel of the same period (*María*), Efraín, who is unable to cure through medical science the hereditary sickness of his beloved María. The third part of Soledad Acosta's novel is built around violence, the hallucinatory battle of Dolores between life and death. Isolated, dead to the world, like 'un árbol carcomido' [a worm-eaten tree], she acknowledges in spite of herself a desperate and visceral love of life, a love present even in her dreams. Water, flowers and books accompany her until the end, acquiring new, aggressive meanings. Even when she runs through the mountains like a wild animal, she carries a pen. She asks her cousin to send her books from Europe because, she says, 'deseo vivir con los muertos y comunicar con ellos' [I want to live with the dead and communicate with them]. It is a chilling view of the act of reading. Her resentment against God and men contrasts with the idealized memory of her unattainable love. Her desire is stronger than her skin and only ends with death. Love keeps her alive and love, which appears with her sickness, kills her. Although the romantic treatment of her love for Antonio seems incongruous in relation to other aspects of her daily life and inner development, which are presented in a more hard and convincing light, her love can be read not only as her acceptance of the female role of dependent and eternal lover, but as the acting out of a deep erotic desire. This desire, although directed to a specific male character, springs from Dolores's impossible and instinctive battle for life.

## Elisa Mújica: Catalina's memory

Elisa Mújica is one of the most distinguished Colombian women writers of this century, although she has not been fully integrated into our literary history. Her name is widely known in cultural circles, but her work is practically unavailable and difficult to classify according to genres. Born in Bucaramanga in 1918, she lived in Bogotá from her childhood. She spent some years in Quito in the 1940s, and in Madrid in the 1950s. She was the first woman to belong as a regular member to the Academia Colombiana de la Lengua. Her writing shows her versatility as critic, her interest in different periods of Colombian and Spanish history, her knowledge of chronicles, her ability as a writer of children's books. Her fiction extends over forty years of Colombian literary history. She published three novels,

*Los dos tiempos* [Two Times] (1949), *Catalina* (1963) and *Bogotá de las nubes* [Bogotá of the Clouds] (1984). Interspersed with the novels she has published three collections of short stories: *Angela y el diablo* [Angela and the Devil] (1953), *Arbol de ruedas* [Wheel Tree] (1972) and *La tienda de imágenes* [The Image Shop] (1987).[4]

When *Catalina* was published, it received all the publicity of the Esso Literary Prize. In fact, the prize went to another novel, but the jury recommended the publishing of Elisa Mújica's *Catalina* 'como tributo de admiración a la mujer colombiana y con el fin de estimular aun más a todos los escritores colombianos'. The phrase 'as a tribute of admiration towards Colombian woman' shows the initial critical reaction to and typical reception of literature written by women: the author and the literary value of her work are ignored, and the work is categorized as the marginal production of a human group that should be 'admired' for being women, not for being writers.

In the first chapter of the novel we find significant clues for the reading of the whole text: the narrator's basic traits and her evolution as character, the *mise en abîme* effect, the different times and spaces that appear in the novel, silence as a thematic and structural device, and violence as a linking recurrent motif. This first chapter functions not so much as prediction but as sudden revelation of everything the text will unfold later. In the first five pages we know that the narrative voice is Catalina's, that she is alive and pregnant, in Bogotá, where she learns about the deaths of her husband Samuel and her lover Giorgio. She cries at the news, and cries for very different reasons, among them loss and guilt, but mainly she cries for her old self, for that 'muchacha borrosa y desprevenida' ['blurred and unprepared girl'] (p. 13), who is gone like her two dead men. We have all the clues to the novel, without understanding them very well: her marriage, her conflictual relationships with her father and her mother, her mother's advice, the *haciendas* and their administrators, the name of her husband's lover, the reference to Bucaramanga (the family's doctor), her grandmother and her green-eyed half-sister, her husband's ambition, the desk of her aunt Catalina (an aunt who shares her name, had a husband and a lover and seems to have committed suicide). For Catalina the character–narrator, 'dejaron de ser inofensivas no solo las personas sino las cosas' ['not only people but things stopped being harmless'] (p. 17) and starting to name things becomes a vehicle to recovering her past. Her desire to tell a story but being unable to do it is thus transformed into an important element of the narrative plot. 'Sin embargo, me habría gustado contárselo' ['However, I would have liked telling him'], she says, thinking about her brother-in-law, but cries instead of talking. A theme that dominates the whole work, the prohibition or inability of talking about certain subjects, produces Catalina's ambiguous narrative situation. We do not know whether she writes or remembers, we do not know who she is addressing in this text, the story of her life. This lack of narratee within the text gives Catalina's voice a tone of amazed introspection, as if she were looking at herself from a distance, oscillating between integration and dissociation. Like another Catalina, the narrator–protagonist of the Mexican María Angeles Mastretta's *Arráncame la vida* (1985), like Celie, the protagonist of the American Alice Walker's *The Color Purple* (1982), like Colometa in the Catalonian Mercé Rodoreda's *La plaça del Diamant* (1962), the text recipient seems to be, in the first place, the protagonist herself. Maybe some critical comments that identify these novels as versions of intimate diaries or epistolary literature derive from this effect of self-addressed narrative. As narrator, Catalina Aguirre very often shows the distance of an omniscient narrator, an 'I' who avoids mentioning herself and withdraws from her very referent. As a result we find a painful and clear mind, with a need to separate herself, as character, from the narrated world. 'En las semanas que siguieron, me vestía, comía, bordaba, caminaba. Lo único curioso consistía en que me miraba hacer esas cosas' ['During the following weeks, I dressed myself, I ate, I embroidered, I walked. The only curious aspect of it all consisted in the fact that I looked at myself doing those things'] (p. 137). 'Me había convertido en una espectadora de mi propia suerte' ['I had turned into a spectator of my own destiny'] (p. 155). Catalina as character sees, lives and registers for the other Catalina, the narrator.

There is much to analyse in the different spaces created by Elisa Mújica. In 1949, in her novel *Los dos tiempos*, she showed a Latin American conscience, building characters linked to political and social events located beyond Colombian borders. Her historical knowledge is clearly related to her exploration of different spaces, an ability she demonstrates in her critical edition of José María Cordovez Moure's *Reminiscencias de Santa Fe y Bogatá*, or her scenes about the old Colonial neighbourhood of Bogotá, *La Candelaria*. *Catalina* is an excellent example of a meaningful and economic handling of multiple significant spaces, in contrast with the limited space the heroine moves through in the narration: apart from the openings signified by the *haciendas* (Las Hojas, her childhood and the happy period of her marriage, Madroñal, her relationship with the forbidden and guilty world of her half-sister) and the final escape to Bogotá, Catalina's life takes place in closed houses and corners:

> Pero era en el rincón de mi cuarto donde bordaba manteles de punto de filtré, que los objetos conocidos de cada día me transmitían la única sensación de seguridad que me quedaba.
> [But it was in the corner of my room, while I embroidered tablecloths with drawn-work, where my everyday, well-known objects granted me the only feeling of security I had left.] (p. 119)

Her limited spaces do not prevent her from knowing and communicating stories and secrets. She let us know about the space of war and politics, the space of power and economic ambition – the appropriation of land through fraud, plunder or marriage – the space of production, which in the region had to do with sugar cane, tobacco, woven hats, business and, in a climactic moment, the discovery of oilfields; the space of nature, the world of *mestizaje* [miscegenation] and superstition, the space of women's leisure and their pastimes – embroidering, learning the language of flowers, collecting postcards, reading romances, visiting and gossiping – the space of desire and its painful interferences, the space of conjugal and family relationships, the space of family stories and the ties of different members of the family with key historical events of the country. In short, after reading *Catalina* we should reconsider what has been called the limited world of a woman's conscience and experience. Elisa Mújica demonstrates in Colombian literature that this so-called limited world involves the access of women – mainly through oral tradition – to all the historical knowledge of their times.

## Marvel Moreno: woman of illusions and elusions

Marvel Moreno has had slow recognition as a writer. She lives and writes in Paris, and her post-garcíamárquez fiction reworks the Caribbean world of her youth in Barranquilla and on the Atlantic Coast, where she was a beauty queen and went through all the steps of socialization in a sexist society. Her first book, the short-story collection *Algo tan feo en la vida de una señora de bien* [Something So Ugly in the Life of a Proper Lady] (1980) is practically unknown in Latin America. A local and badly distributed edition has almost buried a very mature and critical fiction. Her short stories, full of versatility and irony, maintain their value and autonomy beside her long novel, and were very well received in the French translation, *Une tache dans la vie d'une femme comme il faut.*

Her first novel *En diciembre llegaban las brisas* [Breezes Arrived Each December] (1987) was finalist some years ago in one of the Plaza and Janés literary contests, and its publication was eagerly awaited by the small circle of friends and fellow writers who knew of her careful and continuous rewriting of her work. The novel is to be published in French, and early in 1989 she won Italy's Grizane Cavour literary prize, shared with Doris Lessing and Leonid Borodine.

A sort of postmodernist fiction, *En diciembre llegaban las brisas* confronts the reader with all the significant questions of recent literature: an obsessive world, built around temporal and geographical distance; voices that are woven through polyphonic relations deriving from orality and from individual and collective memory; the creation of symbolic, ambiguous and hermetic texts, where information shows through silences and fissures. Bodies break like dolls, and so do the different voices: metaphorical discourse replaces logic. The superimposition of discourses communicates a magical strength to the text, the strength of exploring worlds forbidden to logical discourses. Open, desperate texts are common in contemporary literature. Today's reader falls under the spell of processes and question marks, intertextualities, echoes and mirrors. These questions, common to much contemporary writing, are clearly seen in the treatment given to gender by male and female writers. Gender becomes a central question when the Other – anything that shakes a perfect and human (masculine) order – is explored and analysed. In Colombia, men and women write disturbing texts in which gender is a latent issue. In the case of a huge, woman-written novel like Marvel Moreno's, it is particularly illuminating to read closely the treatment of women and the feminine. The overwhelming succession of female characters and voices results in very complex readings. One of the readings of *En diciembre llegaban las brisas* may be to focus on the way illusions (creations of fantastic worlds that mediate reality) and elusions are combined. Elusions function as mediations that allow critical readings and reconstructions of the text.

Illusions and elusions become apparent already in the cover design of the novel. A porcelain doll – red satin and white embroidered tulle, rigid hand and bent feet – seems to look inside of herself, awkwardly perched on the book cover. Behind these eyes and these pages, dolls and adolescents, devoured and devouring women will start coming up and breaking into pieces, sharing a meaningless world. Definitely, this is not an easy novel. Marvel Moreno has produced a very dense and detailed work, tense with controlled energy, lacking a traditional narrative structure. There are few predictions, no long-term suspense, eluded information abounds, there are no secondary stories neatly organized around a central axis. On the contrary, the stories concatenate, grow like bubbles, acquire volume and life until they blow up and disappear with their protagonists, usually not to be mentioned or integrated again. It is a book that continuously restarts and repeats itself, like the world it reflects.

The main narrative voice seems to be that of a woman who does not focus on herself but accepts the perspective and knowledge of a character-witness: Lina Insignares. Only at the end, in a short epilogue, does Lina speak in the first person, closing the work, placing the book in her past, and underlining her temporal and spacial distance from the narrated material. But not even all the years that have passed, nor the ocean between Paris and Baranquilla, have taken her away from an obsessive world she has been trying to reconstruct, pursuing, mixing and choosing different versions. In other words, she reconstructs an old world believing in the possibilities of remembrance and facing the dark tunnels of memory. Dozens of characters appear and develop, around stories that dissect their most intimate and forgotten past. But curiously Lina, witness and filter of all the stories, is the most elusive character, the one who does not talk about the events of her own life, in contrast with the detailed development received by the rest of the characters. Lina's story is not a bubble put part of the undertow of the whole novel. Accomplice and support of her own generation, she finds alliances among the old and survives as confidante of the most heterogeneous people. As if it were made only of threads, her story results from her voracious absorbing of other people's lives. She is their interpreter and sometimes, like any storyteller and translator, a traitor. But her treason, her telling and retelling, is her most valid act: her word confronts secret memories and confidences, transforming lives into denunciation and transforming her knowledge of curious and individual cases into social experiences.

This is, definitely, a complex novel, whose complexity does not end with one reading. One of its significant contributions is the recovering of a semi-transgressive, feminine world, where intrigue and deception become the weapons of the 'weak sex'. A culture transmitted through gestures and oral tradition teaches survival through cheating, killing, possessing, forgetting and through the obtaining of partial, dubious, and ineffective pleasures. Women's voices dominate the novel, creating and interpreting fantastic inner and projected worlds, part of hallucinated reflexes. But as I said before, fantasy and illusion do not completely explain Marvel Moreno's fiction: her women's voices explore and discover, but they elude as well. Elusions as a kind of mediation allow critical and deconstructive readings, because the texts gain meaning from everything the narrative voices ignore, both about themselves and about the world around them. Marvel Moreno becomes part of a literature of rupture, Colombian and at the same time without borders, a literature obsessed with contemporary reappraisals of gender and history. Like many other unforgettable literary works, *En diciembre llegaban las brisas* offers neither cathartic peace nor escapes from struggle. Neither does it offer easy, pleasant reading: after all, when breezes arrive by the Caribbean sea, the only sticky taste that remains is the taste of salt. And licking salt, an old baptismal rite, may be a step towards wisdom, a step that Lina, the witness, knows how to take. Lina's voice represents the right to breezes, to salt and to writing, and her text, as her author Marvel Moreno knows well, is part of a battle against injustice.

To summarize, the three Colombian writers and three novels considered in this chapter cover more than one hundred years of ignored writing. We are at a stage of identification and evaluation, barely acknowledging the need to rewrite our literary history to take women's writing into account. From Soledad Acosta, Elisa Mújica and Marvel Moreno we can learn that we will not have to make concessions to this new history: it will be full of amazing discoveries.

# Notes

1. Josefa Acevedo de Gómez (1803–61), Soledad Acosta de Samper (1833–1913), Waldina Dávila de Ponce de León (?–1900), Herminia Gómez Jaime de Abadía (1862–1925), María Cárdenas Roa, Elisa Mújica, Flor Romero de Nohra, Rocío Vélez de Piedrahita, Fanny Buitrago.

2. See my introduction to a recent anthology of Acosta's fiction, *Soledad Acosta de Samper, Una nueva lectura* (1988). My reading depends greatly on Doris Sommer's theses on nation and narration, as developed in her work *Foundational Fictions: When history was romance in Latin America* (forthcoming). Sommer studies the relationships between sentimental

romanticism and liberal nationalism in the classical texts that were part of the formation of civil, liberal, and bourgeois states in Latin America after decades of militarism. For her, the erotic in the novel can be a displacement of desire for political peace, and nineteenth-century classical novels were thus integrated into the political projects of building the new nations.

3. I have not been able to find a copy of the English translation but, according to Otero Muñoz's bibliography, the novel was published in New York.

4. For a detailed account of Elisa Mujica's bibliography and criticism, see my article 'Elisa Mújica novelista: del silencio a la historia por la palabra', *Revista de Crítica Literaria Latinoamericana* (Lima), 26, 1987, pp. 123–36.

## Works cited

Acosta de Samper, Soledad, *Novelas y cuadros de la vida sur-americana*, Gante: Imprenta de Eug. Vanderhaeghen, 1869.

Acosta de Samper, Soledad, *Una nueva lectura (Antología)*, Bogotá: Fondo Cultural Cafetero, 1988.

Araújo, Helena, *La Scherezada criolla. Ensayos sobre escritura femenina latinoamericana*, Bogotá: Universidad Nacional de Colombia, 1989.

Araújo, Helena, 'Siete novelistas colombianas', in Gloria Zea (ed.), *Manual de literatura colombiana*, vol. 2, Bogotá: Procultura y Planeta Colombiana Editorial, 1988, pp. 409–62.

Gilard, Jacques, 'Ser escritora en Colombia: cuatro casos de la Costa atlántica', in Clair Pailler (ed.), *Femmes des Amériques*, Toulouse: Université de Toulouse-Le-Mirail, 1986, pp. 209–30.

Hinds, Jr., Harold E., 'Life and Early Literary Career of the Nineteenth-century Colombian Writer Soledad Acosta de Samper', in Ivette E. Miller and Carlos M. Tatum (eds.), *Latin American Women Writers: Yesterday and today*, (Pittsburgh) Latin American Literary Review, 1977, pp. 32–41.

Moreno, Marvel, *Algo tan feo en la vida de una señora de bien*, Bogotá: Editorial Pluma, 1980.

Moreno, Marvel, *En diciembre llegaban las brisas*, Barcelona: Plaza & Janés, 1987.

Moreno, Marvel, *Une tache dans la vie d'une femme comme il faut*, translated by Jacques Gilard, Paris: Editions des Femmes, 1982.

Mújica, Elisa, *Angela y el diablo*, Bogotá: Aguilar, 1953.

Mújica, Elisa, *Arbol de ruedas*, Bogotá: Editorial Revista Colombiana, 1972.

Mújica, Elisa, *Bogotá de las nubes*, Bogotá: Tercer Mundo, 1984.

Mújica, Elisa, *Catalina*, Madrid: Aguilar, 1963.

Mújica, Elisa, *La Candelaria*, Bogotá: Instituto Colombiano de Cultura, 1974.

Mújica, Elisa, *La tienda de imágenes*, Bogotá: Fondo Cultural Cafetero, 1987.

Mújica, Elisa, *Los dos tiempos*, Bogotá: Editorial Iqueima, 1949.

Ordóñez, Montserrat, 'Elisa Mújica novelista: del silencio a la historia por la palabra', *Revista de crítica literaria Latinoamericana* (Lima), no. 26, 1987, pp. 123–36.

Ordóñez, Montserrat, 'Soledad Acosta de Samper: una nueva lectura', in Soledad Acosta de Samper, *Una nueva lectura (Antología)*, Bogotá: Fondo Cultural Cafetero, 1988, pp. 11–24.

Otero Muñoz, Gustavo, 'Soledad Acosta de Samper', *Boletín de historia y antiguedades*, no. 271, 1937, pp. 257–83.

Porras Collantes, Ernesto, *Bibliografía de la novela en Colombia*, Bogotá: Instituto Caro y Cuervo, 1976.
Sontag, Susan, *Illness as Metaphor*, New York: Random House, 1977.

# Griselda Gambaro and the female dramatist: The audacious trespasser[1]

## Catherine M. Boyle

## The role of women: making men not theatre

Why are there so few women dramatists in Latin America? How, asks one of the few successful women dramatists, the Argentinian Griselda Gambaro, do women escape 'enforced anonymity, making men, not theatre'?[2] Where, she asks, echoing the question posed by Virginia Woolf in *A Room of One's Own*, are the sisters of Shakespeare, of Jacques Copeau, Meyerhold, Piscator, not to mention of Latin American male dramatists? How do we talk about women's theatre in Latin America?

We can talk about women's invisibility, about the way theatre has not favoured the development of skills among women, about the narrow limits imposed upon what women are permitted to do. And in doing this we could explore the reasons, suspecting the answers. Yet that approach would only begin to suggest a history of women in theatre, and a history of perceived failure, at that. I have chosen instead to look at a success, to present and study some of the work of one dramatist, Griselda Gambaro.[3] I want to discuss her theatre, a theatre that one critic has described as providing 'new and startling insights' into Latin American society.[4] I want to discuss her theatre because, more and more, the insights she unearths do not speak only for Latin America.

## Women, the doubtful metaphor

It would be wrong to say that there has been no female presence in Latin American theatre. Women have constituted half of the famous husband-and-wife teams who established companies, wrote plays according to the resources of the individual company and became the patrons of both dramatists and actors. There are still important husband-and-wife teams working in Latin America. Undoubtedly, though, it is as actresses that women have had the strongest and the uneasiest presence in the theatre. Playing roles generally created by men, ranging from the intelligent and strong woman – the matriarch – to the spinster, the good-hearted whore or the unfortunate waif, the actress becomes on stage the incomplete, faulty and misleading portrayal of women. More often than not, actresses have represented women in roles that bear little or no resemblance to the reality of women's place in society. The female character has too often been merely an inescapable, if at times intriguing, part of the male world.

In these roles the actress is merely part of a convenient façade. While attention is fixed on the external graces of the actress as she represents recognizably unreal characters, the real voice and expression of women remain muted. If the roles played by the actress are to be more than a sometimes cunningly disguised expression of a male norm and view of the world, these roles must be controlled by another hand, another pen, another social conscience with very real goals for women in society. Until the emergence of a voice that is truly representative of female experience, the relationship between the actress and the roles she plays is bound to be one of conflict.

To write and produce theatre is to hold a certain power, to have power over the word not as the poet or the novelist has, but within a medium that has an immediate, dynamic and potentially subversive interaction with the society in which it is created and staged. It is to have power over the deed, the gesture, the acts of people on stage. It is not a 'feminine' writing, perceived as private, inward-looking, unauthoritative. It is everything that is understood as 'masculine': open, aggressive, authoritative, because woman as dramatist 'provides a text and meanings which others must follow'.[5] She must assume a physical presence that is not normally expected of the poet or the novelist, and publicly assume the voice once paternally tended by men.

There is undoubtedly an emergent female voice in Latin American theatre and it is growing from within the theatre itself. Since the heights of collective creation in the 1960s and early 1970s women's issues have sat, often uneasily because of the difficult relationship between feminism and the genderless *machismo-leninismo*[6] of sectors of the left, alongside other political struggles. Women's voice and demands are becoming public with the growth of women's movements, with growing – if at times still paternalistic – awareness of the crucial role of women in broader-based political movements. And there is a true strengthening of the consciousness of a female experience within different social and political circumstances. This is especially true in the civil wars and unrest of Central America, in the dictatorships of South America, in women's role in creating international awareness of the 'disappeared', of the destroyed families and the premeditated and coldly calculated violence that contributes to the relentless cycles of fear, moral debilitation and authoritarianism. In these circumstances the voice of women has emerged as an expression not only of female experience but of a large spectrum of social experience generally. This political voice is echoed in theatre.

For the dramatist, the common problems of publication, production, audience and the actual existence of and access to theatres combine with more specific and localized problems such as censorship and persecution. The woman dramatist also has to fight against the barrier of her gender, of the label 'female' or, worse still, 'feminist', labels that render her all but invisible – to men and to women. It is for this reason that one of the goals of many Latin American women writers is renewed 'invisibility', a future when the publication, production and criticism of their work will not be hindered by surprise that they can write at all. Whilst still there are certainly more women poets and novelists than dramatists, it is true that women's role in theatre has transcended the merely decorative, and women's voice is beginning to be heard, individually or as part of a team.

## Griselda Gambaro: writer as patient and surgeon

What can the voice of women in theatre be once the step from anonymity and passivity to activity, commitment and command has been taken? Griselda Gambaro, often on the receiving end of such questions, says:

> The contribution we can make as women writers is independent of our sex, and yet will be born of our own identity, which, naturally, also contains our sex. A woman writer assumes her identity in the way she lives, in her personal life, and in this way, will translate that identity implicitly in everything she does.... Our identity comes from our place in the world, from the look we cast over the world, seeking out its richness, its failings, its conflicts.[7]

As a writer Griselda Gambaro has shied away from the label that would almost inevitably exclude her from consideration within the established norm. But she is keen to establish her experience as a woman as the root of her writing.

> In my first works many women challenged the presence of exclusively masculine characters and this, which feminists saw as an offence or a failing, I believe is the most absolute proof that I write as a woman, not only because I am not a man, but because there is no better way to talk about women than to talk about the relationships between men. And the place of women is evident because of their transparent absence. In these plays that were challenged, the world of men was a world marked by incomprehension, egoism, injustice. This is the world where women 'live'.[8]

Griselda Gambaro uses her position as woman dramatist to lay open man's world to communal scrutiny. She analyses the world in which she lives from the essential, glaring and too often ignored truth that it is a world created by men, a clichéd truth whose significance is often obscured by its familiarity. That is not to say that there exists an intention to blame men. Griselda Gambaro does not look for the ubiquitous and unnamed Other at whose door to lay the blame for universal blunders. Her attitude is much less accusatory: she includes herself and each individual in the process that leads to cruel, violent, destructive manipulation of power. She has used the image of the writer as 'both patient and surgeon', someone who 'faces life and death, in order to win life, through words'.[9] These images are not always metaphorical.

Her attitude is more subversive than a purely accusatory one would be, for through it she challenges the male ego. She challenges the male ego by trying to understand not man's power, but his weakness, and not in an abstract but in a concrete sense, studying man's well-hidden incapacity to use power productively. 'I wouldn't say that man is cruel. I say that man, and I still believe this, is a very passive being who finds it difficult to take on responsibility.'[10]

In the one-act play *Decir sí* [Saying Yes] (1978) a man's politeness and anxiety to please have disastrous consequences. On entering a barber's shop, he encounters the Barber who, although only reading a magazine, seems furious at the arrival of a client. The Man immediately assumes a 'conciliatory' attitude, trying – and failing dismally – to make polite conversation. Disconcerted, he makes a half-hearted gesture suggesting that he wants a haircut. The Barber's reply, 'Beard?', totally contradicting the gesture, is accompanied by 'an inscrutable look and a brusque manner'. From then on it is largely the language of gestures that guides the Man's actions. In swift succession he sweeps the floor, cleans the filthy mirror while being forced to agree that it was immaculate, shaves and finally cuts the Barber's hair, while singing, as he is commanded to do. When the Barber sees the dreadful results of the haircut the Man begs for another chance, anguished and in despair in a situation in which he has lost all control:

> I didn't say that I knew how to cut hair! You forced me! I can never refuse when people ask me ... kindly ... to do things. And what does it matter? I didn't cut one of your arms off! If I'd left you with only one arm you could have complained. Or a leg! But to make such a fuss about your hair! What an idiot! No! No, no you're not an idiot! But hair grows in. In a week it'll be down to the ground! (*The Barber points to the chair. The Man, incredulous, accepts the offer, his eyes lighting up.*) Is it my turn? (*He looks behind him as if looking for someone else.*) Are you talking to me? (*The Barber nods.*) Good! Great! Now we're getting somewhere! Everything comes to those who wait! (*He sits down, composed, happy.*) A shave and a haircut! (*The Barber ties the cloth round the Man's neck. He turns the chair round. He takes the knife, smiling. The Man lifts his head.*) I want a good clean cut.
> *The Hairdresser plunges the knife into him.*

*Decir sí* examines a classic Gambaro situation. The Man allows himself to be led step by step into a violent trap. At each point along the way every feeble 'no' becomes an unconvincing but pleading 'yes'. He responds to positive stimulus, desperately changing tack each time he sees that he has annoyed, upset or contradicted the Barber, and reinforcing statements that seem to win the Barber's approval. The Barber is as familiar to us as the intimidating waiter, the shop assistant, the hairdresser whom we allow to convince us that s/he knows exactly what is best for the customer. Gambaro turns a perfectly everyday situation into a process of annihilation. The final scene is one for which the audience has been carefully prepared, it is one which we suspect from the beginning, possessing as we do a mental baggage of barber horror stories but which is nonetheless shocking.

In the theatre of Griselda Gambaro, dramatic tension is developed through a constant friction between what we see and what we hear, what we are requested to believe and what in the end we are forced to believe. The title of *Los siameses* [*The Siamese Twins*] (1967) tells us that the play is about Siamese twins, but the twins have been separated, if they have ever been joined, they do not look like twins and it is only through references to the fact that they were born together, and the three-legged walk they execute on occasion that the notion is kept alive in the audience's mind.

The play begins with Lorenzo rushing out of breath into the room he shares with his physically weaker twin, Ignacio, seemingly having just escaped danger because of a newfound individuality: 'I got away . . . I can run better alone . . . than . . . accompanied' (p. 95). He locks his brother out and, from his side of the door, witnesses the beating Ignacio suffers for a violent attack committed by himself. While Ignacio lies all night in a pool of blood, Lorenzo sleeps, with comfortable 'compassion', on top of their mattresses on the other side of the door. Towards the end of the first act, two policemen, El Gangoso and El Sonriente,[11] appear and, in a grotesquely humourous scene Lorenzo, terrified by the fact that he cannot understand a word El Gangoso says and fearful that this will result in physical violence and arrest, literally fabricates evidence for a crime, for which it is Ignacio who is arrested.

The second act mirrors the first. Ignacio returns from prison, the tensions escalate, and the audience becomes aware that at the root of Lorenzo's hatred and envy is his sexual impotence. Inevitably the police return, this time, to arrest Ignacio for fraud on evidence produced by his brother. Again he is taken to prison, where this time he dies. Lorenzo, who has kept a close watch on the prison, is first in line to become one of the gravediggers and takes on the task with ungracious enthusiasm. Yet, having buried his brother, he accuses him of having died as a deliberate tactic to 'cripple' him, to ruin the rest of his life, to render useless his 'good legs'. For, as Lorenzo sits on the mound of earth that is Ignacio's grave, he finds that he cannot leave, tied finally to his Siamese twin.

One of the most common comments about Griselda Gambaro's theatre is that the victimizer becomes the victim, and that the victim is generally accomplice to his victimization. This is a simplification of the underlying trends in Gambaro's work, where, to borrow her image, nobody is wholly surgeon or patient. *Los siameses* deals with degrees of dependence and complicity, with the ability to handle the rules of a game managed through a chain of delegation of duty and responsibility. As Lorenzo creates the evidence that will damn his brother Ignacio, the latter, who has no access to the rules of the game, pleads with him to stop acting the fool, incapable of grasping the complicity between Lorenzo and the policemen, believing that truth will prevail and that when it does Lorenzo will suffer. Throughout the play Ignacio comes across as being monumentally –stupidly? – understanding and forgiving. He seems to accept the idea of Lorenzo as victim of his uncontrollable envy, an almost animal passion over which he has no control; he is desperately protective of Lorenzo's fear of suffering pain, a fear most splendidly summed up in his awareness of his own vulnerability: 'Look at my skin, Ignacio. It's nothing, scratch it and I bleed,' to which Ignacio replies, *'almost in spite of himself'*, 'Don't be afraid, I'm here' (p. 106). How painfully reminiscent of age-old female experience this is.

Ignacio's one moment of defiance in the play seems to be in death, when the policemen try, 'with barely contained violence', to accommodate his corpse in a cart that is far too small. This recalls a scene in the first act when Lorenzo, explaining why he will not open the door, says that Ignacio will be safer alone, bloody and beaten: 'nobody hits people when they're down. We respect those we kill. I know you're not a corpse. But if you were one you'd be safer' (p. 99).[12] Therein lies a horrible truth about death, the ultimate haven from abuse and, in this instance for Lorenzo and the two policemen, the convenient cleanser of society. Lorenzo's final words as he sits on Ignacio's grave, in the same position as his brother's corpse in the cart, are of dissatisfaction: 'I can never trust you. You've given me worse surprises in life, and now you're dead, and you cripple me' (p. 143). In those words, it seems, Gambaro suggests that killers inevitably learn that murder brings in its trail . . . what? Punishment? Remorse? Regret? Neither is this answer easy.

While burying the corpse Lorenzo had discovered that El Gangoso was, all of a sudden, perfectly intelligible, and that, worse, the policeman did not recognize his 'accomplice'. In the final scene Lorenzo is, simply, scared because he is sitting on the remains of his protection against the violent society whose closeness to him he had previously managed, through Ignacio, to control. Lorenzo's despair is familiar in its self-pity and insincerity. And the memory of the 'outing to the country' to bury the body is too recent to allow us to believe or feel sympathy for Lorenzo as victim, for these are the images that linger:

EL SONRIENTE: We're off to the country. It's bright and sunny. We'll walk slowly, there's plenty of time. Don't think of this as a job. It isn't. The outing should be a pleasure for us all. What a pity the cart hasn't got an engine. We could have ridden along on it. (pp. 138–9)

The country is bare (*pelado*). The two policemen sit on the grass, breathing the country air, and El Gangoso smells a flower. Meanwhile three men, one of whom is the brother of the corpse, dig a grave. The scene is grotesque, it is repugnant and our worst suspicions fear it to be a reproduction of truth. The core idea of this scene is developed in *El campo* [The Camp] (1967) in which Griselda Gambaro not only reveals the countryside as concealing horrors, but re-creates the situation in which this horror is institutionalized.

## The avoidable itch

Every study of *El campo* talks about the ambiguity of the title. This should not blind us to the very real ambiguity of the word 'camp' in the modern Western collective memory and imagination. No longer can we believe that the ambiguity of words is accidental, for we have become too adept at shaping language. And we cannot allow the scope for interpretation of certain key words to dupe us. It is on the obvious duplicity of words and actions and on our stubborn resistance to this that Griselda Gambaro plays in *El campo*.

The protagonist, Martin, goes to a camp in order to carry out a perfectly normal job, but is met by the absurdly named Franco. Franco wears a Gestapo uniform, but has a polite, friendly and considerate manner, despite having a few quirks, like detesting chewing gum, and being preoccupied with the idea that Martin may be a Jew or a Communist; he does not encourage Martin to do the work for which, ostensibly, he is there. At the outset, none of this seems to perturb Martin seriously: the Gestapo uniform, boots and whip are a strange sight, but the affability of his host belies this visual display of potential violence, numbing the newcomer's suspicion that he has entered a concentration camp. Franco describes himself as good and kind, he says that his uniform is no more than a whim. And Martin, in the midst of a place of imprisonment and torture, will, for a long time, not make the step necessary to admit to the essential truth of the place. The jarring sense of normality conveyed in the play is strong precisely because of Martin's inability or unwillingness to give a name to the 'camp' he has entered. He allows himself to believe the affirmations of his host rather than the signs of reality.

In his encounter with the inmate Emma, Martin's ability to subordinate the visual evidence of her state to her verbal assurances and grotesque gestures of normality is equally complete. Emma is dressed in sackcloth, her hair is shorn, she has a terrible itch that she cannot stop scratching, she is branded and has a wound on her hand which, at different times, she and Franco deny exists. She greets Martin with the exaggerated airs of a great concert pianist, even offering a signed photograph, and finds normal the screeches and violent shouting of the children. In her accounts, the camp is really green and fertile, a playground, a place where Franco hunts and children play. Her image of herself, her aura of grandeur, beauty, is evident to the onlooker only in her airs and graces, which are visibly the conscious and painful creation of one whose very survival is guaranteed only by her ability to give the lie to reality. When she gives a concert it is a truly grotesque experience, the piano does not work, only isolated sounds come forth and her 'grand' audience is composed of the inmates of the camp, before whom she is beaten into playing. Yet in her version of the event, it becomes a great concert, for which she is loved and acclaimed.

Emma is used as bait to persuade Martin to leave the camp and to look for freedom, which Martin never fully realizes he has lost. On returning to his home, he discovers that the normal sounds of children playing are extraneous and violent to his ears, and Emma's airs and graces are outrageous as she rejects tea as disgusting muck, hates the sound of happiness, feels her itch subside, but continues to scratch nevertheless. When in an effort to combine, for once and for all, her appearance with the expressed image of herself by putting on a gown, she finds that the people at the camp have packed in her bag another sackcloth.

The entrance in the final scene of prison officers carrying a branding iron who intend to take both escapees back to the camp is at once expected and horrifying. Martin may now, in the false safety of his home, declare that the officers dare not enter his house, he may now claim that they have no right to torture and imprison him, but it is too late. For, before, he had lent them legitimacy. The audience wills an escape, but, like Martin we find out too late that the violence is real, it is premeditated, it is physical torture.

In Gambaro's theatre the words that tell us that violence exists and the words that deny its existence are both revealed as barriers to our awareness of the violence around us. But our tangible horror, provoked by the sight of the branding iron, by the murder of the man in *Decir sí*, by Ignacio's murder and the disposal of his body in *Los siameses*, tells us it does exist. By adopting the attitude that things are indeed fine, while backing away from the actual, real signs of the existence of violence, we are acquiescing to its perpetuation. But, equally true, until threatened the individual cannot grasp the immensity of its existence and force. Words are too inadequate to describe it. Emma scratches at an itch she refuses to identify as lice and dirt. She suggests at one point that the itch may come from within, that really the itch is her responsibility. Martin will soon begin to itch, he will soon bear wounds whose existence he must ignore. And could have avoided.

## The grotesque: privileged point of view of the victim?

One can lie with the mouth but with the accompanying grimace one nevertheless tells the truth.[13]

A tension between appearance and reality, between outward conformity and passivity and inward despair that find their expression in a disturbing intuition that all is not what we say it is, characterizes the writing of

Griselda Gambaro. Her language, it has been said over and again, is the seeming lack of action, the ritualized behaviour, the disintegration of communication that have become the recognized language of the absurd. It is not. Her theatre, this theatre that stretches the everyday beyond its usual boundaries, is an expressin of the grotesque and not of the absurd. For the grotesque is closer to concrete reality than is the intellectualized malaise of the absurd.

Griseldo Gambaro herself places her work more in line with the grotesque and thus in a twentieth-century tradition of Argentinian theatre and narrative. In the theatre the grotesque becomes a true 'magnifying mirror'[14] of the audience and the society in which it is conceived, reflecting not so as to allow the viewer to admire, to shine, to bask in an easily polished image, but so as to magnify, strengthen, accentuate the image until it becomes a painful, sometimes unbearable reflection. It is a theatre that provokes both humour and horror, laughter and tears; 'we feel that this mixture of horror and comedy is "impossible", we cannot be reconciled to it, we may even feel that it is indecent and indicative of a warped mind – but we are unable to shake off the profoundly disturbing effect which it has on us'.[15]

At the heart of Gambaro's dramatization of the grotesque is a distressing instinct that man has no real control: her use of the grotesque undermines the control we need to believe exists over an intuited underlying and terrifying chaos. The notions of control, power and command are central to Gambaro's theatre, for they are subverted as the absurd and finally cruel edifices behind which man hides a fundamental weakness.

It is from a very special position that Gambaro seems to have reached this interpretation, that of the female dramatist. As such she is both 'patient and surgeon': as woman she is supposedly passive, acted upon through the power of men, and as dramatist she is in possession of an instrument of power, of dissection, exploration, for through the public use of the word she assumes an active role, she becomes part of the artifice of command and control. From this position Gambaro asks us to consider that, in seeming contradiction to much of our history, man may not be essentially evil, a congenital usurper of the power of others, but ridiculously and fatally weak. At the root of this position is the awareness that, yes, some people are truly cruel, but that perhaps we have contrived the worst possible scenario, a silently accepted social union of the 'cruel' and those who say 'yes':

> There is always a delegation of cruelty. That is also one of terrible aspects of our history, perhaps of our condition.... And the terrible thing is that power and or cruelty are not abstractions, they are incarnated, that is, there are human beings who are cruel, who have excessive authority. There are human beings who exercise dictatorial power, but why do they have this power? Because there is a complete chain, there is a chain of delegation and nobody takes responsibility for saying 'I am not going to do things that way'.[16]

Gambaro's theatre is a challenge to the word 'yes', so full of social and cultural obligation.

At its most effective Gambaro's theatre forces the audience to peek beyond the protective curtain our intellectual and verbal knowledge of the world provides. The weakness and cruelty of humanity, while expressed and experienced merely as word, is removed from our lives, is false, abstract. Hers is a very humane, modest, but dauntingly ambitious aim: she asks us to see:

> People have lost the sensitivity to be able to see information for what it is. That is to say, the dead are usually numbers, statistics. . . . But if we see all this in a theatre, and we are capable of 'seeing' what death means, war, children, grief and weeping, infinite pain, that moves us in a different way.[17]

It is almost impossible not to think of the suffering of so many Latin American women, of their seemingly endless, sometimes seemingly futile, struggle to make people feel the physical pain of acts gilded in well-phrased reasoning and justifications.

In her writing Griselda Gambaro brings to bear a wealth of female experience, recognizable through her portrayals of a character-type deliberately and cynically perceived as humane, as intrinsically good, yet somehow inherently stupid and (deservedly) outside the rules of the game. She does not glorify this character-type, which is archetypically the façade behind which the victim cowers. As a woman dramatist she subverts the role by examining conceptions of the 'victim'; she recognizes the potential for self-pity upon which the role of victim can be built. In *Los siameses*, Lorenzo is in constant dread, yet somehow there is constant preparation for this role, beautifully summed up at the end of another play, *Sucede lo que pasa* [Come What Will] (1976), when a sister tells her dying brother (who is trying to console her), 'What I'm sorry about . . . [*She can no longer control herself . . ., she cries*] What I'm sorry about is . . . That you're not going to be here when I die!'

These insights are part of what the author has called 'un subtexto anticipatorio'.[18] By this she means that beneath and beyond the apparent meanings of her writing there is another sense, one that, perhaps subconsciously, guides the writer. The subtext of her writing grows from her observation of human conduct, from her observation of the ways in which we bow to what we are expected to be, and from her perception that this lies at the roots of cycles of violence, the repetition of which she can easily foresee.

There is a tendency in the criticism of Latin American literature to eke out the socially specific, to relate the play to concrete events of the time, and to reject works that do not immediately strike the critic, the reader, the spectator as 'relevant'. It is not always directly evident that there is a social or political dimension to Gambaro's theatre, yet there is an uncanny sense of foresight, almost of premonition in her work. *El campo*, for example, was written long before the brutal dictatorships of the 1970s in the southern cone of Latin America, but the sense of oppression, of fear, of epidemic violence is as vivid as if she had already experienced it. *Información para extranjeros* [Information for Foreigners] (1972, as yet unperformed), takes the form of a dramatic tour around various scenes depicting the underlying violence in her country, signs that are dangerous warnings of imminent widespread repression. The 'foreigners' to which this play was directed were not *gringos*, but Argentinians blind to the undercurrents that bode ill. By 1976 Gambaro's country was again in the power of the military.

In the theatre of Griselda Gambaro, the gesture constantly gives the lie to the word, the word constantly belies reality, and 'normality' still seems to reign because we fear the naming of 'abnormality':

I'm no longer accustomed to the spoken word. My gestures deteriorate, because they only grow in weight and meaning when they can be complemented by the words and gestures of others. But nobody speaks amidst this strained silence, nobody names his or her actions or the actions of others, because to name means to discover, to uncover.[19]

What is terrifying in the writing of Griselda Gambaro is the awareness it gives us that though we wish to believe that only other people blind themselves to the real truths of life, we belong body and soul to those others.

# Notes

1. There have been various stages to the writing of this chapter. A first idea was presented at the Women and Creativity in Latin America Conference at the University of Warwick, May 1987, as 'Female Dramatists and the Expression of the Absurd'. A second paper based on similar ideas, 'Griselda Gambaro's View of Man's World: Grotesque', was presented at the Institute of Latin American Studies, University of Glasgow, in March 1989, and caused some consternation among the male members of the audience. The idea of the 'audacious trespasser' is borrowed from Virginia Woolf's *A Room of One's Own*.

2. Griselda Gambaro, '¿Es posible y deseable una dramaturgia específicamente femenina?' p. 18.

3. Griselda Gambaro (born in Argentina in 1928) is undoubtedly one of the most prestigious dramatists in Latin America. In this chapter I concentrate on some of her best-known work, in order to introduce the reader to her writing, and to look at her insights into Latin America, which I believe are born of a specifically female experience. All the translations from Spanish are mine unless otherwise stated.

4. Emilio Carballido, 'Griselda Gambaro o modos de hacernos pensar en la manzana', p. 630.

5. Michelene Wandor, 'The Impact of Feminism on the Theatre' in Mary Eagleton (ed.), *Feminist Literary Theory: A reader*, Oxford: Blackwell, 1988, p. 104.

6. This is a term I encountered in the Uruguayan novelist Mario Benedetti's *Primavera con una esquina rota* [*Spring With a Broken Corner*] (1981).

7. Griselda Gambaro, '¿Es posible y deseable una dramaturgia específicamente femenina?', p. 21.

8. *ibid.*

9. Griselda Gambaro, 'Algunas consideraciones sobre la mujer y la literatura', p. 472.

10. 'Griselda Gambaro: la difícil perfección', p. 28.

11. *Sonriente* means 'smiler', and *gangoso* refers to someone who speaks with a very nasal, moany accent; perhaps 'whinger' would be a close approximation to this meaning.

12. One interviewer remembered the words of a general, 'If this process carries on, we will eventually have peace, but the peace of the cemeteries.' See 'Griselda Gambaro: la ética de la confrontación', p. 15.

13. I borrow this quotation, from Nietzsche, from Oliver Sacks's wonderful description of a group of aphasia sufferers (whom he describes as having 'word deafness' and an enhanced sense of tone and gesture) as they listened to a televized speech by Ronald Reagan. They found the performance hilarious, but 'we normals – aided, doubtless, by our wish to be fooled, were . . . fooled'. See 'The President's Speech', in *The Man Who Mistook His Wife for a Hat*, London: Picador, 1985, pp. 76–80.

14. See Victor Hugo, *Préface de Cromwell*, Paris: Librairie Larousse, 1972, p. 82.

15. See Philip Thomson, *The Grotesque*, London: Methuen, 1972.

16. See 'Griselda Gambaro: la difícil perfección', p. 30.

17. *ibid.*, p. 31.

18. See Griselda Gambaro, 'Algunas consideraciones sobre la mujer y la literatura', p. 471.

19. See Griselda Gambaro, 'The Talks That Never Took Place', p. 135.

# Griselda Gambaro: a bibliography

I have tried to make this bibliography as complete as possible. Naturally, the vast majority of material on Spanish American theatre is written in Spanish and often appears in specialized magazines and journals. I have included as much material in English as I am aware of, although I am sure that this list is by no means complete. Perhaps the greatest disadvantage for readers interested in Griselda Gambaro's theatre who have little or no Spanish, is the fact that few translations of her plays are available, and those that I have read are of poor quality and by speakers of North American English. This in some cases renders them unpresentable as translations in Britain. I hope that this chapter will inspire interest in the women dramatists of Latin America, and that their plays will not be left to 'rust', as Griselda Gambaro puts it. I hope too that we can look forward to new translations and so to new productions. This, more than anything, is my aim in writing this article.

## Plays by Griselda Gambaro referred to

*El desatino*. Buenos A⁚  Sala de Experimentación Audiovisual del Instituto Di Tella, 1965.

*Los siameses*. In Miguel Angel Giella and Peter Roster (eds.), *9 dramaturgos hispanoamericanos del siglo XX*, vol. 2, Canada: Girol Books, 1983, pp. 93–143.

*El campo*. Buenos Aires: Editorial Insurrexit, 1967.

*The Camp*. In William I. Oliver (ed. and trans.), *Voices of Change in Spanish American Theatre*, Austin: University of Texas Press, 1971, pp. 47–103.

*Griselda Gambaro Teatro: Nada que ver. Sucede lo que pasa*. Edited by Miguel Angel Giella, Peter Roster and Leandro Urbina. Ottawa, Canada: 1983.

*Griselda Gambaro Teatro 1. Real envido. La malasangre. De sol naciente*. Buenos

Aires: Ediciones de la Flor, 1985.
*Griselda Gambaro Teatro 2. Dar la vuelta. Información para extranjeros. Puesta en claro. Sucede lo que pasa.* Buenos Aires: Ediciones de la Flor, 1987.
*Decir sí. Hispamérica*, VII, 21, 1978, pp. 75–82.

## Articles by Griselda Gambaro
'¿Es posible y deseable una dramaturgia específicamente femenina?', *Latin American Theatre Review*, 13, 2, 1980, pp. 16–21.
'Algunas consideraciones sobre la mujer y la literatura', *Revista Iberoamericana*, 132–3, 1985, pp. 471–3.
'The Talks that Never Took Place', in Alicia Partnoy (ed.), *You Can't Drown the Fire*, Pittsburgh, San Francisco: Cleis Press, 1988, pp. 134–6.

## Interviews with Griselda Gambaro
'Griselda Gambaro: la ética de la confrontación' (1979), in Miguel Angel Giella, Peter Roster and Leandro Urbina (eds.), *Griselda Gambaro Teatro: Nada que ver. Sucede lo que pasa*, Ottawa, Canada: 1983, pp. 7–20.
'Griselda Gambaro: la difícil perfección' in Miguel Angel Giella, Peter Roster and Leandro Urbina (eds.), *Griselda Gambaro Teatro: Nada que ver. Sucede lo que pasa*, Ottawa, Canada: 1983, pp. 21–37.

## Articles about Griselda Gambaro and women's theatre in Latin America
Boling, Becky, 'From Pin-Ups to Striptease in Gambaro's *El despojamiento*', *Latin American Theatre Review*, vol. 20, no. 2, 1987, pp. 69–75.
Carballido, Emilio, 'Griselda Gambaro o modos de hacernos pensar en la manzana', *Revista Iberoamericana*, XXXVI, 73, 1970, pp. 629–34.
Cypess, Sandra M., 'Physical Imagery in the Works of Griselda Gambaro', *Modern Drama*, XVII, 1975, pp. 357–64.
Cypess, Sandra M., 'La dramaturgia femenina y su contexto sociocultural', *Latin American Theatre Review*, vol. 13, no. 2, 1980, pp. 63–8.
Giella, Miguel Angel, 'El victimario como víctima en *Los siameses* de Griselda Gambaro. Notas para el análisis', *Gestos. Teoría y práctica del teatro hispánico*, vol. 2, no. 3, 1987, pp. 77–86.
McAleer, Janice K., '*El campo* de Griselda Gambaro: una contradicción de mensajes', *Revista Canadiense de Estudios Hispánicos*, vol. VII, no. 1, 1982, pp. 159–70.
Méndez-Faith, Teresa, 'Sobre el uso y abuso del poder en la producción dramática de Griselda Gambaro', *Revista Iberoamericana*, 132–3, 1985, pp. 831–41.
O'Hara, Edgar, 'Cuatro miradas (oblicuas) sobre el teatro argentino', *Revista de Crítica Latinoamericana*, XIII, 25, 1987, pp. 173–83.
Picón Garfield, Evelyn, 'Una dulce bondad que atempera las crueldades: *El campo* de Griselda Gambaro', *Latin American Theatre Review*, summer 1980, pp. 95–102.
Romano, Eduardo, 'Grotesco y clases medias en la escena argentina', *Hispamérica*, 44, 1986, pp. 29–37.

# 11. Assailing the heights of macho pictures: Women film-makers in contemporary Argentina
## John King

As President Raul Alfonsín approaches the end of his six-year term of office and the Radical Party surveys its achievements in the ever-beleaguered political and social arena, one sector in particular can point to years of success and solid achievements: the film industry. Severely censored during the military dictatorship that preceded Alfonsín, cinema has emerged as the most important area of cultural production in Argentina today. It has found success in the home market and, for the first time in the history of Argentine cinema, has consistently reached an international audience. The North American cinema and television trade paper *Variety*, ever sensitive to the marketplace, commented recently on this phenomenon:

> Argentine films currently are one of the darlings of the festival circuit. You see them at festivals from New Delhi to Montreal, from London to San Sebastian. So invites no longer make headlines, since Argentine films have been winning awards at a dizzying rate.... Never before has there been such a mass of tangible approval as in the years since democratic rule returned at the end of 1983. In 1986, the Hollywood Academy sealed the trend with its first Oscar for an Argentine picture, 'The Official Story'.[1]

Recent years have also seen the emergence and widespread acceptance of work by Argentinian women film-makers. Unlike all other areas of cultural life in Argentina (women have played an active role in literature, music, art and theatre),[2] cinema has remained an almost exclusively male preserve. Even today, a recent dictionary of Argentinian film-makers, surveying the work produced in Argentina from 1970 to 1986, lists the names of only five women in a total of 176 directors.[3] Records exist showing that two women made silent films, Emilia Saleny (*La niña del bosque*, 1917; *Clarita*, 1919) and María Celestini (*Mi derecho*, 1920), though the prints have not survived. But then we have to wait until the early 1960s before women reappear, making mainly documentaries (two names of the 1960s are Elena de Azcuénaga and Dolly Pussi). In terms of feature films, María Herminia Avellaneda, Eva Landeck and Narcisa Hirsch have made small-budget fiction films, but it is the work of María Luisa Bemberg, with four major features and a fifth in production, that has caused the main impact in Argentina and abroad. Recently *La amiga*, a film by Jeanine Meerapfel, an Argentinian resident in Germany, has received attention on the festival circuits (it opened in Argentina in April 1989). This chapter surveys two films by Bemberg (*Camila*, 1984 and *Miss Mary*, 1986) and Meerapfel's *La amiga* (1988), which analyse the lives of women in the private and public spheres. Since these works appeared in the last five years of the 1980s and respond to particular industrial, economic and social conditions, it is necessary to place them first within the wider context of Argentinian film production in these years.

## Argentinian cinema since 1983

### Economics

It costs on average $300,000 to make a feature-length film in Argentina. Although this represents a tiny fraction of the budget of a Hollywood film, it is a very considerable sum to be recouped in the domestic market. Film audiences have been shrinking in Argentina, as in every other part of the world: it has been estimated that there has been a fall of 50 per cent between the years 1974 and 1984.[4] The number of cinemas has also halved, from 2,100 in 1967 to 1,100 in 1985. A production costing $500,000 would need to attract an audience of nearly one million in the domestic market, a figure achieved by only a handful of films. Argentinian films receive no protection on the exhibition circuits, with no effective quota system (as for example operates in Brazil, Venezuela or Colombia), to guarantee that a percentage of the films shown locally are Argentinian. Films are largely in the hands of two major exhibition companies, the Sociedad Anónima Cinematográfica and Coll Di Fiore y Saragusti, which control most of the principal cinemas in Buenos Aires. Since money is to be made principally from North American imports, an informal arrangement has grown up whereby the maximum possible number of releases of Argentinian films in mainline houses is about thirty a year (onc a week, not counting holiday periods).[5] All these constraints make film-making a very high-risk business.

This situation is very well analysed in Carlos Sorín's *La película del rey* (1985), which tells of a young film-maker's desperate attempt to tell the story of Orelie Antoine de Tounens, a Frenchman who in 1861 founded the kingdom of Araucania and Patagonia. The Frenchman's deranged Utopian quest is mirrored by that of the film-maker struggling with no money, a dwindling cast and an inhospitable terrain. *La película del rey* is a delightful comedy, but the reality is more serious – despite winning the award for best *opera prima* at the Venice Film Festival, the film is still attempting to cover its costs.

The state, while offering no protection in distribution and exhibition, does advance money to initiate projects. The Instituto Nacional de Cinematografía, ably directed by the film-maker Manuel Antín, has in the Alfonsín years given financial backing to nearly all the major films that have appeared. However this money, which covers about 30–50 per cent of the total costs, is a loan, not a subsidy, and must be repaid. In a country of high inflation, moreover, delays in advancing the loans often mean that the actual sums received are a fraction of their original value. Film-makers are thus constantly demanding more state protection in an economically and politically volatile society.

Increasingly the only way to guarantee the financial viability of a project is to enter into co-production arrangements with other countries, which often means attracting foreign stars. *Miss Mary* by María Luisa Bemberg is a co-production with New World Pictures in the United States and stars Julie Christie. *La amiga* by Janine Meerapfel has German money and stars Liv Ullmann. Both these films have both Argentinian and English versions. Luis Puenzo, the director of *La historia oficial*, which won an Oscar in 1986, has recently completed filming *The Old Gringo* in Hollywood, with a galaxy of North American stars. Bemberg's next feature, based on Octavio Paz's biography of Sor Juana Inés de la Cruz, will probably have a North American actress as the lead, since this is the only way of guaranteeing North American money.

The attractions of such a system of financing projects are obvious, but there are disadvantages too. Spanish television looks to be the new 'saviour' of Latin American cinema since it is pouring money into the Latin American market. As 1992 approaches, it remains to be seen what impact this new 'colonization' makes: forty films are currently in production with Spanish funding. The first films to appear – a series of six entitled 'Amores difíciles', based on García Márquez stories or scripts – are polished and competent but not major works.[6] We are far from the 1960s rhetoric that Latin American cinema should be a 'Third' cinema, an 'Imperfect Cinema', or should express an 'Aesthetic of Hunger';[7] there has been a deliberate move by film-makers across the political spectrum to capture the marketplace. Yet such a strategy raises even more insistently the perhaps unanswerable questions: What is Latin American cinema? What is Argentinian cinema? What discursive practices distinguish these cinemas from the Hollywood mainstream? What languages are appropriate and available to current film-makers?

## Current Argentinian film-making

Argentinians would seem to answer these questions with Borges's celebrated phrase that the patrimony of Argentinian culture is the universe. The films of the last few years reveal a great heterogeneity of styles and themes, which cannot be surveyed here.[8] Two brief points can, however, be made. The first is that after so many years of persecution, direct and indirect censorship, deaths, blacklists and exile, film-makers have shown a great energy and inventiveness in exploring their new freedom – there has been a great desire to make films. Second, many of the films made focus directly or obliquely on the traumas of recent history, traumas denied by the 'official version' of the military dictatorship. The conditions that gave rise to a militant cinema of the 1960s (the Grupo Cine Liberación, Cine de la Base, etc.) no longer exist and, as Silvia Hirsch points out,

> New movies do not call to arms but to a reflection on the society's ills and conflicts. The new film directors do not attempt to provide solutions to socio-political and economic problems, but instead they are interested in presenting diverse aspects of Argentine society and history, which were previously repressed and which must be analysed in order to construct more solid democratic institutions and overcome the tragic past.[9]

Certain films deal directly with recent traumas. The Falklands/Malvinas war provides the context for two major features: Bebe Kamín's *Los chicos de la guerra* (1984) (a film 'not so much about the Malvinas, but rather the portrait of a generation of young people, a sector of the community which was condemned without being guilty')[10] and Miguel Pereira's *La deuda interna*, renamed *Verónico Cruz* (1987), a British–Argentinian co-production, which traces the life of an Andean peasant boy through to his death in the Malvinas.

Yet other analyses have emerged in the last six years, in particular from two women film-makers, María Luisa Bemberg and Jeanine Meerapfel, which add significantly to the discussion of the recent past.

## María Luisa Bemberg
Bemberg, like another radical Argentinian woman of letters, Victoria Ocampo, has used the advantages of her upper-class background productively, to question in art the hegemonic values of the Argentinian aristocracy, in particular the rigid patriarchal codes that suppress any act of rebellion. Her second feature *Señora de nadie* (1982) was made as the military dictatorship was beginning to slacken its grip of rigid censorship, and the film explored as openly as was possible at that time the marginal status of a separated woman. It also includes a homosexual, a detail that caused immense problems for the military personnel in charge of giving out credits at the National Film Institute.

> They told me that it was a very bad example for Argentine mothers and that we couldn't put a *maricón* in the film. The colonel said that he would rather have a son who had cancer than one who was a homosexual, so I couldn't do it.[11]

The film was released on the day before the Falklands/Malvinas war, which reduced the impact of the press notices, but it reached a wide public.

*Señora de nadie* was produced by Lita Stantic, a woman who had been involved with many aspects of radical film-making since the late 1960s.[12] The partnership between Bemberg and Stantic continues, and has its basis in a successful production company, GEA Cinematográfica SA. With the debâcle of the war it became clear that more contentious themes could be explored in cinema, since the military regime was crumbling and large street demonstrations called for the return of democracy. In 1982 Bemberg and Stantic began work on the script of *Camila*, based on the true story of Camila O'Gorman, a girl from the Argentinian aristocracy who eloped with a Jesuit priest during the Rosas dictatorship of the mid-nineteenth century and was executed, with her lover, for sexual immorality and blasphemy.[13] Throughout the year's elaboration of the script, they did not know if they would be allowed to film in Argentina, and signed a co-production contract with Spain to guarantee release in the Spanish market at least. Shooting began, however, the day after Alfonsín's electoral triumph in December 1983 and the project could proceed without fears of censorship. It is not difficult to see where opposition would come from. Elements of the Catholic Church in Argentina are among the most reactionary in Latin America and the Catholic hierarchy had kept largely silent during the years of repression, despite the murder of a number of priests and nuns. Social reforms under Alfonsín, such as the final acceptance of divorce, had to proceed extremely cautiously for fear of a right-wing, Church-led revolt. The film manages to disarm some ecclesiastical criticism by having Camila seduce the priest, but it also makes it very clear that patriarchal values are inscribed in an alliance of large landowners and the Catholic Church. In December 1986, the Church tried to force the state television channel not to show the film over the Christmas period, since it 'undermined' traditional worship.

The film is also transparently clear in its use of history as a commentary on recent events. The dictatorship of Juan Manuel de Rosas has always been viewed by liberal intellectuals as the site of a clash between liberal civilization and autarchic barbarism. The writers of the Rosas dictatorship period, in exile in Chile or in Montevideo – Sarmiento, Echeverría, Mármol – produced a great deal of protest literature, in Manichean terms, including that vertebral nineteenth-century text, *Facundo*. Camila O'Gorman was, of course, their contemporary, but her story would not fit neatly into the River Plate Romantic mode. José Mármol's *Amalia* (1851) offers a heroine who is seen in opposition to Rosas. Rosas receives all the writers' invective and emerges as a strong, evil character. Amalia has to bear the weight of his approval and thus remains as an ethereal cliché of perfect womanhood. In her life Camila O'Gorman subverted such neat Manicheism.

Under the first Peronist regimes (1946–55), liberal intellectuals opposing the government often codified their virulent attacks in references to the Rosas period. Adolfo Bioy Casares's short story 'Homenaje a Francisco Almeyra' is one such case, as are Borges's constant references to

Argentinian history as a cyclical battle between civilization and barbarism. Because of Borges's rabid anti-Peronism, it took him a number of years to realize that the 'gentlemen' (his term) who overthrew the Peronists in 1976 were in fact engaged in a campaign of systematic murder. Just before his death in 1986, Borges went to the trials of the military and came out in tears, stating that the military had been a lot worse than he could have imagined.[14] It was Bemberg, not Borges, who had the imagination to show the horrors of the recent past: the two lovers sacrificed by the Rosas regime clearly symbolize the deaths of so many young people in the 'dirty war'.

Interestingly Bemberg chooses melodrama as her narrative voice. Studies on melodrama in Latin America are in their infancy, but they tend to dismiss the genre as deploying sentimental false consciousness. The best-known study of the period offers a crude critique of films produced in the 1930s and 1940s.

> Commercial Argentine cinema, impregnated with the prevailing pessimism, translated the collective state of hopelessness into a sentimental explosion, thus becoming a hindrance to the development of the people's political consciousness. Taking refuge in a frustrated sceptical individualism, promoting a fatalistic vision of existence and offering eternal sadness as an element of the Argentine character, this cinema is the refuse, the excrescence of a reactionary populism.... God, Fatherland and Home make up the inseparable trinity of social equilibrium in these films.[15]

Such an analysis is too simplistic since it seems to equate melodrama with failed tragedy or failed realism as a second-rate mass cultural form. Christine Gledhill argues that the recovery of realism and tragedy in the early twentieth century as genres dividing off high from low culture, coincided with a re-masculinization of culture:

> The gestural rhetoric of melodramatic acting was displaced by 'naturalist' performance styles. Tragedy and realism focused on 'serious' social issues or inner dilemmas.... Sentiment and emotiveness were reduced in significance to 'sentimentality' and exaggeration, domestic detail counted as trivia, melodramatic utopianism as escapist fantasy and this total complex devalued by association with 'feminised' popular culture. Men no longer wept in public.[16]

Similar prejudices inform Latin American film criticism, but such readings leave out the importance and popularity of melodrama in Argentina, the mass circulation of women's literature that melodrama draws on, sometimes ironically,[17] and also the possibility that this genre can be used as a subversive form or as a way of highlighting emotional effects. Bemberg deploys melodramatic elements very skilfully 'as constituents of a system of punctuation, giving expressive colour and chromatic contrast to the story-line, by orchestrating the emotional ups and downs of the intrigue',[18] in this way putting *melos* back into drama. The spectacle and moral polarizations of *Camila* do not manipulate the audience but instead serve as points of clarification and identification. For as Gledhill notes, the characters of successful melodrama become objects of pathos because they are constructed as victims of forces that lie beyond their control and/or understanding. But pathos, unlike pity, appeals to the understanding as well as to the emotions. The audience is involved with the characters, but can exercise pity only by evaluating signs that the protagonists cannot have access to.[19] The spectator can thus perceive the contrast between the traditional patriarchal family and the Utopian family established by the lovers, between state power and love, and between traditional and progressive Catholicism. When Rosas's *mazorca* gangs of state terror kill and maim, the parallels between them and the anonymous killers of the 'dirty war', in their unmarked Ford Falcons, become inescapable. The film also undermines the stereotypes of women, enshrined in such codes as the nineteenth-century American 'cult of true womanhood', a blend of piety, purity, domesticity and submissiveness, or in the idea of the 'fallen woman', a character who populates literature and film, who must be punished for transgression of sexual mores. *Camila* also allowed Argentinian audiences a form of collective catharsis, enabling them to experience in public emotions that had to remain private during the years of dictatorship. Over 2 million people wept at the story of Camila O'Gorman, which was their own story, an astonishing figure for Argentinian cinema. For many months, the film outgrossed the main Hollywood features *ET* and *Porky*.

With the success of *Camila*, Bemberg found it much easier to attract the co-production money needed in Argentina for any major feature. Her next feature, *Miss Mary*, allowed her to approach a major British actress, Julie Christie, who, following her stardom in the 1960s and early 1970s had deliberately dropped out of Hollywood and had become committed to making films that interested her politically. *Miss Mary* was clearly an interesting project, a chance to explore Anglo-Argentinian relations in the aftermath of war. Christie's presence in Argentina and in the film became an important act of cultural diplomacy, the only diplomacy currently available to the two countries.[20]

The film is told in flashback from 16 October 1945, the day before Perón was released from military captivity as a result of a massive working-class demonstration in his support. From this moment, Peronism became an irresistible force in Argentinian politics, which culminated in Perón's election victory in February 1946. Peronism brought to an end the so-called 'infamous decade' of Argentine history, during which a small group of conservative landowners maintained its power by falsifying elections and banning other political parties. This is the moment and the class that Bemberg, following the melodramatic fireworks of *Camila*, analyses in a cool, dispassionate way. The British nanny and governess were an integral part of the education of upper-class children, especially girls. Boys would often be sent off to public schools in Britain, to Eton or the Catholic schools such as Ampleforth and Downside (the Martínez de Hoz family, for example, are Old Etonians). Bemberg herself had many governesses and at one level the film is

> ... a tribute to those dear old ladies of whom I knew so many as a child myself and with whom one had a love/hate relationship.... They were very conservative, very Victorian, very repressed sexually but usually with a sense of humour and tenderness. I was brought up by these English – or rather Irish – women. My mother preferred them Irish because she wanted to be sure they were Catholics.[21]

Bemberg is also showing the influence of Britain commercially and culturally on the Argentinian oligarchy – the wealth of the large landowners developed through their clientelistic relationship with the British Empire. Sir Malcolm Robertson, the British Ambassador in Argentina, could remark in 1929, 'Without saying so in so many words, which would be tactless, what I really mean is that Argentina must be regarded as an essential part of the British Empire.' By the 1930s, when the film is set, this special relationship was entering into crisis: Britain was losing ground to the United States, which could supply the consumer goods of the second industrial revolution. Britain's attitude in this period, summed up in the Roca–Runciman trade agreement of 1933, was purely defensive: to preserve the dwindling export trade. Significantly all the popular cultural references in the film are to North American films and music.

The Anglo-Argentinian connection is explored in several ways in *Miss Mary*. The landowning father, British-educated, is a cynical chameleon who will support British economic interests, but is clearly prepared to make arrangements with any prevailing political or economic order. The family's patronizing attitude to the rural proletariat, condemned as innocent or noble savages, clearly reflects the prejudices of a Europeanized aristocracy who viewed the *pueblo* as barbarous – a mistake which would allow Peronism to gain almost total support among dissatisfied workers. The Miss Mary character reveals a number of British attitudes to 'other' places and cultures. Miss Mary is protected by her initial unshakable belief in British superiority: the British were never good at promoting their culture abroad (unlike the French), for the values of being British were deemed to be self-evident.[22] Yet Argentina does not fit neatly into an imperialistic vision, as Miss Mary notes early in the film: 'Perhaps you should have gone to India, Miss Mary. There at least it is clear who the natives are.' The British had very hazy ideas about distant Argentina, ideas formed by a series of stereotypes which persist, in different permutations, today. When

Miss Mary is writing home to her mother, disguising her initial distress at the cruelty of her young charges, she paints the following imaginary picture:

> The low white Spanish house has a large patio in which this evening the whole family danced the tango to the sound of throbbing guitars... It was lovely to watch and I will soon be able to dance the tango myself.

In the end, no real dialogue is possible between the two cultures, each retreats into the traditional certainties (which are no longer certain) and the old repressions.

For whilst Anglo-Argentinian relations provide the framework for *Miss Mary*, Bemberg is most successful in developing those interests already explored in *Camila*: the nature of the patriarchal oligarchic family which, in its pursuit of self-interest, in its manipulation of change and in its relentless fixation with appearances, destroys itself, and in particular its women members. The wife Mecha is trapped in a bigoted religiosity and can only retreat into madness. The two girls, despite their strict upbringing, do have a spark of independence. In a telling pre-credit sequence, the little girls are saying their prayers, but once the nanny has tied up their hands in their nightdresses (to prevent any night-time wandering), they cuddle up in bed together singing the latest North American hit, 'Ain't She Sweet'. This independence continues to flourish under Miss Mary, but with the onset of sexuality, when desires can no longer be explained away as childish pranks, the strict, stifling codes are enforced. The eldest girl, who wants to be an actress (a career anathema to the aristocracy, who equated it with prostitution and low-class vaudeville) rebels, but without purpose, into drugs and madness. She is haunted by the sense that her condition is hereditary and fatalistic, as she remarks to Miss Mary: 'Do you think that my family is mad? Do you think we have too much money?' The younger sister is forced into a loveless arranged marriage following a meaningless sexual adventure. Even the brother, who as an adolescent dares to express his desires openly, is eventually assimilated into society's structures, as a military officer and a landowner. The optimism of adolescence is negated by the reality of adult life: there can be no successful 'rite of passage'.

This cold analysis of a class did not have the same popular impact as *Camila*, but it was seen by 500,000 people in Argentina and received worldwide distribution, establishing Bemberg as one of Argentina's leading and most successful film-makers. Her latest project, on Sor Juana, is in pre-production and will again focus on her own life, the struggles of a woman intellectual in a world dominated by male discourses, and the need to create a space for women's creativity, whether in a convent cell in seventeenth-century Mexico or in a bright production company in present-day Buenos Aires.

**Jeanine Meerapfel**

While the two films discussed above have analysed the nature of dictatorship and patriarchal power at two significant moments in Argentinian history, Meerapfel's *La amiga* (1988) focuses on a contemporary issue, the formation and development of the movement of the Mothers of the Plaza de Mayo. It is a remarkable story, which has been the subject of an excellent documentary, *Las madres: the Mothers of Plaza de Mayo* (1985), by Susana Muñoz and Lourdes Portillo, an Argentinian and a Chicana film-maker based in the United States, but this is the first feature film on the topic. A small group of women (initially only fourteen) came together in 1977 (the film begins in 1978) to protest against the disappearance of their children. Blocked through legal bureaucratic channels, they began to demonstrate in the main square in Buenos Aires, opposite the government house, the Casa Rosada. Despite brutal government harassment, the murder of several of their members, including one of their founders Señora Azucena de Vicenti, and the government's attempts to brand them as 'las locas', the movement grew in strength and attracted worldwide media attention to their weekly Thursday-afternoon meetings in the Plaza. These women, none of whom had any previous political experience, had by the early 1980s developed a sophisticated human rights organization. (A similar case of women organizing spontaneously under adversity occurred in Mexico after the 1986 earthquake, when the *costureras* struggled to organize themselves into a union.)[23]

The struggle of the Mothers did not end with the coming to power of Alfonsín. Military leaders were tried for crimes of genocide, but not the junior officers or the rank and file, the torturers or the members of the death squads who might live around the corner from, or share the same restaurants with, their victims. The government opened up many mass graves (the infamous 'No Names' graves), but many Mothers refused to claim these anonymous bones as those of their children, and instead demanded information on their disappearance and justice for their executioners. The Radical Government, constantly menaced by military coups, declared in the mid-1980s an official end, a 'Punto Final', to the military trials, a measure strongly criticized by the Mothers. Today the Mothers are marginalized, sometimes treated with respect but often shamefully branded as an anachronism or as an embarrassment to the government. (It took a British rock star, Sting, to put them centre stage when, in a televized open-air concert in Buenos Aires in 1987, he invited them on to the platform while he sang his 'Cueca a los desaparecidos'. They were also on stage with him during the Amnesty concert in 1988, which was broadcast from Buenos Aires and transmitted all over the world.) Jeanine Meerapfel's film *La amiga*, therefore, deliberately refuses to close the debate on human rights, for as she has said, 'Those who forget their story, repeat their story. Identity is formed by keeping memory alive.'[24]

The friends of the title, María and Raquel, were born in the same working-class Buenos Aires environment in the late 1930s, but grow apart. Raquel becomes an actress, while María remains contendedly married within the *barrio* with three children. The military coup of 1976 shatters this pattern. María's eldest son, a Peronist militant, 'disappears', and she begins the long quest that will lead her to the Plaza de Mayo. Raquel is forced into exile in Germany (from where her parents had fled, escaping the Nazis), labelled as a subversive Jewish actress. The last play in which she appears in Buenos Aires, incurring the wrath of paramilitary groups, who bomb the theatre, is *Antigone*.

*Antigone* has different meanings in the film. At one level it is seen by the military dictatorship as an anti-authoritarian, subversive play. Antigone, the eldest daughter of Oedipus, rebels agains the dictator Creon and buries her banished brother against Creon's will. For this act she is put to death. But on a deeper level we discover that María is an Antigone in reverse. She refuses to bury her son literally, rejecting the bones in the 'No Names' grave, and metaphorically, for she has taken him back into her womb: his struggle has become hers. Graveyards offer a sense of identity, of genealogy, of history, of place, and Raquel justifiably seeks out her ancestors in a German cemetery. But María, like many of the Mothers, rejects the comfort of the tomb, for that implies closure, or acceptance. In a powerful monologue in the penultimate scene of the film, María states, 'Yo fui parida por mi hijo.... Llegué a su corazón.... Llegaron en mi sus deseos, sus sueños de libertad.... Mi hijo no está muerto. ('I gave my son birth... I touched his heart... His desires, his dreams of freedom have come down to me... My son is not dead.')

Through Raquel, the problems of the middle-class intellectual, the artist, the Jew, the nature of exile, are all touched upon, though not in any great detail, for it is the story of María that occupies the emotional and dramatic centre of the film. The spectators are forced to move away from their natural empathy with a middle-class heroine, to recognize the strength of María. At the beginning, Raquel is on stage and, in order to approach her, María must push through a crowd of photographers, journalists and well-wishers. When Raquel returns from exile and seeks out María, who is now the main spokesperson of the Mothers, she must in turn advance through a crowd to the platform on which María is speaking. María occupies the stage of history and articulates a basic intransigent truth – artists and intellectuals, if they are honest, can only strive to find the parables or the appropriate language to convey this truth. As Meerapfel states, 'For me the situation is black and white. Even though intellectuals might relate more to the voice of Raquel, historically there is only one person who is right, the Mother.'[25] Exile, then, is an important theme but the main emphasis remains on those who stayed in Argentina, represented in particular by two notable performances by Victor Laplace as the intellectual chameleon who always makes arrangements with state power, and Federico Luppi, as María's husband, an out-of-work electrician who must face up to the reality that he no longer fills the role of provider and organizer of the family.

The major problem for the film-maker was to find an actress to portray María, and a way of 'translating' the part without being overwhelmed by naturalism. Liv Ullmann was the choice, for a number of reasons. Of course, as in the case of Julie Christie, a big star guarantees co-production money and possible worldwide distribution. But, like Julie Christie, the actress is particularly appropriate for the role. Liv Ullmann's face, her gaze, has been most often used (in particular by Bergman), as demonstrating the 'agony and trauma of being human'.[26] Meerapfel uses the expressive qualities of Ullmann's face, but does not condemn her to inert suffering. María is described on a number of occasions as a 'tanque', a woman too strong for people to understand. This is not a woman to pity. Only the crudest nationalist could demand that an Argentinian play the part. Argentina is an immigrant community, a melting-pot of many different races; moreover, Bergman and Ullmann have been treated as 'honorary' Argentinians throughout their careers, for the Argentinians have been the biggest consumers of Bergman films outside Sweden.

*La amiga* uses its characters in a very controlled way. Sentiment is carefully kept in check and the director's constant use of fades (*fundidos*), especially fades to black, allows a space for spectators to analyse, as well as experience, the emotions expressed. Meerapfel is not interested in being ghettoized as an 'experimental' or a 'woman' or 'Latin American' film-maker: she has found a deceptively simple language whereby 'the spectators can find the points of reference to tell their own story'.[27]

The film begins and ends at an open-air cinema. At the outset, María and Raquel as children are looking at a sentimental Libertad Lamarque musical (Lamarque is one of the superstars of 1940s Argentine cinema). Yet this picture must be seen as a 'wonderful deceit. Something that no longer exists' (Meerapfel). For women are no longer caught in the stereotypes of the 'Woman's Film', that genre created by men in the 1930s and 1940s. They are making their own images, just as the Mothers of the Plaza de Mayo are transforming history. The final shot is of the two women gazing at the blank screen of the deserted open-air theatre, a screen that represents not the blankness of amnesia or forgetfulness, but rather a space waiting to be filled with new stories which bear witness, as do those of Bemberg and Meerapfel, to Argentina's complex past and extremely uncertain future.

# Notes

1. *Variety*, 25 March 1987, p. 85.
2. A recent study analyses the pioneering work of Argentinian women in the cultural field

in the 1920s and 1930s: Beatriz Sarlo, *Una modernidad periférica: Buenos Aires, 1920 y 1930*, Buenos Aires: Nueva Visión 1988.

3. Jorge Abel Martin, *Cine argentino: diccionario de realizadores contemporáneos*, Buenos Aires: Instituto Nacional de Cinematografía, 1987.

4. Octavio Getino, *Cine latinoaméricano, economía y nuevas tecnologías audiovisuales*, Mérida: Universidad de los Andes, 1987, p. 48.

5. Information supplied by Bebe Kamín (conversation with Bebe Kamín, Havana, December 1986).

6. These films have been shown on Spanish television and are receiving worldwide distribution (in Britain, on the BBC).

7. Slogans drawn from theoretical statements by the Argentinian Solanas, the Cuban Julio García Espinosa and the Brazilian Glauber Rocha, included in M. Chanan (ed.), *Twenty Five Years of the New Latin American Cinema*, London: British Film Institute, 1983.

8. For further details see J. King and N. Torrents (eds.), *The Garden of Forking Paths: Argentine cinema*, London, British Film Institute, 1988.

9. Silvia María Hirsch, 'Argentine Cinema in the Transition to Democracy', *Third World Affairs*, 1986, pp. 429–43, here p. 430.

10. Conversation with Bebe Kamín, Buenos Aires, August 1984.

11. 'Pride and Prejudice: María Luisa Bemberg. Interview with Sheila Whitaker' in King and Torrents, p. 117.

12. Conversation with Lita Stantic, Havana, December 1986.

13. The story is also told in a novel by E. Medina, *Una sombra sonde sueña Camila O'Gorman*, Losada: Buenos Aires, 1973.

14. Nick Caistor, 'Argentina: 1976–1983' in King and Torrents, pp. 81–2.

15. Enrique Colina and Daniel Díaz Torres, 'Ideology of Melodrama in the Old Latin American Cinema', in Zuzana M. Pick (ed.), *Latin American Film Makers and the Third Cinema*, Ottawa: Carleton University Film Studies Program, 1978.

16. C. Gledhill, 'The Melodramatic Field: an investigation', in C. Gledhill (ed.) *Home is Where the Heart Is: Studies in melodrama and the woman's film*, London: British Film Institute, 1987, p. 34.

17. On women's literature see Beatriz Sarlo, *El imperio de los sentimientos*, Buenos Aires: Catalogues, 1985.

18. T. Elsaesser, 'Tales of Sound and Fury', in Gledhill, p. 50.

19. Gledhill, *op cit.*, p. 30.

20. Conversation with Lita Stantic and Julie Christie, Havana, December 1986.

21. 'Pride and Prejudice', p. 118.

22. For the influence of Britain on Argentinian culture, see the chapter by J. King in A. Hennessy and J. King (eds.), *The Land that England Lost*, London: Lester Crook, 1989.

23. For an account of the *costureras*' struggle, see Elena Poniatowska, *Nada, nadie: las voces del temblor*, Mexico: Ediciones Era, 1988.

24. Conversation with Jeanine Meerapfel, Havana, December 1988.

25. *ibid.*

26. Liv Ullmann's words. She has a number of sharp things to say in her autobiography *Choices* (London: Weidenfeld and Nicolson, 1985, pp. 22–3), about directors who use her merely as an icon of existentialist suffering.

27. Interview with Meerapfel, Havana, December 1988.

# 12. One woman's cinema: Interview with María Luisa Bemberg
## *Nissa Torrents*

María Luisa Bemberg, the Argentinian screenplay writer, film director and feminist, came from a privileged background. She started filming late in life, for reasons that her films explain with clarity and a dearth of sentimentalism.

Before her first feature, *Momentos* [Moments] (1980), Bemberg had written screenplays for Raúl de la Torre and Fernando Ayala and shot two short films: *El mundo de la mujer* [The World of Women] (1972) and *Juguetes* [Toys] (1978) for which she also wrote the books. Writing, producing and directing her own films was her intention from the beginning, a goal which she attained after her second feature in 1982, *Señora de nadie* [Nobody's Wife].

She receives me in her offices, cool, rather empty, in a quiet district of Buenos Aires. The office is immaculate and the director seems assured. Obviously she is used to interviews and not wasting energy. She is helpful, aware that her profession implies such activities. Talking to her is not difficult.

NT: Your films have a clear theme: women's marginalization in a patriarchal society.

MLB: And their rebellion. They always rebel. Against their husbands and families in *Momentos* and *Señora de nadie*, and in a larger field in *Camila* (1984), against the family, the State and the Church. In *Miss Mary* (1986), the governess, not such a young girl, intends to rebel but, like the other women in the film she is defeated. Nobody makes it. The atmosphere is too oppressive, too rigid. The class pressures are too strong. The mother may have become a good pianist had she been born elsewhere. That is why I have her always playing the same piece by Eric Satie. To indicate the crippling circularity of her existence and also the anguish beyond the placid surface which, to me, is one of the characteristics of this French composer.

NT: She is an Argentinian oligarchic version of Bernarda Alba, more melodramatic than tragic, but like Bernarda she is the actual transmitter of the patriarchal values of which she is the first victim.

MLB: Exactly. My next film is also about a woman who, in spite of great talent, could not escape the pressures of patriarchal society: the Mexican seventeenth-century thinker and poet Sor Juana Inés de la Cruz. Patriarchal society now has eased its hold but it is still very strong. The more we stand up against it the sooner it will finish. Women should not care about social opinion, about what the others think. They should speak up and fight.

NT: But feminism, especially in the non-industrialized countries, continues to be a bourgeois, intellectual movement. Only a handful of the privileged think along feminist lines.

MLB: This is so. Most women in my part of the world are too near poverty, too overburdened by work to think about this type of liberation. But from the actual handful, a bigger movement may develop. It is a slow process. And I do not think it will be easy. Maybe by 2050. . . . No, earlier, by 2005. I like to think that we move forwards, that we do two steps forwards and one backwards. So we are winning. And the women's movement is one of the most interesting in our century.

NT: Because it aims to change the social fabric, social morality and not only class structures and economic practices?

MLB: Yes, and because it involves half of the population of the world.

NT: Divorce is coming to your country after a long hard fight. How do you think it is going to affect women?

MLB: Marriage has always been a form of prostitution, disguised under love and care. Divorce will change this. Women will not be able to feel safe in marriage. They will not consider their certificate as a kind of BA, a meal ticket. After ten, twenty or even forty years, divorce may come. It is a new situation. Previously a husband may have fallen in love outside the home. If he was well off, he would keep another home but the wife was sacred. Her status did not change. Married women were protected by society because of their role within the family. You see, even today, a lot of women, on reaching their forties, get left behind. The husband has become an executive, has travelled and the childhood sweetheart that has not grown in intellect but has done so in kilograms becomes a drag and a hindrance. Insecurity is going to force women to be more careful and not put all their eggs in one basket. There is nothing wrong with being in love but we have to start thinking about ourselves, in the first instance.

NT: In *Miss Mary* you seem to be more generous towards your male characters than in previous films. Is it because repression also touches them?

MLB: Yes. Especially the boy. I think social repression affects us all. But it affects women especially. In particular sexual repression.

NT: *Miss Mary* is a film about the upper class and even within it, a very special group.

MLB: I have always thought that what occurs in the upper classes somehow filters into the middle classes, who transmit it to the lower ones. They are the same values. What happens to the upper class is very significant. Sexual repression is handed down the same way. To me, it is the foremost repression. It is very hard to imagine how a person can be free if s/he is sexually repressed. It is one of the reasons why women have found it difficult to break with the past, to express themselves.

NT: But you have done so.

MLB: Which is why I have to be careful not to think of myself as exceptional.

NT: You are an exception. Cinema is a male preserve. It is a very physical art. You have to rule. As a director you have power and power is not 'feminine'.

MLB: More than power, what frightens women is being exposed to the public eye, to criticism. From childhood we are brainwashed into acceptance. We are supposed to be loved and to be grateful. And making cinema is a transgression, an attempt to follow one's fantasies, which is a male sport. To stand up to criticism, a woman has to feel pretty strong.

NT: And to give orders . . .

MLB: Yes. We have been trained to obey. Also do not forget that part of our transgression is that cinema is a technique, another male preserve. When I decided to direct I read a book by a Russian. I cannot remember the name of the book or the man but he stated, flatly, that directing was a hard job and women could not do it. A bit earlier in my life it might have convinced me but, by that time, I was too hard and I disregarded his advice.

NT: How did you get into films? Not just through reading books?

MLB: I took my first step as a screenplay writer for Raúl de la Torre and Fernando Ayala (two renowned Argentinian film directors). In my contract I stated my desire to be present during the shooting of the films. After my first experience, with De la Torre, I fell in love with the whole thing although, as you know, it is very boring if you don't like it. After repeating the experience with an Ayala film, I realized that if my books were to reflect my ideas entirely, I would have to direct them myself. All directors have their own vision of their work. They interpreted my books and although I know it was legitimate, it was the desire to film my own ideas that took me into directing. I think, also, that I was a born film-maker. As a kid I used to make endless story-boards and direct my sisters and brothers in theatrical performances. I wanted to be an actress. But my family did not back me, though I ended up in New York, eventually, studying acting with Strasberg. It taught me a great deal. How to treat actors, to cuddle them, to feel their loneliness, their need for affection. . . . I was also helped by being a mother. It is not that dissimilar.

NT: Your themes concentrate on the female. You have just spoken about a female directing technique, a womanly film discourse. Does such a language, such a female vision as distinct from the masculine actually exist? Can it be detected and codified?

MLB: They tend to ask me this question. Male directors: Houston, Ford, Hawks and the rest, talk about the male. I talk about the female and everybody is surprised. But, why not? The male is confused with the universal. We have to break this preconception. Male and female are very different and the difference is a source of mutual enrichment. Social use allows the female to be emotional, the male, rational. We have to break this cultural division.

NT: Manuel Puig (the Argentinian novelist and film buff who wrote *The Kiss of the Spider Woman*) talks about the need to make women more masculine and men more feminine.

MLB: I am aware of that. I have tried to put a certain distance between my eye, as director, and the story. Those who are able to see it are conscious of my attitude. I want to go as far as the genre will let me. But I am not a melodramatic person myself. Rather the opposite: cool and ascetic. At my age, at any rate, anything else would be out of place.

NT: *Camila* has many levels. It appeals to a plural audience which is, I believe, the reason why it was so successful.

MLB: I felt that the story had to appeal, basically, to the emotions. I wanted it to be like an opera, passionate. But I spiced it with clues for those who could read them as a send-up of the worse sentimentality: fallen lace handkerchiefs, vivid thunderstorms, rain and tears. Sloppiness had to be avoided but I also knew that I was handling a tragic story – one in which the protagonists could not help themselves – and I did not find it out of place to load some filmic signs with doom.

NT: Like darkening your colours?

MLB: I play with colour to point to the closing stages of the tragedy. I think that it is a pity that prestigious directors avoid the genre.

NT: Some of the best Latin American literature is melodramatic and also some of the best Western productions.

MLB: But people are afraid, justly, of sentimentalism and they're afraid to tread on a dangerous ground which they cannot control.

NT: But to be excessively distant can also be dangerous.

MLB: I try to avoid it but it is difficult to find the right position. I am rather fond of a US show business saying: 'Make them laugh or make them cry, but make them care'. And I tried to follow it in *Camila*, through my heart and through my intellect. In *Miss Mary* my intention was much cooler.

NT: It is a very different film, a fresco. *Camila*, at the end, closed on a note of personal tragedy.

MLB: *Miss Mary* and the class it represented at that point in history was a class which refused all public shows of affection, of sentiment. It is a film about a great emptiness. The lack of spiritual values and tenderness is overpowering. Apparent and actual luxury, but a great void. Form, appearances are all. It did have a great impact on the class I wanted to portray. They found it painful and revelatory. It may look soft but it is not genteel.

NT: There is no pity. Maybe some is spared on the children.

MLB: I wanted to show how society breaks their spontaneity, makes them conform and turns them into empty shells.

The interview took place in one of those luminous autumn afternoons in Buenos Aires. A few days later, the spectre of military terror reappeared with an armed challenge to the democratically elected government of President Alfonsín. Now, with the Argentinian economy in chaos and a new Peronist president, the responsibility of the artist to reveal the structures that underpin shifts in power and the emergence of dictatorships is once again in the limelight.

## María Luisa Bemberg: filmography

1970: *Crónica de una Señora* [The Story of a Lady], screenplay; directed by Raúl de la Torre.
1972: *El mundo de la mujer* [The World of Women], short.
1975: *Triángulo de quatro* [Four-sided Triangle], screenplay; directed by Fernando Ayala.
1978: *Juguetes* [Toys], short.
1980: *Momentos* [Moments].
1982: *Señora de nadie* [Nobody's Wife].
1984: *Camila*.
1986: *Miss Mary*.

## Select bibliography

Barnard, Tim, *Argentine Cinema*, Toronto: Nightwood Editions, 1986.
Burton, Julianne, (ed.), *Cinema and Social Change: Conversations with Latin American film-makers*, Austin: University of Texas Press, 1986.
King, John and Torrents, Nissa, (eds.), *The Garden of Forking Paths: Argentine cinema*, London: British Film Institute, 1988.

# 13. A place for Eve in the revolution: Giaconda Belli and Rosario Murillo
## Patricia Murray

Giaconda Belli and Rosario Murillo are both Nicaraguan revolutionaries previously involved in the struggles against the Somoza dictatorship and now actively working to preserve and sustain the Sandinista revolution of 1979. Despite an extremely privileged upbringing, both women are early characterized by an awareness of the gross injustices in their society and an ardent support for the growing revolutionary movement. As Belli says in 'Canto al nuevo tiempo':

> Sorprendida a los veinte años
> por una realidad
> lejana a mis vestidos de tules y lentejuelas
> volcada a la ideología de los sin pan y sin tierra.[1]

What I find curious is that although Giaconda Belli is heralded as *the* woman poet of the revolution and Rosario Murillo often dismissed as the 'first lady' with bourgeois leanings, it is in Murillo's poetry that we find the revolutionary thrust more fully embodied, whilst Belli remains locked within her own feminine pain of rejection and alienation.

Before contrasting the different responses of Belli and Murillo as women in the revolution, I would like to convey the unique conditions within which each is writing. For there is no other place in the world at this moment where literature and artistic creativity are valued to the degree that they are valued under the Nicaraguan revolution. The belief that a poet is necessary to society, and the dignity and strength such necessity carries with it, is unique to Nicaraguan society, as is the relationship between poetry and ordinary human activity. Poetry *is* regarded as an ordinary human activity, written in local workshops and on the battlefield as well as in private. As Rosario Murillo said on her visit to Britain in 1989:

> We created a Ministry of Culture on the first day of the Triumph. It was a major goal of our Revolution to produce the atmosphere where everyone could create, not simply receive, culture. We did it too;

everyone writes poems, we have literature workshops, painting, theatre, art schools, music schools. All this in a country so seriously affected by US imperialism is nothing less than a miracle. It expresses the incredible joy which is our national characteristic.[2]

The literature beginning to emerge from this awakened creativity is remarkably powerful and coherent, rooted strongly in a people's search for their authentic origins, and a determination to press forward in creating a reality and identity of their own making. Rosario Murillo writes of

> un corazón solitario que se arriesga
> a perderlo todo, a nunca tener nada . . .[3]

and this idealism and courage is to the fore in the feeling of many Nicaraguans that they are reforging, reinventing reality, the reality not only of their own identity but also of the whole country. Michele Najlis, a leading Nicaraguan poet, has said of her job at the Ministry of Interior, 'It was like creating a being, a whole complex organism, out of nothing. As Comandante Borge said, it's as if we're inventing a country.'[4]

The fact of creative artists taking on important governmental positions has occurred in various revolutionary movements in Latin America, but never to the extent that exists in Nicaragua. Sergio Ramírez, the Vice-president, Tomás Borge, the Minister of the Interior, and until recently Ernesto Cardenal as Minister of Culture are just three of Nicaragua's leading writers in key governmental roles. As was revealed on the British TV programme, 'The South Bank Show',[5] the poet and the politician have become kindred souls because the ideals of the poetic imagination are so clearly those of Nicaraguan revolutionary society. But of course it remains a difficult dialectic, and the pressures once felt by the Cuban or Soviet artist to contribute to the daily running of a revolutionary society are constantly felt by the Nicaraguan:

> Quién me dará ahora permiso
> para ausentarme le las cinco reuniones de esta tarde
> para no ir al circulo de estudio
> para dejar de hablar sobre los formularios, las hojas de
>   control y los cuadros,
> a quién puedo explicarle que en mi agenda de esta tarde hay un poema
> que debe completarse.[6]

So are the fears that the revolutionary activity involved in writing will not be appreciated in the face of the more physical struggle of others. Amongst the craftsmen lacking materials, the hospitals without medicines, the struggling *campesiños* and the dying soldiers, Murillo asks in the same poem:

> quién va a creer en la exigencia de un poema
> que también nos reclame
> como si fuera lo único en el mundo
> como si lo estuviera inventando.

But despite the particular pressures of a revolution under threat, it is the mark of Nicaraguan writers that they can conclude triumphantly:

> Hacemos la revolución cuando escribimos un poema.[7]

This self-confidence and sense of personal fulfilment also characterizes Murillo's vision of the triumphant emergence of woman, a vision wholly consistent with the achievements of the revolution and fully integrated into the ongoing revolutionary process. Giaconda Belli, however, despite her role as a leading spokesperson for the revolution, articulates in her poetry a very different female sensibility.

For my comparison of these two poets I will be referring principally to Belli's *De la costilla de Eva* and to Murillo's *En las espléndidas ciudades*. I very much regret that my knowledge of the earlier books of poetry by both writers is limited to what I can read in the Sandinista newspaper *Barricada* or the odd magazine, as I found it impossible to find these editions, even during time spent in Nicaragua. One can only hope that criticism such as this can help penetrate the inertia of the publishing industry and generate enough interest for the earlier works to be reprinted, or at least that new material will be made available by publishers/distributors outside Nicaragua. Because neither the poetry of Belli nor Murillo is very widely known outside Nicaragua, I will quote extensively from both.

Giaconda Belli is a popular symbol of the revolution both within Nicaragua and with Western admirers of her work. Her interviews reveal her to be a passionate and caring person struggling to be simultaneously mother, poet and revolutionary worker.[8] It is easy to see why her poetry should so appeal to a Western audience, and why at first it shocked many Nicaraguans. There is, initially, a new liberation of expression, the voice of a new woman passionate and free:

> Yo he amado hombres hermosos,
> violentos, dulces, tristes y joviales.
> En todos he buscado la luna,
> los flujos y reflujos, la marea.
> Yo he sido un volcán desparpajado
> arrojando lava
> y una gaviota volando a ras del agua.[9]

Her personal honesty reflects the reality of changing sexual and emotional relationships:

> He visto partir tanta gente
> tanta gente se ha llevado pedazos de mi piel.[10]

Her sexual explicitness embraces and celebrates the physicality of love:

> amo la escondida torre
> que de repente se alza desafiante
> y tiembla dentro de mí
> buscando la mujer que anida
> en lo más profundo de mí interior de hembra.[11]

This 'new' woman guides her partner through the extended adventure and revelation of love in highly accomplished erotic poetry, where she teaches him how to arouse her senses so that she can enjoy and take part as fully as he:

> Repasa muchas veces una extensión
> Encuentra el lago de los nenúfares
> Acaricia con tu ancla el centro del lirio
> Sumérgete ahógate distiéndete
> No te niegues el olor la sal el azúcar
> Los vientos profundos cúmulos nimbus de los pulmones
> Niebla en el cerebro
> Temblor de las piernas
> Maremoto adormecido de los besos.[12]

And in 'Pequeñas lecciones de erotismo' the act of love experienced is one without shackles, without barriers, without domination, where each shares equally in the other and reaches a transcedent state of ecstasy:

> Aspira suspira
> Muérete un poco
> Dulce lentamente muérete
> Agoniza contra la pupila extiende el goce
> Dobla el mástil hincha las velas
> Navega dobla hacia Venus
> Estrella de la mañana
> – el mar como un vasto cristal azogado –
> duérmete náufrago.[13]

Together with 'Reglas del juego para los hombres que quieran amar a mujeres', 'Pequeñas lecciones de erotismo' revolutionizes social convention, particularly the traditionally passive and servile role of the woman, and demands that the Nicaraguan man take his revolution into the home:

El amor de mi hombre
no le huirá a las cocinas,
ni a los pañales del hijo,
será como un viento fresco
llevándose entre nubes de sueño y de pasado,
las debilidades que, por siglos, nos mantuvieron separados
como seres de distinta estatura.[14]

All this is consistent with Giaconda Belli's work with the Nicaraguan Women's Association (AMNLAE) and her public struggle against *machismo*. And this apparent stance as a 'feminist' has undoubtedly added to her popularity with the Western women who have visited Nicaragua and with other admirers of her poetry. Rosario Murillo, on the other hand, like many Nicaraguans, rejects feminism as the opposite of *machismo*, an extreme at the other end of the spectrum that should also be avoided.[15] She feels, for instance, that exclusively female organizations such as AMNLAE deny men the opportunity to understand important situations of inequality and to work together to change them. However much this may contradict our own experience, we must understand that to a large number of Nicaraguans – women and men alike – feminism represents an ideology originating in 'developed' countries that has little to say about the reality of Nicaragua or Nicaraguan women. Consequently, very few Nicaraguan women, even those active on women's issues, will call themselves feminists even though these same women will put forward positions that would be considered feminist, that is, they promote the just and equal participation of women in all aspects of society. In her role as revolutionary spokesperson Murillo, as well as Belli, has stressed a concern about women and in promoting women's rights. In their poetry both explore hidden and previously repressed areas of the female psyche in an attempt to carve an authentic place for women in the revolution. That, to me, is feminist.

Another factor in the response to the poetry of Belli and Murillo is the highly personalized nature of Nicaragua's revolution. Its leaders and spokespersons are close to and intimately known by the people; some personalities will seem more preferable to others, and favourites will emerge. And of course as the *compañera* of President Daniel Ortega, Rosario Murillo's privileged position as 'first lady' of Nicaragua exposes her to more intense public evaluation.[16] All this tends to militate against a fair and analytic assessment of the respective poets, so that complex and meaningful differences that wrestle below the surface are often missed. I would like now to return to the texts and look at those differences.

Beyond the few, though undoubtedly intense, moments of strength and liberation captured in 'Reglas del juego . . .' and 'Pequeñas lecciones . . .' the poems of Giaconda Belli are more typically characterized by pain and fear. At times it is just a hint of sadness which casts a shadow over an otherwise evocative and joyful memory. In 'En la doliente soledad del domingo', for example, a vivid description of recent pleasure revolves around

> mi cuerpo
> que fue ávido territorio de tus besos[17]

The sense of loss that wavers around the word 'fue' is what provokes this 'sad solitude'. At others, though, the pain is unremitting as Belli wrestles with her own insecurities.

The first dialectic to crack the surface of the 'new' woman is that between independence and dependence. If we compare Belli's 'Anoche' with Murillo's 'En el bosque hay un pájaro . . .' we can see that both use images of guerrilla warfare as metaphors for the act of making love. Murillo compares lovemaking with the calm in between guerrilla battles:

> amó la revolución, amó la vida
> con sus ojos de agua, limpios, ilusionados
> con su ingenuo corazón de estrella
> su abrazo dulce, como la calma entre combate y combate,
> en Bismona, Zelaya, antes del amanecer.[18]

On the other hand, Belli's comparison, in direct contrast to the relaxed tenderness of 'Pequeñas lecciones . . .,' evokes struggle and violence:

> Anoche tan sólo
> parecías un combatiente desnudo
> saltando sobre arrecifes de sombras
> yo desde mi puesto de observación
> en la llanura
> te veía esgrimir tus armas
> y violento hundirte en mí . . .[19]

Though one of the most erotically accomplished of Belli's poems, 'Anoche' is disconcerting in its dependence upon male activity, even violent male activity, for motivation – the woman only seen from a position of 'observación'. Indeed many of her poems often begin as petitions to some outside being – 'Vestime de amor/que estoy desnuda' ('Petición'); 'Devuélveme mi corazón, viajero' ('Devoluciones') – revealing a constant dependence on others, a propensity to wait for others to act rather than acting herself. In 'Vigilia', Belli describes her contentment in the gradual awareness of the beauty of life, but laments:

> El amado no llega.

and in the end becomes almost the Victorian heroine waiting patiently for her knight in shining armour:

> Esa que sólo espero habrá de levantarse
> de la niebla y el vapor
> hacerse hombre y venir a habitarme.[20]

The woman, it is true, struggles in Belli's poetry, but mostly against male abandonment:

> y fui aquella mujer que te llamaba
> sin que jamás tu voz le respondiera.[21]

Even her moments of joy are clouded by 'la certeza del futuro dolor'. In 'Fronteras', for example, she awakes content but then immediately embarks on a destructive process of self-alienation:

> y tus ojos tienen un algo de lejano
> un algo de otras tierras
> de otros jardines
> de otros seres que algún día te llevaron.

She becomes almost hysterical in an effort to convince herself that the day will not come when her lover will leave:

> quiero tocarte para pensar que estás aquí
> pensar que no va a existir ese día en que te irás
> pero el día ese existe.[22]

Then come the inevitable tears: 'me dan ganas de llorar'.

Tears overflow in the poetry of Giaconda Belli as she cries disconsolately, feeling alone, alienated and useless:

> que, inútilmente,
> cavo tenaz, enfurecida, incapaz,
> llorando en mi espanto,
> esta última trinchera.[23]

Her anger does not inspire reassessment or change but is classically unproductive in that it turns in on herself and she finds refuge only in reminiscences:

> Este sueño que vivo,
> esta nostalgia con nombre y apellido,
> este hurucán encerrado tambaleando mis huesos,
> lamentando su paso por mi sangre . . .
> No puedo abandonar el tiempo y sus rincones.[24]

At times, then, Belli resembles more a Freudian case history in hysteria,[25] or the hopelessly grieving female locked within the bourgeois walls of María Luisa Bemberg's *Miss Mary*, than she does a woman of the revolution. She has none of the inherent strength that Rosario Murillo draws upon:

> La vida que es el amor
> y un beso cuando ya dejamos de creer en los besos.[26]

This is the strength and conviction of the revolutionary 'new' woman who recognizes even in her own menstrual cycle the manifestation of revolutionary rebirth:

> Vivo una renovación de la sangre
> – cada veintiocho días –
> porque soy mujer y amo y me doy cuenta
> y cada veintiocho días nazco nueva[27]

And it is because she, as a woman, has such a strong affinity with the revolution that Murillo can confidently assert:

> Se inventaron una mujer y un hombre[28]

In this vision both man and woman stand shoulder to shoulder and are not dependent on stereotypes:

> La revolución es un hombre soñando bajo un alero
> una mujer armada vigilando la noche[29]

Belli, on the other hand, praises specifically 'esta nueva raza de hombres'[30] whilst her women are dependent on the reflected glory and bravery of their men:

> Vendrá la guerra, amor
> y yo me envolveré en tu sombra invencible[31]
>
> y viajara hasta siempre
> en la eternidad de la primigenia mirada de los héroes[32]

Rather than forge a self-sufficient existence for herself, Belli cultivates a life of self-sacrifice and self-denial. 'Sin palabras' is the ultimate reflection of this process, where the poet invents for herself a huge tree under which she sits – 'bajo su sombra' – performing all manner of favours in the hope of a response, but receiving only continual rejection:

> pero no me hablaba . . .

In the final stanza she explains how she learnt so many things for his sake, stripped herself of so many other needs:

> que olvidé hasta cómo me llamaba,
> olvidé de dónde venía
> olvidé a que especie de animal pertenecía[33]

As Murillo forges a new and invincible identity, Belli denies what little identity she may have left, indeed evoking the desire to disintegrate within the existence of her lover:

> Estar como una ola
> encrespada en el suave
> murmullo de tu sangre.

Both Belli and Murillo invoke the figure of Eve in their collections of poetry. Belli titles her edition *De la costilla de Eva* while Murillo includes in her edition a series of poems entitled *Eva después del paraíso*. Belli's Eve, however, despite the tentative sectioning of her edition into 'De la fuga' 'Del renacer' etc., is quite clearly a prelapsarian Eve, where life is simple, where she is adored by her lover and has no complicated worries:

> Ser este animalito dulce
> que te busca con los ojos abiertos
> y piensa que la vida es hermosa, intensa,
> inesperadamente nueva.[34]

This is also a theme of her earlier books of poetry where she clings to the received role of woman as someone who looks after and cares for the male:

> Yoy soy tu cama,
> tu suelo,
> soy tu guacal
> en el que te derramás sin perderte
> porque yo amo tu semilla
> y la guardo.[35]

Murillo's Eve is different. In *Eva después del paraíso*, she begins with the shock of the Fall and of sudden solitude in poems of startling brevity and poignancy:

> Tiemblo
> Cuando escucho el silencio.[36]

'El silencio' is a recurrent theme throughout Murillo's poems, a solitude at first frightening and daunting, but something to be cultivated if one is to fully understand oneself and draw strength from within. As we shall see, there is a clear progression in Murillo's Eve poems, whereas Belli remains locked within the pain of 'sad solitude'.

Murillo's Eve, unlike her man-made biblical ancestor, has not been rejected by Nature and, unlike Belli, she does not grieve alone. Indeed, female emotional states are always harnessed to the natural world and to natural cycles in Murillo's poetry so that even grief and solitude become communal and uplifting:

> En junio,
> los jasmines caen sobre la noche
> mudos, como mi tristeza.[37]

> ¡Cómo llora la noche en mis espaldas
> Cómo la soledad me envuelve, me aprisiona
> Cómo mientras te amo
> y los pájaros enmudecen ante mi ventana![38]

Throughout the course of the poems Eve chides an unidentified Adam with her extraordinary good sense and sensitivity:

> Hombre, de qué nos sirven las noches
> si hemos abandonado el amor[39]

She decides not to dwell too long on the pain of lost encounters, and her efforts to reforge a new identity and reality for herself are implicitly allied with the thrust of the Sandinista revolution. Woman is firmly told to

> Levanta ya los ojos
> camina el día sin pedazos de polvo
> no te quedes allí, mujer
> como un santo con las manos cortados
> ajeno y sordo ya
> a los milagros.[40]

And it is the stereotypically 'fallen' Eve – Eve with experience and knowledge – who is exalted:

> ... Eva después del paraíso
> sin pasado posible, sin futuro posible,
> sola, en la revolución...[41]

For only a woman fully whole and self-reliant in this way can truly integrate into the revolutionary process, and it is this lack of wholeness, this fear of 'aloneness', which prevents Belli's similar psychic integration.

Describing the period when she was becoming increasingly involved with the revolutionary movement in Nicaragua, Rosario Murillo has said, 'I began to feel I could live a life of love which transcended personal love.'[42] But for Giaconda Belli the process has not been one of transcendence but of division, and she sees her own alienation in the context of 'problems of transistion' where people are

> inmersos en el amor colectivo
> pero solos de piel.

and where the fact that

> Amo a un hombre.
> Sé que el me ama,
> pero grandes soledades y distancias que mi mano no alcanza
> nos separan.[43]

is symptomatic of the gulf that still exists between the sexes. Belli identifies this gulf as the remains of *machismo* and of male insecurity, for despite the many real social changes in Nicaragua Belli believes that there are still a great many unresolved aspects:

> The whole emotional part. Because while, on the one hand, professional women are recognised and stimulated in their work – and I think there's a great deal of liberation in Nicaragua in this respect – on the emotional side, a great many old patterns are maintained. The woman who has won her place in society – in ways in which only men did previously – now lives like a man, but alone. Because what happens? The ordinary man sees her as an 'equal' and therefore not as a woman. Because his idea of a woman is not yet that of 'equal'.... I've spoken to many of the compañeros about this problem. And they realise it's a problem, they understand that it's a manifestation of machismo, of their own insecurity. But they don't yet know how to deal with it, really.[44]

But the manifestations of *machismo*, real as they are in Nicaragua, do not explain the gulf that exists in Belli's poetry. More consistent with the underlying current of her poems is her own admission of insecurity:

> And I think it's a problem for women, too, because sometimes you think you are very liberated. When somebody might try to establish a relationship with you, which is not traditional with you, you might feel they are not treating you the right way. I was saying to a friend that we have points of reference in the past but we don't have points of reference towards the future. And it's hard to know what you really want. And you have all this programming in your head that affects your whole way of behaviour.[45]

This is what lies at the core of Belli's poetry. For although she is a consistent and convincing spokesperson for the revolution and at the forefront of Nicaraguan women's struggles against male *machismo*, in her poetry she reveals her own insecurities, her own clinging to points of reference in the past. Sometimes she wishes to escape these problems of transition and return to the security of class origins and a happy childhood:

> Rodeame de gozo
> que no nací estar triste ...

> Volver a refrescarme de brisa risa,
> reventada ola
> ma sobre las peñas de mi infancia[46]

She recognizes that these memories are constraints, that she is hidden behind a façade that must be penetrated:

> El hombre que me ame
> debera saber descorrer las cortinas de la piel[47]

But the implication remains that only man, in his devotion, can break down these barriers.

Significantly, the one poem which stands out in Belli's collection as not being male-orientated is the one in which the female emerges strong and independent and a fully integrated revolutionary. 'Seguiremos naciendo' conveys Belli's feeling of having given birth to her daughter's consciousness as she watches her being initiated into the Sandinista youth:

> Ven y dame la mano
> esa tu mano joven, militante.
> Ahora que nos unen Revolución y sangre
> enfrentarmos juntas
> este futuro de guerra y de victoria.

It is a rebirth that will be replenished through future reproduction:

> y cuando amés a un hombre
> y también brote vida de tu vida,
> naceremos otra vez,
> muchas veces,
> prolongando roja nuestra bandera;[48]

This sense of the generations of women and an immense feeling of solidarity within a collective female identity is very strong in Murillo's poetry. In 'Daguerrotipo de Madre' she traces the steps of a woman that could be those of Mary, the mother of Jesus, but at the same time could be those of a modern Nicaraguan mother. In the final stanza we learn that they are the same woman, sharing the same experience:

> Una mujer, un corazón, una estrella,
> se levanta apurada con el dolor
> encendido, con el dolor del hijo que
> se entrega al sacrificio del alba.[49]

To a very large extent, Murillo has learnt her strength from other women, from the example of other women through history, and from the women

around her. In 'Aprendiendo a retomar las palabras', Murillo tells of the
sorrow and courage of Lidia through the death of her son Camilo, and how
much she herself learnt from Lidia's example:

> Vos me contaste...
> Cómo aprendemos a retomar las palabras
> a practicar el amor todos los días
> a renacer en cada gota de lluvia.
> Vos eras la madre
> que me contabas con los ojos brillantes
> el nacimiento del hijo.[50]

When Murillo speaks, then, she is the voice of generations of women,
generations of strength and fortitude that make up her character:

> ... estos viejos ojos de mujer
> que siempre descubren el mundo
> diferente.[51]

She ends her series of poems *Eva después del paraíso* with the triumphant
woman literally emerging from this collective identity. 'Blanca, como un
enorme lirio' presents a multi-faceted identity seen from varying angles and
perspectives, past and present. The poem begins with the poetic voice
speaking directly to the dramatic character:

> La muerte desapareció hoy entre tus ojos

Then both poetic voice and character become one:

> Hoy envié una carta a la muerte, sin sellos, sin destinatario,

Finally, the poetic voice stands back to look admiringly at the woman –
herself/other women – who grows out of the collective female identity
mirrored in herself to become the 'new' woman, the revolutionary woman,
who must reforge her world anew:

> Ella se puso su vestido verde
> sorprendida lanzó la última mirada a los espejos
> y, como quien no sabe nada,
> salió sin rumbo, sin señas particulares,
> pensó tal vez, antes de cerrar la puerta
> que atrás quedaba una mujer extraña
> con una nueva deliciosa piel
> el cabello revuelto
> entre los ojos
> la boca fresca

> miles de pecas oscuras
> y unas ganas infinitas de amar
> deshaciendo las piernas.[52]

The poems of Giaconda Belli, by contrast, do not grow out of the strength of a collective female identity, and the ecstatic integration into the revolutionary process achieved in 'Seguiremos naciendo' is not sustained, so that she will soon become the lonely, isolated individual who can only lament:

> Estoy muriéndome de frio.[53]

There is no doubt that such moments of grief and solitude often produce poetry that is both tender and erotic, but the emotional state itself is ultimately unproductive and alienating. On the other hand, Murillo manages to draw strength from the fact that woman is sensitive to such spiritual and emotional upset:

> ¡Una mujer no puede desconocer el temblor de las hojas
> no debe desconocerse!
> Siempre hay alguien temblando en el temblor de una hoja
> siempre hay ojos entrecerrados, desengrando la tierra
> y una mujer es la tierra
> y raíces, árboles, estaciones.[54]

In this way she emerges as triumphant and transcendent as the earth itself, dependent on no one but her own inner grace.

It is ironic that Giaconda Belli ends 'Furias para danzar' by opposing the qualities associated with the mythical Penelope:

> esta mujer que cantó
> contra Penélopes
> para un sordo Ulises navegante.[55]

In fact, her poetry remains the articulation of a suffering, waiting woman, firmly supporting the revolution she helped to make possible, but unable to find in it the permanent fulfilment that Rosario Murillo so obviously conveys in 'Confesión':

> La revolución, el amor, la lluvia de todos los días
> esta canción que acabo de escribirte
> con el ritmo de ayer y la certeza de hoy
> con la seguridad infinita de mañana.[56]

Women in Nicaragua are emerging as strong and triumphant as the revolution they helped to forge, even bourgeois first ladies like Rosario

Murillo. But centuries of male dependence and received illusions are not easy to unlearn, and some will feel the pain of transition.

## Biographical information

### Giaconda Belli

Giaconda Belli, born in 1948, was educated in Europe and the United States and studied advertising in Philadelphia. She married at eighteen, making what her family considered to be a 'good marriage', and had two children by this marriage. At twenty, whilst working in an advertising agency, she met Camilo Ortega[57] and became increasingly involved with the FSLN (Sandinista Front for National Liberation), though without her family knowing. Her political activism led to the break-up of her marriage and to her necessary exile from Somoza's Nicaragua. From December 1975 she worked with the Solidarity Committee in Mexico, and with the Foreign Affairs Commission of the FSLN in Costa Rica. Her status as a poet by this point gave her the opportunity to be heard by intellectuals abroad and she worked building support for the Sandinista cause in Europe. Since the revolution of July 1979, Giaconda Belli has worked on the Sandinista newspaper *Barricada*, on elections and in the Ministry of Planning. She has three children and works for the Association of Nicaraguan Women (AMNLAE) and for the national Nicaraguan broadcasting companies. She is a popular poet in Nicaragua and has recently published her first novel.

### Rosario Murillo

Rosario Murillo, born in 1951, was, like Belli, educated in Europe. She returned to Managua to work initially as a language teacher. She also married the husband chosen for her and had two children. At the age of seventeen she started working as a journalist for *La Prensa*, then the main opposition newspaper, and started to study politics, art and philosophy. Two years later she joined the FSLN and worked as an underground courier, then as one of its professional leaders in the final two years of the struggle. Since the revolution she has been the General Secretary of the Writers Union in Nicaragua, the editor of *Barricada*'s cultural supplement *Ventana*, and was elected a full member of Nicaragua's National Assembly in the general elections of 1984. Until recently she was the General Secretary of the Sandinista Cultural Workers Union (ASTC), and since its abandonment has become director of the new Institute of Culture (IC). She is the *compañera* of Daniel Ortega, President of Nicaragua, and between them they have eleven children. She has recently completed her sixth book of poems.

## Appendix: English translations of texts cited

Translations are by Susan Bassnett, unless otherwise stated.

[Note 1]      born at twenty to a reality
distant from my organdy and sequin dresses:

to the ways of those with no bread, with no land,
['Song to the New Times', translated by Electa Arenal]

[Note 3]   a solitary heart that risks its all
to lose, to never keep a single thing...

[Note 6]   Who is going to give me permission now
to miss those five meetings this afternoon
to stay away from the study group
to stop discussing documents, identity forms and pictures,
who can I tell about the poem in my diary this afternoon
that is still half finished?

[Note 7]   who is going to believe that a poem has needs
and also makes demands on us
as though it were alone in the world
and were creating that world itself?

We make the revolution when we make a poem.

[Note 9]   I've loved handsome men,
gentle, violent, sad and cheerful men.
I've looked for the moon in all of them,
for ebbs and flows, for tides.
I've been an unruly volcano
pouring out lava
and a seagull skimming across the sea.

[Note 10]   I've seen so many people leave,
people taking parts of me away.

[Note 11]   I love the hidden tower
that can suddenly rise defiantly
and quiver inside me
seeking out the woman who dwells
in the depths of my inner femaleness.

[Note 12]   Go over the length of me again
seek out the lake of waterlilies
let your anchor caress the centre of the lily
sink down let yourself drown spread out
don't ignore the smell the salt the sweetness
the deep winds great clouds from the lungs
mist in the brain
a trembling in the legs
a tidal wave put to sleep with kisses

[Note 13]   Breathe, sigh
die a little
die slowly, sweetly
let your dying eyes linger, your cheeks pull tight
double the masthead swell the sails
jointly steer a course for Venus
star of the morning
– the sea a great quivering crystal –
sleep after shipwreck.

[Note 14]    My loving man
will not flee from kitchens
or his babies' nappies.
He will be like a fresh breeze
blowing through clouds of dreaming and the past
scattering the faults that through the ages kept us separate
like creatures of different kinds.

[Note 17]    my body
the parched soil of your kisses

[Note 18]    I love the revolution, I love life
with its limpid eyes like pools, filled with illusion
with its childlike starry heart
its sweet embrace, like the calm between battles
in Bismona, Zelaya, just before daybreak.

[Note 19]    Tonight so alone
you're like a naked warrior
leaping over reefs of shadow
I, from my observation post
on the plain
saw you brandishing weapons
and thrust yourself violently into me...

[Note 20]    my loved one does not come.

What I most long for must rise up
out of the mist and smoke
to become a man and come to dwell in me.

[Note 21]    I was that woman who called you
though your voice never answered her.

[Note 22]    and there is a hint of distance in your eyes
a hint of other lands
of other gardens
of other beings who will one day take you from me.

I want to touch you to believe that you are here
to believe the day will never come when you will leave
although that day is here already.

[Note 23]    that, uselessly
crying with fear
doggedly, furiously, helplessly
I dig this last trench.

[Note 24]    This dream I live
this nostalgia with a name and title
this sealed-in storm that rattles my bones
mourning as it courses through my blood...
I can't let go of time and all its crannies.

[Note 26]    Life that is love
and a kiss when we've just stopped creating through kisses.

[Note 27]      I live a renewal of blood
               every twenty-eight days
               because I am a woman and in love and aware
               and every twenty-eight days I am reborn.

[Note 28]      Woman and man are invented.

[Note 31]      War will come and love
               and I shall wrap myself in your invincible shadow

[Note 32]      and travel to forever
               in the eternity of that first sight of our heroes.

[Note 33]      but he did not speak to me...

               so that I forgot even my own name
               I forgot where I came from
               I forgot what species I belonged to.

[Note 34]      To be like a wave
               rippling in the soft
               murmur of your blood

               To be this little soft creature
               searching for you with open eyes
               and think that life is good and vibrant
               new in unhoped-for ways

[Note 35]      I am your bed,
               your ground,
               I am your vessel
               into which you can pour yourself without loss
               because I love your seed
               and protect it.

[Note 36]      I tremble
               when I hear silence.

[Note 37]      In June
               the jasmine flowers fall at night
               as silent as my sorrow.

[Note 38]      How the night weeps behind me!
               How loneliness enfolds, imprisons me!
               How, even while I love you,
               the birds fall silent outside my window!

[Note 39]      Man, what good are nights to us
               if we have rejected love?

[Note 40]      Lift up your eyes,
               walk the day without pieces of dust
               do not stay there woman,
               like a handless saint
               distanced and deaf
               to miracles.

[Note 41]     ... Eve after Paradise
              with no possible past, no possible future,
              alone, in the revolution ...

[Note 43]     steeped in collective love
              but alone inside their skin.

              I love a man.
              I know he loves me,
              but great solitude and distances that my hand can't grasp
              keep us apart.

[Note 46]     Surround me with pleasure
              I wasn't born to be sad ...

              Turn back to refresh myself in a laughing breeze,
              a breaking wave
              the sea over the rocks of my childhood

[Note 47]     The man who loves me
              will need to know how to open the curtains of being.

[Note 48]     Come and give me your hand
              your young, fighting hand.
              Now we are joined by blood and Revolution
              we can face together
              this future of war and victory.

              and when you love a man
              and then when life comes out of your life,
              we'll be born yet again,
              many times over,
              keeping our flag coloured red.

[Note 49]     A woman, a heart, a star,
              rises up purified by searing pain
              with the pain of a son who
              surrenders to be sacrificed at dawn.

[Note 50]     You told me ...
              How we learn to take back words
              to put love into practice every day
              to revive with every drop of rain.
              You were the mother
              whose eyes shone when you told me about
              the birth of your son.

[Note 51]     ... these old woman's eyes
              that keep discovering the world
              anew.

[Note 52]     Death disappeared from your eyes today.

              Today I sent a letter to death, with no stamp and no address

She put on her green dress
surprised she cast a last look in the mirrors
and, like someone who knows nothing
she went out silently, in no special way,
perhaps she thought before she locked the door
that she was leaving an unknown woman behind her,
with soft fresh skin
and ruffled hair
between her eyes
her mouth fresh
thousands of dark freckles
and an infinite longing for love
making her limbs dissolve.

[Note 53] I am dying of cold...

[Note 54] A woman can't disown the way leaves tremble,
she must not disown it!
There is always someone trembling along with that leaf,
there are always half-closed eyes, disengaging with earth
and woman is the earth
and roots, trees, seasons.

[Note 55] this woman who sang
against Penelopes
for Ulysses, the deaf sailor

[Note 56] Revolution, love, everyday rain
this song I've finished writing for you
with the rhythm of yesterday and the certainty of today
with the infinite security of tomorrow.

# Notes

1. 'Canto al nuevo tiempo', in *Amor insurrecto*, p. 132 (text from *Envío*, May/June 1988).
2. See the *Guardian*, 18 May 1989: interview with Victoria Brittain.
3. 'La sobreviviencia, lo unico que tengo y vamos a cantar...', in *En las espléndidas ciudades*, p. 111.
4. *Risking a Somersault in the Air*, p. 113.
5. The programme entitled 'Nicaragua – Poets as Politicians', was transmitted on 27 March 1988.
6. Rosario Murillo, 'Es cierto que estamos construyendo el mundo', in *En las espléndidas ciudades*, p. 40.
7. Rosario Murillo, 'Confesión, in *En las espléndidas ciudades*, p. 43.
8. See *Risking a Somersault in the Air*, pp. 144ff, where Giaconda Belli talks about the difficulty of being both poet and revolutionary; also *Nicaraguan Women: Unlearning the alphabet of submission* (WIRE) interview where Belli discusses trying to bring up children within a revolutionary ideology when the father lives in the United States, with all the fascination that would imply for a child coping with the shortages of war-torn Nicaragua.
9. Giaconda Belli, 'Furias para danzar', in *De la costilla de Eva*, p. 83.
10. Giaconda Belli, 'Fronteras', in *De la costilla de Eva*, p. 87.

11. Giaconda Belli, 'Definiciones', in *De la costilla de Eva*, p. 59.

12. Giaconda Belli, 'Pequeñas lecciones de erotismo', in *De la costilla de Eva*, p. 101.

13. *ibid.*, p. 103.

14. Giaconda Belli, 'Reglas del juego para los hombres que quieran amar a mujeres mujeres' in *De la costilla de Eva*, p. 43.

15. See Rosario Murillo, 'El feminismo es reaccionario': *Ventana (Barricada)*, 28 September 1985.

16. Her flamboyant dress, for instance, irrationally perceived as a symptom of bourgeois leanings.

17. Giaconda Belli, 'En la doliente soledad del domingo', quoted from *Mujer en Nicaragua*, Managua: Editorial Nueva Nicaragua, 1984, p. 24.

18. Rosario Murillo, 'En el bosque hay un pájaro . . .', *En las espléndidas ciudades*, p. 65.

19. Giaconda Belli, 'Anoche' in *De la costilla de Eva*, p. 79.

20. Giaconda Belli, 'Vigilia', in *De la costilla de Eva*, p. 38.

21. Giaconda Belli, 'In Memoriam', in *De la costilla de Eva*, p. 30.

22. Giaconda Belli, 'Fronteras', in *De la costilla de Eva*, p.87.

23. Giaconda Belli, 'Signos', in *De la costilla de Eva*, p. 54.

24. Giaconda Belli, 'Esta nostalgia', in *De la costilla de Eva*, p. 23.

25. 'Hysterics suffer mainly from reminiscences', said Breuer, who worked with Freud on *Studies on Hysteria* (1893–5).

26. Rosario Murillo, 'En mi país hay hombres que cantan a la noche . . .', in *En las espléndidas ciudades*, p. 13.

27. Rosario Murillo, 'Mujer en la Revolución', in *En las espléndidas ciudades*, p. 49.

28. Rosario Murillo, 'Sólo tibios carbones al alba desnuda', in *En las espléndidas ciudades*, p. 32.

29. Rosario Murillo, 'Batiendo sombras', in *En las espléndidas ciudades*, p. 27.

30. Giaconda Belli, 'Los portadores de sueños', in *De la costilla de Eva*, p. 132.

31. Giaconda Belli, 'Canto de guerra', in *De la costilla de Eva*, p. 19.

32. Giaconda Belli, 'Saludo al eclipse en tiempo de guerra', in *De la costilla de Eva*, p. 49.

33. Giaconda Belli, 'Sin palabras', in *De la costilla de Eva*, p. 31.

34. Giaconda Belli, 'Acontecimientos', in *De la costilla de Eva*, p. 67.

35. Giaconda Belli, 'Yo soy', in *Amor insurrecto*, p. 51 (quoted from *Envío*, May/June 1988).

36. Rosario Murillo, 'Tiemblo', in *En las espléndidas ciudades*, p. 84.

37. Rosario Murillo, 'En Junio', in *En las espléndidas ciudades*, p. 86.

38. Rosario Murillo, 'Cómo llora la noche en mis espaldas', in *En las espléndidas ciudades*, p. 87.

39. Rosario Murillo, 'Hombre de qué nos sirven las noches' in *En las espléndidas ciudades*, p. 89.

40. Rosario Murillo, 'Canción Antigua' in *En las espléndidas ciudades*, p. 98.

41. Rosario Murillo, 'Eva después del paraíso, in *En las espléndidas ciudades*, p. 108.

42. *Observer*, 7 May 1989: interview with Cynthia Kees.

43. Giaconda Belli, 'Problemas de la transición', in *De la costilla de Eva*, p. 77.

44. See *Risking a Somersault in the Air*, pp. 153–4.

45. Interview in *Nicaraguan Women* (WIRE).

46. Giaconda Belli, 'Petición, in *De la costilla de Eva*, p. 25.

47. Giaconda Belli, 'Reglas del juego . . .', in *De la costilla de Eva*, p. 41.

48. Giaconda Belli, 'Seguiremos naciendo', in *De la costilla de Eva*, p. 112.

49. Rosario Murillo, 'Daguerrotipo de Madre', in *Mujer en Nicaragua*, p. 25.

50. Rosario Murillo, 'Aprendiendo a retomar las palabras', in *Ventana (Barricada)* 21 February 1981.

51. Rosario Murillo, 'El poder de los espelos', in *En las espléndidas ciudades*, p. 112.

52. Rosario Murillo, 'Blanca, como un enorme lirio', in *En las espléndidas ciudades*, p. 135.

53. Giaconda Belli, 'Esta nostalgia', in *De la costilla de Eva*, p. 23.

54. Rosario Murillo, 'En mi pequeño, pequeñito ser', in *En las espléndidas ciudades*, p. 115.

55. Giaconda Belli, 'Furias para danzar' in *De la costilla de Eva*, p. 85.

56. Rosario Murillo, 'Confesión', in *En las espléndidas ciudades*, p. 44.

57. Brother of Daniel Ortega, killed in the struggles against Somoza.

# Bibliography

## Giaconda Belli
*Sobre la grama*, 1974.
*Línea de fuego*, 1978.
*Truenos y arco iris*, 1982.
*Amor insurrecto* (anthology), 1984.
*De la costilla de Eva*, Editorial Nueva Nicaragua, 1987.
*La mujer inhabitada* (novel), Editorial Nueva Nicaragua, 1989.

## Rosario Murillo
*Gualtayán*, 1975.
*Sube a nacer*, 1977.
*Un deber de cantar*, 1981.
*Amar es combatir*, 1983.
*En las espléndidas ciudades*, Editorial Nueva Nicaragua, 1985.

## In translation
*From Eve's Rib*, (translated by Steven F. White). To be published in the USA by Curbstone Press.
Belli, Giaconda, 'Reglas del juego para los hombres que quieran amar a mujeres', translated as 'The man who loves me', and 'Canto al nuevo tiempo', translated as 'Song to the New Times', both in *Nicaraguan Women: Unlearning the alphabet of submission*, New York: WIRE, Fall 1985.
Hopkinson, Amanda (ed.), *Lovers and Comrades: Women's resistance poetry from Central America*, London: Women's Press, 1989. Both Belli and Murillo are represented in this anthology.

## Interviews with/articles on Belli and Murillo
Margaret Randall (ed.), *Risking a Somersault in the Air: Conversations with Nicaraguan writers*, San Francisco: Solidarity Publications, 1984. Chapter on Giaconda Belli.
*Nicaraguan Women: Unlearning the alphabet of submission*, New York: WIRE (Women's International Resource Exchange), Fall 1985. Poems by, and interview with, Giaconda Belli.
*Envío*, May/June 1988 (*Envío* is the monthly magazine of the Instituto Histórico Centroamericano, IHCA, an educational centre for the Jesuits in Central America, published in Spanish, English, French and German). Article on the poetry of Giaconda Belli, entitled 'Mujer y poesía, clave de la nueva cultura Nicaraguense'.

I know of no literary articles on the poetry of Rosario Murillo. Recently two very short interviews appeared in the *Observer*, 7 May 1989, with Cynthia Kees; and the *Guardian*, 18 May 1989, with Victoria Brittain.

See *Ventana*, the cultural supplement of *Barricada* from 1979 onwards. Various poems and articles by Belli and Murillo were first published here.

In England the Nicaragua Solidarity Campaign (NSC) holds copies of *Envío*, *Barricada* (*Ventana*), and other Nicaraguan publications. The NSC is looking into the possibility of distributing the works of Belli and Murillo in Britain.

# Index